Contemporary Gulf Studies

Series Editors
Steven Wright
College of Humanities and Social Sciences
Hamad bin Khalifa University
Doha, Qatar

Abdullah Baabood
College of Humanities and Social Sciences
Hamad bin Khalifa University
Doha, Qatar

Salient Features:

- The Gulf lies at the intersection of regional conflicts and the competing interests of global powers and therefore publications in the series reflect this complex environment.
- The series will see publication on the dynamic nature of how the Gulf region has been undergoing enormous changes attracting regional and international interests.
- The series is managed through Gulf Studies Center at Qatar University, which has emerged as the leading institution within the Gulf region offering graduate degrees in Gulf Studies at both masters and doctoral level.

Aims and Scope:

This series offer a platform from which scholarly work on the most pressing issues within the Gulf region will be examined. The scope of the book series will encompass work being done on the member states of the Gulf Cooperation Council (GCC): Saudi Arabia, Oman, United Arab Emirates, Qatar, Bahrain, Kuwait in addition to Iraq, Iran and Yemen. The series will focus on three types of volumes: Single and jointly authored monograph; Thematic edited books; Course text books. The scope of the series will include publications relating to the countries of focus, in terms of the following themes which will allow for interdisciplinary and multidisciplinary inquiry on the Gulf region to flourish:

Politics and political development
Regional and international relations
Regional cooperation and integration
Defense and security
Economics and development
Food and water security
Energy and environment
Civil society and the private sector
Identity, migration, youth, gender and employment
Health and education
Media, literature, arts & culture

More information about this series at
http://www.palgrave.com/gp/series/15318

Andreas Krieg
Editor

Divided Gulf

The Anatomy of a Crisis

Editor
Andreas Krieg
Defence Studies Department
King's College London
London, UK

ISSN 2524-602X   ISSN 2524-6038   (electronic)
Contemporary Gulf Studies
ISBN 978-981-13-6313-9   ISBN 978-981-13-6314-6   (eBook)
https://doi.org/10.1007/978-981-13-6314-6

Library of Congress Control Number: 2019930399

Cover credits: eStudio Calamar image
Cover designed by Fernando Tatay, shutterstock.com

This Palgrave Macmillan imprint is published by the registered company Springer Nature
Singapore Pte Ltd.
The registered company address is: 152 Beach Road, #21-01/04 Gateway East, Singapore
189721, Singapore

ACKNOWLEDGEMENTS

This edited volume came together during the course of the 2017 Gulf Crisis as an attempt to provide the first holistic academic account of a crisis that in the West had widely been misunderstood. This book is the result of sieving through the narratives that were soon to define the new post-factual reality not just of the stand-off between Qatar and its neighbours but more importantly also define the new reality of relations between all actors in the region. In the first eighteen months of the Gulf Divide when this book was written, tensions started to escalate between the Gulf monarchies involved and its citizens that would increasingly suck external observers, among them academics, analysts and journalists, into the conflict. While for most of us the war over narratives remained limited to social media attacks, trolling and botting, others fell victim to the increased clamp down on the freedom of speech particularly in the blockading countries. Therefore, this book developed amid a climate of repression on civil liberties in the Gulf that has been unprecedented, making it almost impossible to reach out to analysts and writers working in Saudi Arabia, the United Arab Emirates or Bahrain. I would hereby like to express my hope that the conditions for the freedom to think, speak and assemble will improve as the Gulf Divide becomes a depressing yet tolerated new reality.

I would also like to express my gratitude to all contributors without whom this book would not have been possible. Their valuable input to this book made this idea come to life over a busy period where all of us were drawn to daily, new developments and escalations in what was to become the most severe Gulf crisis to date. A special thanks goes to Steven Wright and Abdullah Baabood whose support for this edited volume in the *Contemporary Gulf Studies* series of Palgrave was instrumental to get this project off the ground. Their constant support in the writing, editing and production phase was of great help to me as an editor.

I also would like to thank all the various journalists, analysts, diplomats, ministers and officials from the Gulf and the West whose empirical input into writing this book has helped me to triangulate findings, rumours and narratives in an effort to produce a book that tries to stay focused on the facts while admitting that truth remains a subjective reality in a highly polarized context such as the current Gulf Divide.

Finally, I would like give a special thank you to my wife Zohal and my daughter Amalia who had to endure my impatience and fatigue throughout the editing process in the summer of 2018. Their love and support has helped me to stay sane when trying to get submissions in on time for the various deadlines.

CONTENTS

Notes on Contributors

Mohammed Hashem Al-Hashemi is a Qatari youth advocate and doctoral student at Brunel University London, researching youth empowerment and national capacity building in Qatar. Previously, Mohammad founded several youth initiatives and was a member of several advisory boards. He has obtained a master's in development studies from School of Oriental and Asian Studies (SOAS) and worked as a government and public affairs advisor for ExxonMobil.

Maryam Al-Kuwari is a Ph.D. candidate in the Institute of Arab and Islamic Studies at University of Exeter. She holds a master's degree in Middle East Politics from SOAS, University of London. Since graduation, Maryam has been working as a Teaching Assistant (TA) in the Department of International Affairs at Qatar University, where she had been teaching and assisting faculty in researches about the Gulf region. In addition to working as a TA, Maryam is active in community development. She co-founded a number of initiatives and dedicates a lot of her time to several campaigns in Doha, Qatar.

Dr. Hamad Al-Muftah holds a Ph.D. in Digital Diplomacy from the University of Bradford. His research interests are public and digital diplomacy on which he published a number of conference papers and journal articles. He is currently doing a master's in Policy Leadership at Georgetown University. Hamad holds a master's in international strategy and diplomacy from the London School of Economics (LSE). He also holds an M.B.A. from the University of St. Thomas in Houston Texas, a master's in computer and Information Networks and a bachelor's degree in Telecommunication Engineering, both from the University of Essex.

Dr. Abdullah Baabood is the former director of the Center for Gulf Studies at Qatar University. Prior to joining Qatar University, he spent several years as Director of the Gulf Research Center at the University of Cambridge. His academic and research interests focus mainly on the economic, social and political development of the GCC countries and their external relations. He had several publications on these topics. He graduated with a master's in business administration (M.B.A.), a master's in international relations (M.A.) and a doctorate in international political economy from the University of Cambridge.

Dr. Ali Bakir is an Ankara-based political analyst and researcher. He previously worked as a senior consultant on Qatar-Turkey relations, a senior researcher in the "International Strategic Research Organization/ Center for Middle East and Africa Studies", and an analyst in "AIWA Group". Bakir holds a Ph.D. in Political Science/International Relations from Beirut Arab University. He writes extensively on Middle East politics and great powers rivalry with a particular focus on the foreign policies of Turkey, GCC countries and Iran. Bakir is a distinguished commentator and a frequent guest on many Arabic and Turkish TV channels.

Dr. Sébastien Boussois, Ph.D. is an associate researcher at the *L'Observatoire sur le Moyen-Orient et l'Afrique du Nord* (Université du Québec in Montréal), and Université Libre in Bruxelles (ULB), focusing in his research on the Levant and GCC geo-politics. Sébastien is also an international consultant for different Euro-Arab foundations and has authored numerous books and publications on Israeli-Palestinian issues, on Euro-Arab relations, terrorism and radicalization. He previously held a position at the MEDEA Institute and ULB in Brussels. Sébastien Boussois has a developed a unique political awareness of the wider Middle East lecturing on International Affairs across the region. He is often invited to comment on current Middle East affairs in francophone newspaper and broadcast media.

Giorgio Cafiero is the CEO of Gulf State Analytics, a leading geopolitical risk consultancy based in Washington, DC. He is a frequent contributor to Middle East Institute, Atlantic Council, Carnegie Endowment for International Peace, Middle East Policy Council, Al Jazeera,

New Arab, Qatar Peninsula, Al Arabiya, Gulf Daily News, Al Monitor, TRT World, and LobeLog. Throughout Cafiero's career, he has spoken at international conferences and participated in closed door meetings with high-ranking government officials, diplomats, scholars, business-men, and journalists in GCC states, Iran, Turkey, and Egypt. From 2014 to 2015, he worked as analyst at Kroll. Cafiero holds an M.A. in International Relations from the University of San Diego. Follow him on Twitter @*GiorgioCafiero*.

Dr. Christopher M. Davidson has taught at Durham University in England, Kyoto University in Japan, and Zayed University in the United Arab Emirates. He is presently a visiting fellow at Leiden University College, The Hague, and an associate fellow at the Royal United Services Institute in London. He is the author of several books and other scholarly works on the comparative politics of the Arab world, most recently Shadow Wars: The Secret Struggle for the Middle East. Beyond academia, he has also written for the *New York Times, The Guardian, Foreign Policy, Foreign Affairs*, and other such publications. He has briefed a number of governmental organizations including Britain's Foreign Office, British Intelligence (GCHQ), NATO Intelligence, and the Dutch and New Zealand foreign ministries.

Anas El Gomati is the founder and current Director General of the Tripoli-based Sadeq Institute, the first public policy think tank in Libya's history established in August 2011. Anas is also the research director for the security & governance programme at the institute. He has held sev-eral positions across the Middle East and Europe, as a visiting fellow at the Carnegie Middle East Centre in Beirut, Lebanon and visiting lecturer at the NATO Defence College in Rome, Italy. He is a frequent commen-tator on Libya & the MENA region on Al Jazeera, BBC, France 24, Sky News. His research focuses are primarily on the security sector, foreign policy, and violent extremism.

Dr. Jeremias Kettner earned his Ph.D. in International Relations from the Free University of Berlin, where he also did his master's degree in political economy and politics in 2010. His doctoral studies exam-ined the evolution of foreign relations between Germany and Qatar. He is specialised in German and European foreign politics and foreign trade promotion towards the Middle East, in particular the Arab Gulf

States (GCC). Jeremias works as a consultant and has an affiliation with the Free University. In addition, Jeremias is a member of the German Council on Foreign Affairs (DGAP), Germanys leading foreign policy think-tank, where he served as Vice-President for the Young DGAP from 2011 to 2013. In 2015, he was appointed as a Global Shaper of the World Economic Forum and served as Vice-Curator at the Global Shapers Hub Hamburg from 2016 to 2017. Jeremias is a regular speaker at international conferences in the fields of foreign politics, Middle Eastern Studies and Cultural Diplomacy.

Dr. Andreas Krieg is an assistant professor for Defence Studies at King's College London currently seconded to the UK Defence Academy. In his research Andreas has combined his regional expertise of the Middle East with the wider field of Security Studies. He has looked at violent non-state actors and unconventional means of warfare in the twenty-first century. As an expert for Middle East security more generally and Gulf security in particular, Andreas has employed his regional and subject-related expertise providing strategic and operational risk consultancy to a variety of commercial and governmental organizations operating in the MENA region. He most recently published a book with Palgrave titled *Socio-Political Order and Security in the Arab World*.

Dr. Neil Quilliam is a Senior Research Fellow with the Middle East and North Africa (MENA) Programme at Chatham House. He is Director of Chatham House's Future Dynamics in the Gulf project and previously directed its Syria and Its Neighbours policy initiative (2015–2017). Before joining Chatham House 2014, Neil served as Senior MENA Energy Adviser at the Foreign and Commonwealth Office (FCO), Senior Analyst at Control Risks, London, and Senior Programme Officer at the United Nations University, Amman. Neil has lived in Saudi Arabia, Jordan and the United Arab Emirates, and has travelled extensively around the MENA region, working on a variety of development, education and research projects. He has published a number of books and articles on international relations and political economy of Syria, Jordan, Iraq and the Gulf Cooperation Council states. Neil was the first recipient of the Prince of Wales and King Faisal Foundation Scholarship in 1998. He received his Ph.D. in International Relations from the University of Durham in 1997.

Dr. Kristian Coates Ulrichsen is the Fellow for the Middle East at Rice University's Baker Institute for Public Policy. He holds a Ph.D. from the University of Cambridge and is the author of five books, including *Insecure Gulf: The End of Certainty*, *Qatar and the Arab Spring* and *The Changing Security Dynamics of the Persian Gulf*, all published by Hurst.

Dr. Steven Wright is an Associate Professor of International Relations and an Associate Dean for Academic Affairs and Research, in the College Humanities and Social Sciences at Hamad bin Khalifa University in Qatar. He previously served as an Associate Dean, in addition to the Head of the Department of International Affairs, at Qatar University. His areas of research focus are on the international relations and political economy of the Arab Gulf states, energy geopolitics, in addition to U.S. foreign policy towards the Gulf region. He has held research fellowships at the London School of Economics (LSE), Exeter University and also at the University of Durham. He received his undergraduate degree in Social and Political Science from the University of London, and his graduate degrees in International Relations from the University of Durham.

Glossary

AKP	Justice and Development Party
ATQ	Anti-Terror Quartet
CENTCOM	US Central Command
EU	European Union
FDI	Foreign Direct Investment
GCC	Gulf Cooperation Council
GDP	Gross Domestic Product
GIMI	Global Investable Market Indexes
GNA	Government of National Accord in Libya
GNC	General National Congress in Libya
HbK	Hamad bin Khalifa al Thani (Father Emir of Qatar)
HoR	House of Representatives in Libya
ISIS	Islamic State in Iraq and Syria
KSA	Kingdom of Saudi Arabia
LNG	Liquified Natural Gas
MbN	Mohammad bin Nayef al Saud
MbS	Mohammad bin Salman al Saud (Crown Prince of Saudi Arabia)
MbZ	Mohammad bin Zayed al Nahyan (Crown Prince of Abu Dhabi)
MENA	Middle East and North Africa
MESA	Middle East Strategic Alliance
MoU	Memorandum of Understanding
NATO	North Atlantic Treaty Organization
PMF	Popular Mobilization Forces

QIA	Qatar Investment Authority
QNA	Qatar News Agency
S&P	Standard & Poor's
UAE	United Arab Emirates

CHAPTER 1

Introduction

Andreas Krieg

The idea of a divided Gulf takes me back to summer 2014. At that time, I was still seconded to the Qatari Armed Forces in Doha. My academic colleagues had departed already into their well-deserved summer holiday while I stayed behind to finish several projects. My students, all mid-ranking military officers from Qatar, were unable to leave the country as the entire military remained on high alert amid a diplomatic crisis that had begun several months earlier. In March 2014 Saudi Arabia, the United Arab Emirates (UAE) and Bahrain had withdrawn their ambassadors and severed diplomatic ties with Doha over Qatar's support for opposition groups and dissidents during the Arab Spring—most notably groups linked to the Muslim Brotherhood.

What for many looked like a mere diplomatic dispute over interests to be settled within the parameters of the Gulf Cooperation Council (GCC) actually had taken a turn for the worse. Aside from the fact that the move to withdraw the ambassadors of three fellow GCC members was unprecedented in the thirty-year history of the GCC, withdrawn from the public eye, tensions particularly between the leadership in the UAE and Qatar had heightened over the spring going into the summer. The reason that my military students were unable to leave

A. Krieg (✉)
Defence Studies Department, King's College London, London, UK
e-mail: andreas.krieg@kcl.ac.uk

© The Author(s) 2019
A. Krieg (ed.), *Divided Gulf*, Contemporary Gulf Studies,
https://doi.org/10.1007/978-981-13-6314-6_1

1

the country to go abroad for the holy month of Ramadan, was that Emirati fighter jets repeatedly probed the Qatari air force by penetrating Qatari air space without warning, just to turn around before being intercepted. In the Ministry of Defence in Doha there were serious concerns that the Emirates could take military action—something that contradicted everything I had read, learned and experienced in the Gulf. Conventional wisdom had been that *Khalijis* are a homogenous group of people, united by family, tribal, linguistic and religious ties—a group that would not go to war with one another despite empirical evidence to the contrary. The GCC had been hailed as an intergovernmental organization resting on a firm foundation of a united people where ambitions for economic, political and societal integration could not be undermined by any dispute or divergence between the ruling elites. Yet, as it turned out the debate about regional integration had been a mere façade in the years following the Arab Spring and leading up to the 2014 diplomatic crisis.

The 2014 diplomatic crisis was seemingly resolved with the signature of two consecutive Riyadh agreements between Qatar and its neighbours, brokered by the 'old' establishment of Saudi Arabia under the late King Abdullah. While relations were restored on the surface, strategic disagreements particularly between Abu Dhabi and Doha did not seem to fade. Although Qatar gradually withdrew their support for opposition groups in Libya, Egypt, Syria and Yemen, the strategic rift over how to manage socio-political relations in the region post-Arab Spring, remained in place. For many hidden behind joint GCC declarations and summits was a deeper ideological divide over beliefs, worldviews and values. At the heart of the rift between Qatar and its neighbours stands a value-based conflict, namely a clash of two diametrically opposed belief systems about how to organize socio-politics in the Middle East after the Arab Spring.[1] At the heart of this conflict over narratives are two GCC countries, which have since the 1990s developed into two alternative poles of power to Saudi Arabia: Qatar and the UAE. Here, it is mostly the Qatari approach to the Arab Spring, promoting political pluralism with the help of non-state actors that clashes with the Emirati advocacy for a centralized strong state situated in the region of authoritarian stability. In this soft-power battle over narratives, which has spilled over to

---

[1] Roberts, D. (2017). Qatar and the UAE: Exploring Divergent Responses to the Arab Spring. *The Middle East Journal*, 71:4.

almost every post-Arab Spring conflict from Libya over Egypt to Yemen, Doha and Abu Dhabi appear on two ends of the spectrum.[2]

Meanwhile, social and political transformations ongoing in Saudi Arabia under the leadership of the new King Salman bin Abdulaziz and his son Mohammad bin Salman al Saud (MbS), had set the kingdom on a different path. Consensual decision making within the wider Al Saud family had given way to an increased centralization of power under the then deputy Crown Prince MbS.[3] Against the backdrop of the ambition to fundamentally transform the kingdom, the king's son proved to be an impulsive and impatient decision maker eager to use any means necessary to prepare the conservative monarchy for the twenty-first century. Plagued by internal sectarian, religious and socio-economic rifts, the kingdom was increasingly portrayed as the sick man on the Gulf whose failure to reform the almost century-old redistributive system would have detrimental consequences for the survival of the regime. Under immense pressure to reform the ultraconservative Saudi society, MbS turned to Abu Dhabi for inspiration of how to bring a society built around eighteenth-century values into the twenty-first century. The emerging personal relationship between MbS and the Crown Prince of Abu Dhabi and de facto ruler of the UAE Mohammad bin Zayed al Nahyan (MbZ) developed more and more into an alliance based on mutual interests, ideologies and values—a development that would bring Saudi Arabia and its evermore omnipotent then deputy Crown Prince closer to the Emirates.

Hence, when the Qatar News Agency (QNA) was hacked on 23 May 2017,[4] releasing fabricated statements by Qatar's Emir Tamim bin Hamad al Thani, Qatar had already been somewhat isolated from its peers in Riyadh and Abu Dhabi. The released statements of the Emir hailed Qatar's relationships with Iran, expressed understanding for both Hezbollah and Hamas, and suggested that the new U.S. President

[2] Krieg, A. (2017). The Saudi-Emirati Axis: United Against Gulf Unity. *Middle East Eye*, 7 December 2017. http://www.middleeasteye.net/columns/united-against-gulf-unity-saudi-emirati-axis-1609002553.

[3] Kechichian, J. (2017). The Politics of Succession in Saudi Arabia: A Struggle for Primogeniture. In K. Ulrichsen (ed.). *The Changing Security Dynamics of the Persian Gulf*. London: Hurst.

[4] Kirckpatrick, D.D. and Frenkel, S. (2017). Hacking in Qatar Highlights a Shift Toward Espionage-for-Hire. *The New York Times*, 8 June 2017.

Trump would not last long in office.[5] Despite robust denials by the Qatari leadership, news outlets based in Saudi Arabia and the UAE were quick to disseminate the ostensible QNA press releases. To many Gulf observers, it dawned that the Gulf Crisis might go into its next round.[6] More so, what commenced with the QNA hack quickly developed into the worst crisis since the inception of the GCC in the early 1980s. The coalition of four under the leadership of Saudi Arabia and the UAE were ready to escalate to previously inconceivable levels.

Less than two weeks after the cyberattack on the QNA, on 5 June, the coalition of Saudi Arabia, the UAE and Bahrain cut diplomatic ties with Qatar not only withdrawing their ambassadors but more importantly cutting off all transport links to the emirate. As a peninsula importing the majority of foodstuff, building material and other essentials via its only land border with Saudi Arabia or via the Emirati port of Jebel Ali near Dubai, Qatar suddenly appeared to be isolated not just diplomatically but more importantly logistically.

At first sight, the allegations made by the quartet suggested that this crisis was the result of an interest-based conflict, one between Doha and Abu Dhabi over market shares, one between Qatar and the Saudi kingdom over power and hegemony in the region, or allegedly one over the fight against terrorism and relations with Iran. While Saudi Arabia raised allegations that Doha had built too intimate relations with the Islamic Republic, the UAE claimed that Qatar had become a regional hub for terror financing and radicalization. Ignoring the fact that Saudi Arabia had long been the primary ideological and financial supporter of global jihadism and overlooking the statistics of the Emirates' far greater trade volume with Iran, the blockading countries quickly got bogged down in a war of alternative facts.

At a second glimpse, commentators were quick to label the crisis a relationship conflict, namely a conflict over personalities and the individual interests of the ruling families.[7] The rivalries between the Al Thanis of

---

[5] Maclean, W. (2017). Gulf Rift Reopens as Qatar Decries Hacked Comments by Emir. *Reuters*, 24 May 2017.

[6] Ibid.

[7] The Economist. (2017). A Family Feud: Saudi Arabia Cuts Off Qatar. *The Economist*, 10 June 2017; Kirckpatrick, D.D. (2017). Journalist Joins His Jailer's Side in a Bizarre Persian Gulf Feud. *The New York Times*, 1 July 2017; Ramesh, R. (2017). The Long-Running Family Rivalries Behind the Qatar Crisis. *The Guardian*, 21 July 2017.

Qatar and the Al Nahyans of Abu Dhabi are as old as the disputes between the Al Thanis and the omnipotent Al Sauds in neighbouring Saudi Arabia. The decade-old game of thrones had more recently boiled down to a clash of personalities between Tamim bin Hamad, Qatar's Emir, Mohammad bin Zayed, Crown Prince of Abu Dhabi and de facto ruler of the UAE, and Mohammad bin Salman, Crown Prince of Saudi Arabia.

Few, however, connected the dots to the underlying ideological differences between Doha and its neighbours. Most notably, the fundamentally opposed visions in Doha and Abu Dhabi on how to rebuild the Arab World after years of uprisings, revolutions and civil wars, appear to divide the GCC states. Particularly in the Emirates, Qatar's foreign and security policy has been securitized, namely framed as a fundamental threat to regional and national security.[8] Qatar's support, whether material or ideological, of non-state actors in a region of weak statehood, has been perceived by Abu Dhabi as threatening its own Jeffersionian vision of a secular strong state with centralized power in a region of authoritarian regimes.[9] While none of the Gulf monarchies qualify as democracies, their visions for a socio-political reconstitution of the Arab World after the Arab Spring nonetheless displayed considerable nuance. Under Hamad bin Khalifa, the father Emir, Qatar developed a particular appetite to employ soft power to challenge the myth of authoritarian stability in the Arab World through education, youth empowerment and the support for dissident organizations, of which many were linked to political Islam. Arguably the most resilient state in the region, Qatar had the luxury to look beyond its own borders to tackle social injustice and advance an agenda of political pluralism in the face of mass protests and uprisings in 2010. With the collapse of regimes in Libya and Egypt as well as the strategic weakening of regimes in Syria and Iraq, the regional centre of gravity had shifted to a divided Gulf where states were looking for ways to translate financial and economic power into political influence. The 2011 NATO-led military operation in Libya, substantially supported by Qatar and the UAE, demonstrated not just the reach of more confident players in the Gulf, but also the diametrically opposed nature of their worldviews, values and interests.

[8] H.E. Yussuf al Otaiba, UAE Ambassador to the United States on Charlie Rose. (2017). Qatar and the Middle East, broadcasted 26 June 2017. https://charlierose.com/videos/30799.

[9] Roberts, D. (2016). Mosque and State: The United Arab Emirate's Secular Foreign Policy. *Foreign Affairs*, 18 March 2016.

Despite the fact that the countries of the GCC share a common legacy, ethnicity, religion and language, the deceptive homogeneity of the Gulf Arabs has not prevented conflict to occur between the relatively young states of whom many achieved full independence only in the second half of the twentieth century. As state nations rather than nation states, nationalism has long been a top-down effort by the monarchies to instil an invented sense of identity, which in recent years has increasingly tried to replace an inclusive form of '*Khaliji*' identity with a more exclusive one.[10] Within this competitive environment Freud's thesis about the 'narcissism of small differences' appears to provide an explanation for regional disintegration. According to Freud 'it is precisely those communities that occupy contiguous territories and are otherwise closely related to each other…that indulge in feuding and mutual mockery'.[11] The war over words that preceded and perpetuated the 2017 Crisis appears to coincide with Freud's observations about the hypersensitivity to details of differentiation between otherwise quite similar communities.

Thus, while identity politics have widened the imagined gap between the Arab states of the Gulf, the silence of the GCC has reinforced the observation that the Gulf lacks a sustainable institutional framework that could help bridge the gap. The growing division in the Gulf has been a manifestation of the crisis of the GCC as an organization, which for long has been criticised of failing to move the ambitious plans for regional integration forward.[12] The long-held view that individual state interests and values in the Gulf take precedence over the community as a

[10]Lawson, F.H. and al-Naboodah, H.M. (2012). Heritage and Cultural Nationalism in the United Arab Emirates. In A. Alsharekh and R. Springborg (eds.). *Popular Culture and Political Identity in the Arab Gulf States.* London: Saqi Books; Partrick, N. (2009). *Nationalism in the Gulf States.* Kuwait Programme on Development, Governance and Globalisation in the Gulf States, 5. London School of Economics and Political Science, London, UK; Partrick, N. (2012). Nationalism in the Gulf States. In D. Held and K. Ulrichsen (eds.). *The Transformation of the Gulf: Politics, Economics and the Global Order.* London: Routledge.

[11]Freud, S. (2004). *Civilization and Its Discontents.* Trans. David McLintock. New York: Penguin Books (Chapter V).

[12]Pinfari, M. (2009). Nothing But Failure? *LSE Crisis States Working Papers Series* No. 2 Paper No. 45, 2009; Tripp, C. (1995). Regional Organizations in the Arab Middle East. In L. Fawcett and A. Hurrell (eds.). *Regionalism in World Politics: Regional Organization and International Order.* Oxford: Oxford University Press (p. 293); Ulrichsen, K. (2017). Is the GCC Worth Belonging to? *Chatham House Expert Commentary,* 20 June 2017. https://www.chathamhouse.org/expert/comment/gcc-worth-belonging.

whole, was confirmed by the means by which Saudi Arabia and the UAE bypassed the GCC Secretariat in Riyadh in the months prior to the 2017 Crisis. Any mechanism of conflict resolution or mediation were ignored to bring about what was believed to be a quick solution to a fundamental disagreement that had weighed heavily on the community of six since the previous crisis in 2014.

Instead of finding a consensual solution within the framework of the GCC, the UAE and Saudi Arabia consulted the Trump administration for its support of what both states presented as a move against terror finance and Iranian expansionism—two buzzwords that resonated well with the new White House. Informal, personal relationships that had been forged already in 2016 between key advisors of the new President and the crown princes of the kingdom and the Emirates, were supposed to pave the way for an isolation of Qatar.[13]

What once was the most resilient part of the otherwise unstable Middle East, has now become itself a region of geo-strategic concern as the new Middle Eastern powerhouses on the shores of the Gulf appear to confront each other directly. The implications of this crisis for the wider region and the world are multifold. Regional powers striving for more influence in the Middle East have welcomed the crisis as a means to expand their regional footprint. Iran has been able to pose as a saviour amid Qatar's logistical impasse, allowing food to be delivered to the emirate via ports and airports in the Islamic Republic. Russia has enjoyed courting from both sides of the Gulf Crisis allowing the Kremlin to experience a rapprochement with traditional US allies.[14] For the Trump administration the crisis is consequently a foreign policy disaster as much of its regional policy depended on a strong and united GCC.[15] Both in terms of countering terrorism and Iranian expansionism, the Trump administration had hoped that under Saudi leadership the GCC could develop into a more proactive regional partner that was able and willing to take over more responsibility in the Middle East.

---

[13] Henderson, S. (2017). Meet the Two Princes Reshaping the Middle East. *Politico Magazine*, 13 June 2017.

[14] Issaev, L. (2017). Russia and the GCC Crisis. *Al Jazeera Opinion*, 13 June 2017. http://www.aljazeera.com/indepth/opinion/2017/06/russia-gcc-crisis-170613073826800.html.

[15] Krieg, A. (2017). Barking Dogs Seldom Bite: Trump and the Middle East. *Insight Turkey*, 19:3.

Hence, in light of the complex underlying dynamics shaping the Gulf divide, this book is a first attempt to unpack the various critical dimensions of the Qatar Crisis as a crisis, which fundamentally reshapes the nature of regional integration in the near future. The book presents the first academic attempt to challenge the commonly propagated binary view of this conflict. It will be argued that the Gulf Crisis is a multipolar conflict that has been simmering for many years amid the changing distribution of power and influence in the wider region and the Gulf in particular after the Arab Spring. As the centre of gravity of the wider MENA region has shifted from the old power houses in North Africa and the Levant to the shores of the Gulf, these developing states find themselves with the financial, economic and political capital to shape the future of a region in upheaval. Amid a process of building nation states within a global network society, the Gulf monarchies have embarked on experimental foreign and security policies far beyond the immediate boundaries of the regional security complex of the Gulf. Imagining communities, inventing national myths and raison d'états, as well as developing national brands and narratives, the Gulf monarchies are in the formative years of state and nation building while the global and regional order is fundamentally shifting. As the West seemingly changes its nature of engagement in the MENA region, as the old regimes are disintegrating across the Arab World and as the boom years of the hydrocarbon sector seem to be over, the Gulf stands at a crossroads. The all-for-one mentality has given way to more politically and economically competitive national narratives as the GCC states compete for foreign investments, skilled labour and external protection in a globalized world.[16]

Against this new contextual background, this book intends to look to what extent the Gulf divide is a product of a more competitive security environment in the Gulf as new security narratives are on the rise. Although the war over narratives, which began with the hack of Qatar's New Agency in May 2017, was built around existing security frames of 'Iran' and 'terrorism', a deeper look at the structural security concerns of the GCC countries suggests that internal socio-political and socio-economic concerns might equally shape perceptions of security in the monarchies.[17] In particular in Saudi Arabia, Bahrain and Oman,

---

[16] Ulrichsen, K. (2017). Introduction. In K. Ulrichsen (ed.). *The Changing Security Dynamics of the Persian Gulf*. London: Hurst.

[17] Ibid.

the rentier bargain appears to be under immense stress, exacerbating senses of insecurity. Across the Arab shores of the Gulf, the future of socio-political organization arguably depends on the ability of the monarchies to reform the redistributive system to achieve both public and regime security, which ought to be increasingly seen as two sides of the same coin.[18] Within this volatile climate where all Gulf States to a varying degree are preparing for the post-hydrocarbon era, Qatar and the UAE appear to be two countries best prepared to weather the storm.[19] Yet, their expeditionary ambitions excelled by hydrocarbon wealth have put both countries in direct competition as Saudi Arabia more often than not has taken a backseat throughout the Arab Spring.

This book intends to explain the Gulf Crisis in the context of the transformation of the Gulf in the early twenty-first century with new alliances and power balances emerging.[20] At the heart of this book lies the question of how the changing global and regional order has facilitated or even fuelled the 2017 Crisis, which will be perceived as the most recent climax of a long ongoing crisis in the Gulf, which had been simmering since 2011 and is rooted in historical feuds that go back to the 1800s. While contextualizing the crisis historically, the book tries to look beyond historic events to identify underlying patterns of identity security employed in state and nation building in the Gulf.[21] It will look at how the various strategic narratives of these states have divided the relatively homogenous community of *Khalijis*. As the new regimes have looked inwards to prioritize domestic security concerns, collective regional integration has been neglected and with it the one institution that had been set up to manage collective security concerns: the GCC.[22] The consequent competition over ideas, resources and global public attention has

[18] Krieg, A. (2017). *Socio-political Order and Security in the Arab World*. London: Palgrave.

[19] Krieg, A. (2016). Gulf Security Policy After the Arab Spring. In J.M. Rickli and K.S. Al Mezaini (eds.). *The Small Gulf States: Foreign and Security Policies Before and After the Arab Spring*.

[20] Ulrichsen, K. (2011). *Insecure Gulf*. London: Hurst (p. 63).

[21] Kinninmont, J. (2015). *Future Trends in the Gulf*. Chatham House Report. London: Chatham House (p. 55ff.).

[22] See Legrenzi, M. (2015). *The GCC and the International Relations of the Gulf*. London: I.B. Tauris.

shaped the post-Arab Spring reality across the region. External actors such as the United States have been unable or unwilling to play the role of a mediator in recent years, intensifying Gulf competition by delegating more regional responsibility to the infant states on the Gulf.[23]

Thereby, dissecting the truth from the narrative becomes a very difficult task amid the ongoing war of words. With more official statements made by Gulf governments, and an apparent boost of transparency, one would imagine that writing about the Gulf Crisis in the twenty-first century should be more straightforward. Even direct access to high profile sources and interviews do not necessarily allow the researcher an unbiased view on actual events. As both sides of the Gulf divide invest heavily in information and influence campaigns overseas, targeting media outlets, think tanks and state officials, academic rigour is required here to achieve an attainable level of objectivity. Through triangulation of information and data, this book tries to move beyond the clash over narratives to produce a balanced account of the dynamics that divide the Gulf.

Book Outline

The book commences with a chapter on securitization in the Gulf after the Arab Spring. Seeing regimes being toppled by dissident crowds feeling economically, socially and politically disenfranchised, the Arab monarchies directed their attention towards reforming the struggling rentier state model that had long guaranteed a degree of socio-political stability. Ulrichsen shows that new dimensions of security have dominated regime considerations amid the rise of an outward looking, tech-savvy and globally connected generation of youth who although better educated than previous generations can no longer rely on the socio-economic certainties of the rentier state and expect more social and political liberalization. This chapter will set the security context within which to understand the 2017 Gulf Crisis.

Chapter 3 looks at the important role of the tribe in the modern history of the GCC. Tribes have been influenced by the sweeping developments that have influenced the region, including rapid modernization, the wars in the Gulf, the Arab Spring, and most recently, the GCC crisis. Al Kuwari claims that these events have tested the existence, structure,

---

[23]Krieg, A. (2016). Externalizing the Burden of War: The Obama Doctrine and US Foreign Policy in the Middle East. *International Affairs*, 92:1.

functionality and relevance of the tribe within the modern state and on the regional levels in multiple ways. In some cases, moreover, tribes have also been at the core of political challenges and crises facing the state. Not so long ago, the tribe was a central social, economic and political unit in Gulf communities, and it was even a core component in the process of state building in the modern state in the region. This chapter intends to answer whether the tribe has become the weak link? Or even worse, has the tribe become a Trojan horse that undermines the legitimacy and stability of the state?

Al-Hashemi builds on Freud's concept of the narcissism of small differences in Chapter 4, showing how the regimes of the Gulf have in recent years tried to foster top-down identity building as a means to attain socio-political legitimacy. While in the past national identity in the Gulf was defined consensually in reference to wider Gulf identity, efforts to invent new senses of communal belonging are often antagonistic in character vis-à-vis neighbouring communities. As the first crisis in the Gulf exceeding the boundaries of a feud between royal families, the 2017 Crisis can be defined as the first truly public crisis polarizing the people of the Gulf along previously defined national narratives. Although outsiders might argue there is more between the Gulf States that unites them than divides them, the 2017 Gulf Crisis has arguably driven a wedge not just between the states but the people of the Gulf.

In Chapter 5, Davidson looks at the rise of two worldviews in Doha and Abu Dhabi since the 1990s embodied by two individuals whose vision for the wider region could not be more diametrically opposed: Hamad bin Khalifa al Thani and MbZ, respectively. The efforts by both leaders to reform their countries to escape the Saudi sphere of influence, set Qatar and the UAE on two different paths that for the first time clashed in Libya in 2011. While Qatar somewhat naively saw the Arab Spring as an opportunity to rid the region of authoritarianism, the UAE feared that Qatar's support for opposition groups and non-state actors could undermine the myth of authoritarian stability. MbZ's vision for secular, centralized strong states in the Middle East was at odds with Qatar's harbouring and support for activists from the Islamist camp. It is this dispute over worldviews and ideologies between Qatar and the UAE that is arguably at the heart of the Gulf rift.

Chapter 6 illustrates how conventional and social media have been employed to maintain the crisis momentum through distorted facts, false accusations and fabricated information. I show, as the first crisis in the era of alternative facts, the 2017 Gulf Crisis was triggered by a hacking incident, which spread false statements attributed to Qatar's Emir via the QNA—statements that were quickly disseminated via media based in Saudi Arabia and the UAE. After the embargo against the gas-rich emirate was put in place, the crisis reached a monotonous stalemate that was accompanied by an ever escalating war over narratives as the 'anti-terror quartet' and later also Qatar started to invest heavily in PR and lobbying firms in a campaign to win the hearts and minds of not just the people of the Gulf but the Western public as well. Amid the absence of a diplomatic rapprochement, communication between Abu Dhabi and Riyadh on one side and Doha on the other, was maintained indirectly via social media sites, blogs, broadcast media and the international press. All that while the Trump White House, at least initially, amplified the joint Saudi-Emirati narratives, in direct contradiction to statements released by the State and Defence Department.

In the following chapter Quilliam looks at the social, political and economic reforms underway in Saudi Arabia under King Salman and his son Mohammad bin Salman. Against the backdrop of the ambition to fundamentally transform the kingdom, the young Crown Prince has proven to be an impulsive and impatient decision maker eager to use any means necessary to prepare the conservative monarchy for the twenty-first century. Plagued by internal sectarian, religious and socio-economic rifts, Saudi Arabia appears increasingly like the sick man on the Gulf whose failure to reform the almost century-old redistributive system would have detrimental consequences for the survival of the regime. MbS has turned to Abu Dhabi as a role model for reforming a conservative society. The emerging personal relationship between MbS and MbZ has created an alliance based on mutual interests, ideologies and values. The Gulf Crisis has served both leaders with a means to advance their interests ridding the Gulf of Qatar as an inconvenient partner whose activities and rhetoric could challenge any reform initiatives within the fragile kingdom.

In Chapter 8, Cafiero looks at Donald Trump's presidency as the key variable in the Qatar crisis 2017. As a security guarantor of all GCC members, the US, under the leadership of President Obama, played an important role in thwarting further action from being taken against Qatar by Saudi Arabia, the UAE, and Bahrain during the Gulf crisis of 2014. In 2017, however, Cafiero argues the Saudi and Emirati leadership saw an invaluable opportunity to finally settle scores with Qatar given that Trump sat in the Oval Office and had previously indicated his preference for a new US foreign policy that rejected many pillars of his predecessors' approaches to international affairs. As the chapter will show, based on Trump's staunch opposition to Iran as an influential power in the Middle East, as well as his rhetoric against the Muslim Brotherhood, Riyadh and Abu Dhabi (mis)calculated that the new US administration would buy an anti-Qatar narrative and interpret the blockade as a sign that Washington's Arab allies were serious about cooperating with the US in the struggle against violent extremism.

Chapter 9 examines the crisis from a political economy perspective, with particular attention to the various macro-economic implications of the crisis, in addition to the role of Qatari LNG. At an economic level, Wright makes the case, Qatar has proved resilient despite its trade, currency, and macro-economic indicators all coming under pressure in the wake of the crisis. In terms of Qatar's LNG exports, the global and diversified nature of Qatar's energy strategy meant that the crisis has had no discernible effect on its current energy policy, but longer-term, there are clear implications stemming from this crisis that work against both Qatar and the blockading GCC states. While the blockade may not have had any immediate impact, one conclusion that can be reached is that it has served to close the door to any future use of gas to drive regional integration. This has longer-term negative implications for Qatar, as the Gulf market was poised to be an important future market for Qatar given the transformational changes taking place in the global gas market and the rise of competing LNG powers which include the United States, Australia and Russia.

Chapter 10 looks at the role of the GCC as an intergovernmental organization, conceived and designed at a time when Saudi regional hegemony had to be protected against Iranian expansionism. Today, Baabood asserts, while external security concerns about Iran's covert operations in the region still feature widely in the security rhetoric of the Gulf States, the domestic security dimension relating to potential dissidence and violent non-state actors allegedly can no longer be served collectively by the GCC; the reason being that the organization has never been greater than the sum of its parts. Each member state appears to take a different approach to liberalization, political opposition and the activities of non-state actors. The fact that Saudi Arabia and the UAE have ignored the organizational mechanisms for conflict resolution to deal with their grievances over Qatar's policies shows that the trust in the organization appears to have vanished. The other small states of Kuwait and Oman have looked in distress to the actions taken against Qatar by one group of member states against another member state fearing that GCC membership might not shield them from the bullying of its bigger neighbours.

Chapter 11 will look at the ripple effects of the Gulf Crisis felt in Northern Africa. On basis of the case study of Libya, El Gomati illustrates how the competition between the Qatari and the Emirati vision for a post-Arab Spring order has exacerbated the polarization of the conflict and the rift running throughout the country. Years before the 2014 Gulf Crisis, Libya had already experienced how both Doha and Abu Dhabi were fighting a proxy war on the shores of the Mediterranean. While Qatar eventually suspended aid for the revolutionary forces, the UAE forcefully continued to shape the post-revolutionary environment in direct violation of the UN arms embargo. Today, the UAE's proxies are not only fighting jihadist terrorists but any group that opposes the authoritarian ambitions of General Hafter. All that under the pretext of 'fighting terrorism'—a narrative that was developed in Libya but has since been applied in the Gulf Crisis.

In Chapter 12, Bakir examines how bilateral relations between Qatar and Turkey evolved over time within Turkey's broader Middle Eastern and Gulf strategy in parallel to Ankara's great shift from a more ideal foreign policy that depends on vast soft power to a more realistic one equipped with hard power. The Arab uprisings paved the way for the two countries to achieve a high level of alignment over interests, values and ideology. However, the rise of common challenges, unconventional threats and the change in the security environment amid the attempts to reformulate the region in the post-Arab uprisings era upgraded their bilateral relations in an unprecedented way. As Turkey regained self-confidence in Erdogan's period, Ankara has been taking a more assertive stance across the Middle East, including the Gulf. By demonstrating that it has the will and the capability to utilize its hard power, Ankara's decision to deploy its military forces in Qatar played a major role in depriving the Saudi-led bloc from militarily escalating the crisis. In this sense, this chapter highlights Turkey's motives, implications and what it has to gain from getting involved in the divided Gulf.

In Chapter 13, Boussois looks at the role of Iran amid the ongoing Gulf Crisis. As the GCC, once conceived as a bulwark against a post-revolutionary Iran, increasingly degenerates into a divided intergovernmental forum, Iran appears to benefit from Gulf disunity. In face of a joint Saudi–UAE-led initiative to reconsolidate the Gulf around their narratives, Qatar, Kuwait and Oman might be more inclined to develop their own autonomous policy towards the Islamic Republic. This chapter will look at how Iran might be able to develop new relationships on the Arab side of the Gulf. Nonetheless, although providing Qatar with an umbilical cord amid the embargo, the small emirate has not opted to further integrate policies with Iran beyond the dimensions of trade and hydrocarbon exploration. The question then is whether Iran can actually develop a new more sustainable relationship with its Arab neighbours as the GCC remains divided.

In the next chapter, Al-Muftah explains at how Qatar has employed public diplomacy to handle the crisis and counter the war by narrative waged by the quartet. This chapter intends to show how public diplomacy in its various dimensions has been employed by Qatar to maximize its soft power to win over the hearts and minds in the Western public sphere in what could be defined as a war over narratives. This chapter particularly focuses on the utility of public diplomacy as a force multiplier of conventional diplomacy, to pave the way for de-securitizing the issue of Qatar's alleged terror finance and amicable relationship with Iran to counter what the blockading countries, and the UAE especially, had tried to frame as an extraordinary security issue. Al-Muftah concludes that Qatar has been rather successful in undermining the allegations, which had served as justification by its neighbours to impose the blockade.

The last chapter continues to look at how Qatar's soft power might have shaped the response by its European partners to the Gulf divide. Kettner examines how Germany, France and the UK have responded to the internal Gulf rift and explains how these different responses came about. This chapter looks at both economic and security interests, as well as ideologies, values and personal interests in determining how the leading countries in Europe dealt with both Qatar and the main protagonists of the blockade, Saudi Arabia and the UAE. The chapter indicates how the three Gulf states have been able to translate their soft power into political influence within the three different domestic contexts of Berlin, Paris and London. The extremely supportive approach towards Qatar taken by Germany can thereby be explained by a unique set of circumstances Kettner demonstrates.

THE CONTEXT

This edited volume brings together leading researchers of the Gulf to shed light on the fundamental rift dividing the six GCC members. As will be argued in this volume, the 2017 Gulf Crisis does not exclusively revolve around a feud between Qatar and its neighbours but is more fundamentally founded on a more competitive climate that has shaped the Gulf since the Arab Spring. For the first time, an academic volume looks at the underlying dynamics dividing what has long been regarded as a very homogenous and unified group of states. Thereby, as the GCC countries have grown into regional powerhouses shifting the Arab World's centre of gravity from Northern Africa and the Levant to the Arabian Peninsula, the implications of this crisis is a matter of concern for anyone interested in the wider Middle East. In fact, due to the expansive foreign, security and economic policies of the GCC members in recent decades, the Gulf Crisis affects the wider international relations of the Gulf. While previous crises in the Gulf have appeared merely on the fringes of the global news cycle, the 2017 Qatar Crisis has drawn extensive political, scholarly, journalistic and civil societal attention to a region, which remains widely under-researched and misunderstood. Amid an ongoing war over narratives principally between Doha, Abu Dhabi and Riyadh, this volume intends to provide a nuanced, academic view on what has become a highly polarized crisis. For scholars and policymakers alike, it is important to understand the context within which Gulf tensions have evolved in recent years finding its most recent climax in the 2017 Qatar Crisis. Thereby, this volume goes beyond the literature's narrow binary view of Gulf security limiting its focus on tensions between the Arab GCC countries and Iran. While concerns about Iran's activities in the Levant, Iraq and the Arabian Peninsula still shape securitization in the Arab Gulf states, this volume makes the case that Iran as the securitized 'other' fails to effectively foster negative integration within the GCC. This novel approach to the Gulf in crisis addresses aspects of identity security, socio-political transformation, institutional decay as well as great power politics.

As such this book is situated within a nascent literature on the internal and external affairs of the Gulf monarchies. Traditionally the Gulf literature has focused on the Persian Gulf holistically as a region shared by the Arab Gulf monarchies of the GCC, Iraq and Iran.[24] From a

---

[24]Kechichian, J. (2001). Unity on the Arabian Peninsula. In J. Kechichian (ed.). *Iran, Iraq and the Arab Gulf States*. New York: Palgrave.

narrow, realist point view the Gulf monarchies appeared on the fringes of regional power politics between Saddam's Iraq, the Islamic Republic and US superpower interests.[25] When in the 2000s the literature focused more explicitly on the GCC states as independent players, the monarchies were pitted against Iran in a widely binary view of Arab versus Persian spheres of interests.[26] The Gulf monarchies were presented as part of a US and Saudi-led security umbrella, the GCC, where the smaller states were seen as passive followers of Riyadh and its interests.[27] Overall, the six GCC countries were presented as a group of states being shaped by rather than shaping global or regional dynamics. Instead, the insecurities emanating from the Iran-Iraq War, the subsequent two Gulf Wars or 9/11 dominated the security agendas of the Gulf monarchies who were believed to be side-lined by great power politics.[28] Beyond Saudi Arabia, the small Gulf monarchies were not given much attention as independent players.[29]

While some authors addressed the looming hydrocarbon crisis and the implications of dropping oil prices on internal security already in the 1990s,[30] the widening of the literature's focus on Gulf affairs only really occurred after the Arab Spring—which is where this book commences. Suddenly, domestic security concerns resulting from diminishing hydrocarbon rents became factors impacting the resilience of the monarchies in a region where the idea of authoritarian stability increasingly appeared as a myth.[31] At the same time, the former small states of the Gulf, most

---

[25] Al Alkim, H.H. (1994). *The GCC States in an Unstable World*. London: Saqi.

[26] Cordesman, A. (2003). *Saudi Arabia Enters the 21st Century*. Washington, DC: Praeger; Cordesman, A. (2005). *Saudi Arabia: National Security in a Troubled Region*. Washington, DC: Praeger Security Intl.; Fuertig, H. (2002). *Iran's Rivalry with Saudi Arabia Between the Gulf Wars*. Reading: Ithaca Press.

[27] Gause, G. (2010). *The International Relations of the Persian Gulf*. Cambridge, UK: Cambridge University Press.

[28] Wright, S. (2007). *The United States and Persian Gulf Security: The Foundations of the War on Terror*. Reading: Ithaca Press.

[29] Kemrava, M. (ed.). (2011). *International Politics of the Persian Gulf*. Syracuse, NY: Syracuse University Press.

[30] Gause, G. (1994). *Oil Monarchies: Domestic and Security Challenges in the Arab Gulf States*. New York: Council on Foreign Relations; O'Reilly, M.J. (1999). Oil Monarchies Without Oil: Omani & Bahraini Security in a Post-oil Era. *Middle East Policy Council*, 6:3.

[31] Gause, G. (2011). Why Middle East Studies Missed the Arab Spring: The Myth of Authoritarian Stability. *Foreign Affairs*, 90:4.

importantly the UAE and Qatar, had emancipated themselves from Saudi hegemony in an effort to shape regional affairs—no longer just as junior partners of the United States. Exploiting the effects of globalization in the Arab World, the Gulf monarchies had become self-confident actors autonomously engaging in independent foreign and security policies, which would not adhere to the binary view of Arab versus Persian spheres of influences.[32] As the centre of gravity shifted to the shores of the Gulf after the Arab Spring, the literature took a more nuanced approach to the region. In his writing, Ulrichsen demonstrates how the Gulf monarchies' gained confidence, amid local hyper-development and wider regional decay, started to redefine their status in the region and more globally.[33] More importantly, as the regional context within the GCC became more competitive, a new introverted and exclusive form of nationalism was on the rise, potentially pitching family and tribal members on opposite sides of arbitrary borders against each other.[34] Identity politics, internal security considerations, pressure on the rentier state system and a more hostile regional security environment amid a perceived withdrawal of the United States, have paved the way for more autonomous and self-interested policies in the Gulf in the last decade. Against this backdrop, this book is trying to make sense of the 2017 Gulf Crisis as part of a greater regional rift that has increasingly divided the Gulf since the beginning of the Arab Spring.

[32] Legrenzi, M. (2011). Introduction. In M. Legrenzi (ed.). *Security in the Gulf: Historical Legacies and Future Prospects*. London: Routledge.

[33] Ulrichsen, K. (2011). *Insecure Gulf*. London: Hurst; Ulrichsen, K. (2017). Introduction. In K. Ulrichsen (ed.). *The Changing Security Dynamics of the Persian Gulf*. London: Hurst.

[34] Partrick, N. (2012). Nationalism in the Gulf States. In D. Held and K. Ulrichsen (eds.). *The Transformation of the Gulf: Politics, Economics and the Global Order*. London: Routledge.

CHAPTER 2

Perceptions and Divisions in Security and Defense Structures in Arab Gulf States

Kristian Coates Ulrichsen

INTRODUCTION

This chapter explores how threat perceptions in Gulf Cooperation Council (GCC) states evolved during and after the Arab Spring upheaval that began in late-2010 and reconfigured regional security dynamics in the Gulf. Responses to the political unrest that swept the wider region in 2011 varied sharply as officials in Doha, Riyadh, Abu Dhabi, and Dubai reacted in very different ways to the cascading pushback against authoritarian misrule in large parts of the Arab world. Although policies were determined on an individual basis toward each of the states that experienced regime fall in 2011, bitter new fault-lines emerged over the pace and direction of the political transitions that unfolded. This process accelerated in and after 2013 as Saudi Arabia and the United Arab Emirates (UAE) formed regionally interventionist policies designed to reassert authoritarian control and outflank the participatory openings of 2011.

The focus of this chapter therefore is on the ways in which ruling circles in different Gulf States adapted to the volatile post-2011 security

K. C. Ulrichsen (✉)
Rice University, Houston, Texas, USA
e-mail: k.ulrichsen@cantab.net

© The Author(s) 2019
A. Krieg (ed.), *Divided Gulf*, Contemporary Gulf Studies,
https://doi.org/10.1007/978-981-13-6314-6_2

landscape and shaped policymaking accordingly. How was foreign and security policy formulated and what factors determined whether issues became 'securitized'? This chapter draws upon constructivist approaches that emphasize the importance of analyzing what motives and policy goals state elites and social actors consider when constructing local and regional security agendas and defining threat perceptions and policy responses, especially in the context of the Gulf monarchies where decision-making remains highly personalized and generally restricted to a small circle of senior officials.[1]

This chapter also assesses the shifting balance between the GCC as an institution and individual national capitals as the process of securitizing very different forms of threats widened the gap between Qatar and its three neighboring detractors into a chasm by 2017. Although the six GCC states experienced numerous territorial disputes and other rivalries over the past century, they retained enough of a common security economic and security interest to make the GCC the most durable and functionable regional organization in the Arab world in the decades after its formation in 1981. After the initial diplomatic spat of 2014 and the subsequent blockade of Qatar in 2017, ties of trust among GCC member-states and societies have been shattered in ways that may take years, if not decades, to repair.

CONCEPTUALIZING 'SECURITY' IN GCC STATES

Processes of 'securitization'—that is, how issues become constructed as threats to security, by whom, and for what reason—encapsulate the importance of agency—especially among the small, closed-door circles of decision-making in Gulf States—in defining and shaping policy responses to specific issues. As the very *idea of security* itself is a relative and relational concept it is subject to interpretation.[2] At a global level, the

---

[1] Notable contributions include Wendt, A. (1999). *Social Theory of International Politics.* Cambridge: Cambridge University Press; Buzan, B. and Waever, O. (2003). *Regions and Powers: The Structure of International Security.* Cambridge: Cambridge University Press; and Price, R.M. (2008). *Moral Limit and Possibility in World Politics.* Cambridge: Cambridge University Press. For the Gulf specifically, see Ulrichsen, K.C. (2011). *Insecure Gulf: The End of Certainty and the Transition to the Post-oil Era.* London: Hurst.

[2] Kelstrup, M. (2004). Globalization and Societal Insecurity: The Securitization of Terrorism and Competing Strategies for Global Governance. In Stefano Guzzini and Dietrich Jung (eds.). *Contemporary Security Analysis and Copenhagen Peace Research.* London: Routledge (p. 108).

'War on Terror' launched by the George W. Bush administration in the aftermath of the September 11, 2001 attacks on the United States represented an example of securitization and enabled the United States to set aside international norms and structures to combat the terrorist threat that they perceived Al-Qaeda presented.[3]

An additional factor pertinent to the examination of security policy in GCC countries—as in many other states in the Middle East and in regions of the world, especially in non-democratic settings—is the alignment between *national security* and *regime security* when the two are frequently conflated in leaders' minds. Determining the intersubjective pressure points when considerations of security and threat perception— whether at the domestic, regional, or international level—are drawn up casts light, as Keith Krause has pointed out, on "*the more elusive notion of 'survival' ... especially when the referent point is not the state, but the 'nation' or other identity group.*"[4] In settings where ruling families regarded regime security and national security as two sides of the same coin, perceived threats could appear as much from internal societal contestation as against external aggression by neighboring or regional states.[5]

Internal and external aspects of (in)security came together in the two Saudi incursions into Bahrain in 1994, briefly, and, more substantively, in 2011, to assist the Bahraini government during periods of domestic unrest. In the 1994 iteration of the Saudi intervention, the powerful Saudi Minister of the Interior, Prince Nayef bin Abdulaziz Al Saud, declared on a trip to Bahrain's capital, Manama, that the security of Bahrain and Saudi Arabia was inseparable and, left unspoken, acknowledged that a threat to any one of the ruling families in the Gulf was, ideationally, a threat to them all.[6] In 2011, as 1000 Saudi Arabian National Guardsmen drove across the King Fahd Causeway in armored personnel

[3]Buzan, B. (2006). Will the "Global War on Terrorism" Be the New Cold War? *International Affairs*, 82:6 (p. 1103).

[4]Krause, K. (1998). Theorizing Security, State Formation and the 'Third World' in the Post-Cold War World. *Review of International Studies*, 24:1 (p. 135).

[5]Halliday, F. (2005). *The Middle East in International Relations: Power, Politics and Ideology.* Cambridge: Cambridge University Press (p. 175).

[6]Fakhro, M. (1997). The Uprising in Bahrain: An Assessment. In Gary Sick and Lawrence Potter (eds.). *The Persian Gulf at the Millennium: Essays in Politics, Economy, Security, and Religion.* London: Macmillan (p. 184).

carriers accompanied by 500 military policemen from the UAE, a Saudi official was quick to emphasize that *"Bahrain will get whatever assistance it needs. It's open-ended."*[7]

Policy formulation and decision-making in all six GCC states are highly concentrated within elite circles of policymakers clustered around the King, Emir, or Sultan. Decisions are taken 'at the top' and are passed downward for implementation by government ministries such as Foreign Affairs and Defense, which, in some cases, are rarely consulted in the process. A case in point was the abrupt Saudi decision in October 2013 to decline to take up one of the ten rotating non-permanent seats on the United Nations Security Council a day after being elected to the vacancy reserved for the Asia-Pacific group of nations. The Saudi Mission to the United Nations campaigned for the seat and the sudden decision to reverse course stunned the Saudi diplomatic corps both in New York and in Riyadh who had only hours before celebrated the achievement. Indeed, the Saudi Ambassador to the United Nations, Abdullah al-Muallimi, initially told the New York Times that

> We take this election very seriously as a responsibility to be able to contribute to this very important forum to peace and security in the world…Our election today is a reflection of a longstanding policy in support of moderation and in support of resolving disputes by peaceful means.[8]

At least some members of the foreign diplomatic community in Riyadh suggested the volte-face was a decision taken by King Abdullah and his advisers without meaningful consultation with the Ministry of Foreign Affairs.[9]

[7]Miller, R. (2016). *Desert Kingdoms to Global Powers: The Rise of the Arab Gulf.* New Haven, CT: Yale University Press (p. 211).

[8]Worth, R. (2013). Saudi Arabia Rejects U.N. Security Council Seat in Protest Move. *New York Times*, 18 October 2013. https://www.nytimes.com/2013/10/19/world/middleeast/saudi-arabia-rejects-security-council-seat.html.

[9]Author conversations with diplomats from Australia, Canada, Sweden, and Norway, Riyadh, March 2014.

'Personalization' vs. 'Institutionalization' in Decision-Making

The personalized nature of policymaking in Gulf capitals influenced heavily the shape and speed of regional cooperation through the creation of the GCC in 1981 and its subsequent evolution. While Emir Isa bin Salman Al Khalifa of Bahrain hailed the GCC as a river that would *"irrigate the path of the future where it meets with the streams of good and aspires to the coasts of glory,"* the subsequent evolution of the GCC illustrated the practical challenges of aligning policy among six ruling elites unwilling to devolve real power to their own peoples let alone each other.[10] The GCC came together in a matter of months in early 1981 after several years of inconclusive talks and competing visions of what form a regional organization should take, and the impetus for its creation was provided more by the external shocks of the Islamic Revolution in Iran in 1979 and the Iraqi invasion of Iran in 1980 than by any meaningful regional consensus about the path forward for the organization.

Foreign Ministers of all eight states in the Gulf (the six future GCC states plus Iraq and Iran) met in Jeddah in July 1975 to discuss a Saudi proposal for a collective security agreement in the Gulf, and a further meeting of the eight countries took place in Muscat in November 1976 where regional security arrangements were again discussed. Both meetings broke up without agreement and served more to highlight the difficulty of aligning the eight littoral states when it came to sensitive issues of defense, security, and foreign policy.[11] Even after the toppling of the Shah in 1979 and the start of the first Gulf War in 1980 removed Iraq and Iran from consideration in the proposed regional arrangement, differences among the six Arab Gulf states remained. When representatives of the six states met in Kuwait in February 1981 they had before them three very different proposals from Kuwait, Oman, and Saudi Arabia that emphasized, respectively, economic integration, military cooperation, and collective security.[12]

---

[10] Miller, *Desert Kingdoms to Global Powers* (p. 9).

[11] Jones, J. and Ridout, N. (2015). *A History of Modern Oman*. Cambridge: Cambridge University Press (pp. 185–186).

[12] Abdulla, A. (1999). The Gulf Cooperation Council: Nature, Origin, and Process. In Michael Hudson (ed.). *Middle East Dilemma: The Politics and Economics of Arab Integration*. New York: Columbia University Press (pp. 154–155).

Little more than three months after the initial meeting in Kuwait the GCC was formally launched at a summit in Abu Dhabi on May 25. The speed with which the new organization was drawn up—along with the compromises between the three competing visions of coordination—meant that key issues of institutional design were left unaddressed. Writing in 1999 about the creation and early years of the GCC, Emirati political scientist Abdulkhaleq Abdulla observed that *"Its nature and what it stands for was hardly clear at the outset, and it is certainly no clearer today,"* in part because the hasty formation of the GCC reflected *"not so much sober thinking as…an immediate* ad hoc *reaction to the turbulent regional events of 1979–80."*[13] The GCC was neither a political union nor a military alliance and the six member-states have been reluctant to grant supranational powers to the General Secretariat based in Riyadh. Moreover, the requirement for unanimity (rather than majority voting) on substantive matters at the Supreme Council (of rulers) and the Ministerial Council meant that individual countries (i.e. rulers) had veto power over policies they did not approve of.[14]

Two further impediments to the accrual and consolidation of authority at the regionwide GCC-level were the imbalance in size and power between Saudi Arabia, on the one hand, and its five smaller neighbors, on the other, as well as the nature of decision-making in all six of the monarchies that made up the GCC. At various times in the twentieth century, Saudi leaders exhibited expansionist designs in the Arabian Peninsula, against Kuwait in the 1920s, Qatar in the 1930s, and Oman and Abu Dhabi in the 1950s.[15] Although the majority of border and transboundary disputes were resolved prior to the formation of the GCC, they left a legacy of residual wariness in other Gulf capitals over expressions of Saudi power and influence within the organization. In 2009, Saudi officials placed restrictions on Emirati citizens entering the Kingdom using UAE identification cards that featured a map including

[13] Ibid., pp. 153–154.

[14] Legrenzi, M. (2011). *The GCC and the International Relations of the Gulf: Diplomacy, Security and Economic Coordination in a Changing Middle East.* London: I.B. Tauris (p. 35).

[15] For a good overview of mid-twentieth century territorial claims and counter-claims, see Morton, M.Q. (2013). *Buraimi: The Struggle for Power, Influence and Oil in Arabia.* London: I.B. Tauris.

as Emirati contentious territory claimed by both sides.[16] Several months later, in March 2010, a short yet sharp naval clash was reported to have occurred as the UAE navy opened fire on a Saudi patrol vessel and forced its surrender after it strayed into disputed water.[17]

The failure of efforts between 2011 and 2013 to first broaden and then deepen the unity of the GCC illustrated the other characteristic of the organization's four-decade existence, namely the inability to reach consensus on 'big ticket' issues, especially if they related to defense, security, or foreign policy. King Abdullah of Saudi Arabia surprised fellow Gulf rulers with his May 2011 call for Morocco and Jordan to apply for associate GCC membership as the matter had not been discussed beforehand.[18] When King Abdullah's suggestion to broaden the GCC failed to gain traction he subsequently proposed to deepen the GCC into more of an integrative political entity at the December 2011 GCC Summit in Riyadh. However, a subsequent midyear 'Consultative Summit' in Riyadh in May 2012 ended without an agreement as the most the six states could agree on was to refer the issue of union to a committee for further consideration. The outcome was a blow to the Saudis who had played up the talk of (and prospects for) union in the run-up to the meeting, just as they did eighteen months later before the December 2013 Summit in Kuwait.[19]

The Arab Spring and the End of Consensus

Developments since 2011 have gravely weakened, if not shattered, the notion of collective self-interest that underlay the decision to establish the GCC back in 1981 and provided a baseline of cooperation ever since.

[16] Anon. (2016). FACTBOX: Rivalry and Differences Between Saudi and UAE. *Reuters*, 6 April 2010. https://www.reuters.com/article/gulf-union/factbox-rivalry-and-differences-between-saudi-and-uae-idUSLDE63405T20100406.

[17] Spencer, R. (2010). Naval Battle Between UAE and Saudi Arabia Raises Fears for Gulf Security. *The Daily Telegraph*, 26 March 2010. http://www.telegraph.co.uk/news/world-news/middleeast/unitedarabemirates/7521219/Naval-battle-between-UAE-and-Saudi-Arabia-raises-fears-for-Gulf-security.html.

[18] Hamdan, S. (2011). Gulf Council Reaches Out to Morocco and Jordan. *New York Times*, 25 May 2011. http://www.nytimes.com/2011/05/26/world/middleeast/26iht-M26-GCC.html.

[19] Ulrichsen, K.C. (2015). *The Gulf States in International Political Economy*. Basingstoke: Palgrave Macmillan (p. 202).

Until 2011, and throughout the three major wars in the Gulf between 1980 and 2003 (the Iran-Iraq War, the Gulf War, and the US-led invasion of Iraq) all six Gulf States had retained enough of an agreement about a common threat perception to overcome periodic instances of intra-GCC friction, such as Saudi and Emirati opposition to and efforts to reverse the 1995 succession of Qatar's Emir Hamad bin Khalifa Al Thani or the Emirati withdrawal from the GCC monetary union project in 2010. However, the cathartic upheaval of the Arab Spring and the role of Islamist groups in political transitions in North Africa underscored the dramatic divergence in threat perceptions that conditioned policy responses in Doha and the new Abu Dhabi-Riyadh-Manama axis in and after 2011.

In 2011, the Qatari leadership of Emir Hamad bin Khalifa Al Thani and Prime Minister Sheikh Hamad bin Jassim Al Thani responded to the outbreak of protests at authoritarian rule in North Africa by supporting—cautiously at first and then more openly—the calls to hold political leaders to account. Rolling coverage by the Doha-based and Qatar-funded *Al Jazeera* media group spread the demonstrators' message and galvanized protestors elsewhere as the initial demonstrations in Tunisia spilled across the region.[20] Uniquely in the Middle East, Qatar faced no real prospect of economic or political upheaval and was able to approach the 'Arab Spring' in a very different way from virtually every other regional state, including its neighboring GCC states, which all faced varying degrees of political or economic unrest in 2011. This included Saudi Arabia, which faced persistent protests in the Eastern Province, Bahrain, which experienced a full-blown uprising, and the UAE, where policy hawks in Abu Dhabi constructed a threat to national security from a petition for (modest) political reform to justify a security crackdown on opposition and human rights activists.[21]

In common with many others in the region and around the world, Qatari officials (and Al Jazeera) were slow to recognize the swelling protest movement in Tunisia until it reached the capital and posed an imminent danger to Ben Ali. Even the calls on social media for an Egyptian day of action on January 25, 2011 initially received relatively little

---

[20]Lucas, R. (2014). The Persian Gulf Monarchies and the Arab Spring. In Mehran Kamrava (ed.). *Beyond the Arab Spring: The Evolving Ruling Bargain in the Middle East*. Oxford: Oxford University Press (p. 316).

[21]Ibid., pp. 318–325.

attention, and as the demonstrations that triggered the eighteen-day revolt against Mubarak began Al Jazeera was airing a sports documentary.[22] However, almost as soon as the magnitude of what was developing in Egypt became apparent, the leadership in Qatar rapidly acknowledged the seismic shifts in the regional landscape and adjusted their policies accordingly. They were assisted by Al Jazeera, which became *"a focal point for audiences everywhere to share in revolutionary protest"* through its iconic round-the-clock coverage of the unfolding revolution in Cairo's Tahrir Square.[23]

Three factors made such a rapid change in Qatari policy possible. The first was the highly concentrated core of decision-making that was detailed in general terms above. This restricted circle of policymaking responsibility interacted with the personalized structure of power in Doha to enable a sudden shift in direction without having to filter proposals through layers of bureaucracy or seek legislative approval. Qatar's small size was also a factor that played to its advantage as it meant there were fewer vested interests or competing factions within policymaking circles than in larger polities such as Saudi Arabia at that time. This was connected to the second explanation for Qatar's greater freedom of action, namely the lack of domestic constraints on policymakers as described above. Elite decision-making structures unencumbered by significant domestic demands greatly facilitated the reorientation of Qatari policy after January 2011. Together, they intersected with the third factor, which was that the early 'direction of travel' of the Arab uprisings aligned with the grandiose international 'branding' of Qatar as an innovative and dynamic new actor in the Middle East seeking a global stage to announce itself as such.[24]

The Arab Spring provided an opportunity for Qatari leaders to mark themselves and their country as distinct from more obviously authoritarian counterparts across the region, and to make a high-profile stand for 'universal norms' such as political and human rights and freedom of expression, at a minimal apparent cost to themselves. The same went for Al Jazeera, which experienced its CNN-style 'breakout moment' with

[22] Lynch, M. (2013). *The Arab Uprising: The Unfinished Revolutions of the New Middle East*. New York: Public Affairs (p. 90).

[23] Ibid.

[24] Ulrichsen, K.C. (2014). Qatar and the Arab Spring: Policy Drivers and Regional Implications. *Carnegie Endowment for International Peace*, Paper 224 (p. 10).

its no-holds-barred coverage of the latter stages of the Egyptian revolution and the subsequent uprising against Colonel Gaddafi's dictatorial regime in Libya. During the first few giddy weeks of the Arab Spring, when for a time at least it seemed that virtually anything might be possible, it seemed that the whole world was watching Al Jazeera. Through its association with Qatar, this effectively meant that the emirate was able to shape some of the narratives emerging within and about the Arab Spring.

The combination of these abovementioned factors allowed Qatari officials to view the Arab Spring more of an opportunity rather than a challenge. Having just, one month earlier, astounded international opinion by winning the race to host the 2022 FIFA World Cup, Qatar's name recognition and confidence was at its peak. The projection of influence took place both directly, through the words and actions of Qatari leaders and indirectly, through Al Jazeera's coverage of the uprisings. The result was that, especially during the chaotic early months of the Arab Spring, Qatari diplomacy was at the forefront of attempts to bring together the regional and international dimensions of policy responses to the Arab Spring, as both the Emir and the Prime Minister vocally championed an approach that prioritized 'Arab solutions to Arab issues,' especially during the run-up to the multinational intervention in Libya in March 2011.[25]

Both Qatar and the UAE participated alongside NATO and other non-NATO forces in the No-Fly Zone in Libya that was set up in March 2011 and culminated in the ousting of Colonel Gaddafi by Libyan militia forces in August 2011 and his grisly death two months later. Emirati leaders nevertheless approached the Arab Spring—and the Libyan intervention—from a standpoint that was virtually diametrically opposed to their Qatari counterparts. Jean-Marc Rickli observed the Emirati response to the Arab Spring from the vantage point of a post at the Institute for International and Civil Security at Khalifa University in Abu Dhabi and argued that

> the fall of Mubarak in Egypt was a wake-up call…that traditional Western support could no longer be taken for granted and that more efforts would

---

[25] Ulrichsen, K.C. (2016). The Rationale and Implications of Qatar's Intervention in Libya. In Dag Henriksen and Ann Karin Larsen (eds.). *Political Rationale and International Consequences of the War in Libya*. Oxford: Oxford University Press (p. 123).

have to be invested in managing their strategic alliances while at the same time taking care of their own security.[26]

Rickli—who moved from the UAE to a post based at Qatar's Joint Command Staff College in 2013—argued also that the budding rivalry between the UAE and Qatar—which grew exponentially between 2011 and 2013—added another dimension to the UAE's decision to join the Libyan No-Fly Zone to at least reciprocate.[27]

Under the firm leadership of Crown Prince Mohammed bin Zayed Al Nahyan of Abu Dhabi, the authorities in Abu Dhabi adopted a 'zero-tolerance' approach toward the Arab Spring and the prospect of protests domestically as well as regionally. Mohammed bin Zayed's task was facilitated by the decline of his older half-brother, UAE President Sheikh Khalifa bin Zayed Al Nahyan, who suffered a debilitating stroke in January 2014 and withdrew from public life, and the consolidation of Abu Dhabi's financial influence across the UAE after the 2008 global financial crisis, which hit Dubai especially hard. The death in October 2010 of Ras al-Khaimah's longstanding ruler, Sheikh Saqr bin Mohammed Al Qassimi, also became important in retrospect as it removed the protection hitherto provided by the veteran sheikh to adherents of a local Islamist organization in the UAE loosely linked to the Muslim Brotherhood. Taken together, these developments meant there were far fewer constraints to the rise of a hard-security 'clique' clustered around Mohammed bin Zayed as the Arab Spring unfolded.[28]

Although the significance of Sheikh Saqr's death only became clear in retrospect, the fact that it took place less than three months before the onset of the Arab Spring removed a significant obstacle to the State Security's subsequent decision to dismantle *Al-Islah*, the Ras al-Khaimah based Islamist group, once and for all. Evidence also began to accumulate during 2010 that members of *Al-Islah* were attempting to break out

---

[26] Rickli, J.-M. (2016). The Political Rationale and Implications of the United Arab Emirates' Military Involvement in Libya. In Dag Henriksen and Ann Karin Larsen (eds.). *Political Rationale and International Consequences of the War in Libya*. Oxford: Oxford University Press (pp. 146–147).

[27] Ibid., pp. 147–148.

[28] Ulrichsen, K.C. (2016). Evolving Power Dynamics in the United Arab Emirates. *Houston Chronicle*, 1 March 2016. https://blog.chron.com/bakerblog/2016/03/evolving-power-dynamics-in-the-united-arab-emirates/.

of their long-held stronghold in Ras al-Khaimah and lay the foundations for a national campaign that would focus on social and political issues in the UAE. A Public Relations Committee in Ras al-Khaimah attempted to coordinate the actions of members and sympathizers across the seven emirates and reach out to the broader Emirati community. At around the same time, moreover, members of *Al-Islah* began to get involved in calls for political reform and agitate increasingly openly for a widening of the democratic opening initiated in 2006.[29] Thus, several members of the Public Relations Committee were heavily involved in the preparation of a petition submitted to the UAE President, Sheikh Khalifa bin Zayed, on March 3, 2011. Signed by 133 Emirati individuals, including many members of *Al-Islah*, the two articles in the petition called for elections to the Federal National Council (FNC) and for the body to be granted regulatory and supervisory powers.[30]

Beginning in 2011 but escalating in 2012, the UAE authorities arrested dozens of people whom they suspected of harboring Islamist sympathies and placed 94 of them on a mass trial in 2013 that found 69 of them guilty of attempting to overthrow the government and given jail sentences that ranged from seven to fifteen years without the right to appeal.[31] Simultaneously, senior Emirati officials portrayed the UAE as standing on the frontline of a regionwide campaign against the Muslim Brotherhood. The charge against *Al-Islah* and other groups perceived to be linked to the Muslim Brotherhood was led by the outspoken director general of the Dubai Police Force, General Dhahi Khalfan Tamim. In March 2012 Tamim suggested (without providing supporting evidence) that he had information about a Brotherhood plot to take control of the Gulf monarchies: *"My sources say the next step is to make Gulf governments figurehead bodies only without actual ruling. The start will be in Kuwait in 2013 and in other Gulf states in 2016."*[32] Remarkably, Tamim

[29] Author Interviews, December 2015.

[30] Freer, C. (2015). The Muslim Brotherhood in the Emirates: Anatomy of a Crackdown. *Middle East Eye*, 17 December 2015. http://www.middleeasteye.net/essays/muslim-brotherhood-emirates-anatomy-crackdown-1009823835.

[31] Anon. (2013). UAE Sentences 69 in Al-Islah Trial. *Gulf States Newsletter*, 37:950, 4 July 2013 (pp. 7–8).

[32] Anon. (2012). Islamists Plot Against Gulf, Says Dubai Police Chief. *AFP*, 25 March 2012. https://gulfnews.com/news/gulf/kuwait/islamists-plot-against-gulf-dubai-police-chief-1.999524.

also suggested, "*they* [the Muslim Brotherhood] *are also secret soldiers for America and they are executing plans to create tension.*"[33]

In late-2012, after major political protests in Kuwait over a change to the electoral law, the UAE foreign minister, Sheikh Abdullah bin Zayed Al Nahyan denounced the Brotherhood as "*an organization which encroaches upon the sovereignty and integrity of nations*" and called upon fellow ruling families in the Gulf to join a coordinated crackdown on the group.[34] In yet another interview in 2012, Dhahi Khalfan Tamim warned that "*if the Muslim Brotherhood threatens the Gulf's security, the blood that will flow will drown them.*"[35] Tamim subsequently returned to the anti-Brotherhood theme in April 2013 when he labeled them 'dictators' and added that "*they want to change regimes that have been ruling for a long time, but they also want to rule forever ... We have evidence this group was planning to overthrow rulers in the Gulf region.*"[36]

In this atmosphere of deep polarization, a regional 'rivalry' between the UAE and Qatar took root as officials in Doha and Abu Dhabi competed for influence and supported very different groups in the post-transition political reordering. This was most immediately apparent in Libya, where both the UAE and Qatar provided critical Arab support to the NATO-led military intervention, and in Egypt, where the turbulent period of post-Mubarak politics presented policymakers with the UAE with an initial challenge in the form of a Muslim Brotherhood government in Cairo backed heavily by Qatar. Once, however, the presidency of Mohammed Morsi was ousted by a military coup led by General Abdel-Fatah al-Sisi in July 2013, the UAE—and Saudi Arabia—responded quickly to mobilize large amounts of political and financial support that far exceeded Qatar's support to the Morsi government. Significantly, Saudi Arabia joined with the UAE to slam shut the participatory windows that had opened in Egypt in 2011 and, after Salman succeeded Abdullah as King in January 2015 a close relationship developed

[33] Ibid.

[34] Black, I. (2013). Emirati Nerves Rattled by Islamists' Rise. *The Guardian*, 12 October 2013.   https://www.theguardian.com/world/on-the-middle-east/2012/oct/12/uae-muslimbrotherhood-egypt-arabspring.

[35] Gresh, A. (2015). Dubai's Police Chief Speaks Out. *Le Monde Diplomatique*, 19 May 2015. https://mondediplo.com/outsidein/dubai-s-police-chief-speaks-out.

[36] Brotherhood Sowing Subversion in Gulf States. *Reuters*, 3 April 2013. https://www.jpost.com/Middle-East/Muslim-Brotherhood-sowing-subversion-in-Gulf-states-308530.

between Mohammed bin Zayed in Abu Dhabi and Prince (later Crown Prince) Mohammed bin Salman in Riyadh.[37]

REGIONAL POWER PLAYS AND THE QATAR CRISES

Both rounds of the Qatar dispute—the nine-month withdrawal of the Saudi, Bahraini, and Emirati Ambassadors from Doha in 2014 and the later blockade that began in 2017—have demolished any remaining notion of a common threat perception in Gulf security. The legacies of the 2014 and 2017 ruptures are both profound and polarizing at the level of individual states as well as for the GCC as an organization. The hardening of positions and creation of a 'zero-sum' mentality has occurred as mutual trust and confidence has been decimated. Qataris rightly question how and why they could rebuild faith in their immediate neighbors while the leaders of the 'GCC-3' in Manama, Abu Dhabi, and Riyadh have convinced themselves of Qatar's bad faith in negotiating agreements to resolve bilateral tensions. Officials in the GCC, moreover, have failed to prevent three member-states turning against a fourth for the second time in little more than three years, and have been conspicuously absent from every stage of the current crisis since it erupted in May–June 2017.[38]

The 2014 rift in the GCC began in March as Saudi Arabia and the UAE declared the Muslim Brotherhood to be a terrorist organization and, along with Bahrain, withdrew their Ambassadors from Qatar on the unverified ground that they had been unable to prevent Doha from agreeing "*on a unified policy...to ensure non-interference, directly or indirectly, in the internal affairs of any member state*" of the GCC. In addition, the trio claimed also—citing the Qatari leadership's perceived support for Muslim Brotherhood affiliates in Syria and North Africa but without providing any actual evidence to back up their rhetorical assertion—that they had appealed to Doha "*not to support any party*

[37] Bianco, C. and Stansfield, G. (2018). The Intra-GCC Crises: Mapping GCC Fragmentation After 2011. *International Affairs*, 94:3 (p. 634).

[38] Ulrichsen, K.C. (2018). The Gulf Impasse's One-Year Anniversary and the Changing Regional Dynamics. *Gulf International Forum*, 30 May 2018. https://gulfif.com/the-gulf-impasse/.

aiming to threaten security and stability" in the Gulf.[39] Three months earlier, in late-November 2013, King Abdullah of Saudi Arabia had pressured Qatar's young new Emir, Sheikh Tamim bin Hamad Al Thani, to sign a document pledging 'non-interference' in neighboring countries' affairs and to 'change Qatar's ways' in a regional power play unprecedented—at that time—in the modern history of the Gulf States.[40]

The 2014 diplomatic spat lasted nine months until it was resolved by an agreement in late-November in which Qatar made several concessions and the three GCC states agreed to return their Ambassadors to Doha in time for the annual GCC Summit set to take place there in December. The concessions included the relocation of several Egyptian members of the Muslim Brotherhood to Turkey and the removal of two Emirati dissidents who had been given refuge in Doha after the UAE's crackdown on domestic Islamists in 2012, the closure of the Egyptian branch station of Al Jazeera, the enforcement of the GCC Internal Security Pact, which Qatar had been the first to ratify in August 2013, the dispatch in September 2015 of 1000 members of the Qatar Armed Forces to join the Saudi-led coalition in Yemen and defend the Saudi border against rebel Houthi attacks, and close cooperation with GCC partners on matters of intelligence and policing.[41] These were meaningful acts by the new Qatari leadership that exhibited a willingness to acknowledge and address the perceived grievances of its three regional adversaries, and yet still they proved insufficient to Qatar's detractors.

By the time the 2017 iteration of the row began with the renewed withdrawal of the three countries' ambassadors from Doha in June, accompanied this time by their Egyptian counterpart and an economic and trade blockade of Qatar, the so-called 'Anti-Terror Quartet' accused the Qatari leadership of violating both the spirit and the letter of the Riyadh Agreement that ended the 2014 dispute. By 2017, however,

[39] Malek, C. (2014). UAE Recalls Envoy from Qatar over 'Interference'. *The National*, 5 March 2014. https://www.thenational.ae/uae/government/uae-recalls-envoy-from-qatar-over-interference-1.452598.

[40] Stephens, M. (2017). The Arab Cold War Redux: The Foreign Policy of the Gulf Cooperation Council States Since 2011. *The Century Foundation*, 28 February 2017. https://tcf.org/content/report/arab-cold-war-redux/.

[41] Ulrichsen, K.C. (2017). Qatar: The Gulf's Problem Child. *The Atlantic*, 5 June 2017. https://www.theatlantic.com/international/archive/2017/06/qatar-gcc-saudi-arabia-yemen-bahrain/529227/.

the Saudi Arabia–Bahrain–UAE triumvirate came to perceive Qatar as a
hostile entity and direct threat to their concepts of national and regional
security. Rather than any one trigger, several factors came together to
alter the geopolitical climate in the Gulf as the new Trump administration appeared willing to pursue regional policies that aligned closely with
the interests of its declared partners in Riyadh and Abu Dhabi, due in
no small part to a concerted outreach campaign by Saudi and Emirati
leaders and their surrogates to shape the thinking of key members of the
White House team as they took office.[42]

CONCLUSION

There is therefore a need to reframe academic debates on Gulf security which have, in the past, remained heavily dependent on realist and
neorealist considerations of the balance of power and balance of threat
in the framing both of regional security agendas and subsequent policy
responses. Balance of threat theory as developed by Steven Walt held
that states would determine and modify alliances based on their threat
perception from other states, which itself was a function of aggregate
strength, geographical proximity, offensive capabilities, and offensive
intentions. Aspects of this are clearly discernible in the creation of the
GCC in May 1981 as a defensive response to the perceived threats to
regional security after the twin shocks of revolution in Iran and war with
Iraq. Balance of power and balance of threat assessments continue to feature high on national and regional security agendas in the Gulf as evi-
denced by the Saudi and UAE-led coalition that intervened militarily in
Yemen in March 2015 to prevent the further empowerment of Houthi
rebels backed ostensibly (in their view) by Iran, and in their decision to
cast their blockade of Qatar in 2017 as a response to a perceived threat
to regional security and stability.

And yet, scholars of Gulf security affairs confront a paradox whereby
regional security agendas often follow the remorseless assessment of
balance of power considerations even as decision-making structures
remains highly personalized and open to intersubjective interpretation.
The enduring dynamic among GCC states, as well as their immediate

---

[42]Butler, D. and LoBianco, T. (2018). The Princes, the President, and the Fortune
Seekers. *Associated Press*, 21 May 2018. https://www.apnews.com/a3521859cf8d4c-
199cb9a8567abd2b71/The-princes,-the-president-and-the-fortune-seekers.

neighbors Iran, Iraq, and Yemen illustrates the importance of integrating constructivist approaches to security that focus on narratives and identities in shaping and reshaping policy agendas. A constructivist approach to regional security in the Gulf encompasses the environment within which policymakers (and publics) must operate as they analyze how and why issues become constructed as threats to security or not. Reactions to the Arab Spring in 2011, the gradual disintegration of governing authority in Yemen both before and after the start of the Yemen War in 2015, and the two disputes with Qatar in 2014 and 2017 all thrust contrasting interpretations of regional stability to the forefront of policy responses to the multiple threats to regional security.

The announcement in December 2017 of a bilateral new Saudi–Emirati partnership, which met for the first time in June 2018 as the Saudi–Emirati Coordination Council, is an additional shift away from the common approach to regionwide issues that at least characterized the GCC in spirit if not always in practice. The formation of the new coordination council crystallizes the new power axis in the Gulf around a hyper-hawkish spine that runs from Riyadh to Abu Dhabi and is more exclusionary than inclusionary—to the extent that it appears to exclude Bahrain, the third Gulf member of the anti-Qatar group, entirely. Officials in Oman and Kuwait, meanwhile, acknowledge that they also could face pressure from Saudi Arabia and the UAE as they approach and eventually undergo their own transition to new leadership in coming years. Moreover, for a collection of six states that traditionally guarded their autonomy in both domestic and foreign affairs, the assertive stance of, and apparent intolerance by, the Crown Princes of Saudi Arabia and Abu Dhabi, to distinct regional approaches may well target Kuwait and Oman at some future point.[43]

Other chapters in this volume will explore the contours and dynamics of the Gulf crisis that erupted in June 2017. For the purposes of this chapter, it is sufficient to state that a breakdown of trust among the six GCC states and confidence in the GCC as an organization is likely to be generational and probably fatal to the chances of the organization re-cohering in any meaningful way. The primacy of personalized decision-making and the fact that both Qatar and Saudi Arabia are

[43] Riedel, B. (2018). Is the GCC Dead? *Al-Monitor*, 18 June 2018. https://www.al-monitor.com/pulse/originals/2018/06/gcc-dead-saudi-arabia-qatar-dispute-salman-mbs.html.

led by ruling figures in their thirties—along with the possibility that Mohammed bin Zayed may easily lead the UAE for several decades after he eventually becomes President—means the discord is likely to cast a long and bitter shadow across the Gulf. Moreover, the anger and recrimination that the crisis has created on both sides of the divide—augmented by the criminalization in Bahrain and the UAE of sympathy for Qatar—has torn at the social fabric of Gulf societies hitherto bound closely together by tribal and familial ties, and created discord, even enmities, that may persist for years, if not decades, to come.[44]

[44] Al-Serkal, M. (2017). Qatar Sympathizers to Face Fine, Jail. *Gulf Times*, 7 June 2017. https://gulfnews.com/news/uae/government/qatar-sympathisers-to-face-fine-jail-1.2039631.

CHAPTER 3

Tribe and Tribalism: The Trojan Horse of GCC States?

Maryam Al-Kuwari

INTRODUCTION

After decades of independence and state building, tribes in most countries in the Middle East were at least in theory, believed to have been subdued, losing power, and in response to the processes of modernisation, becoming part of a nostalgic past. This assumption, however, has been challenged by the events of the Arab Spring. The revival of the tribes and of bloody tribalism was ultimately a reason for concern throughout the region, even in the GCC countries which had historically adopted a transformational model where the state gradually stripped the tribe of its power and replaced it as the source of identity and the legitimate provider of security and benefits to society. As Castells (2000) argues, however, regardless of the means, all state identities are coerced at the expense of the identities that they ultimately replace.[1] Indeed, while building national identities has been a challenge that faced all

---

[1] Castells, M. (2000). Globalisation, Identity and the State. *Social Dynamics*, 26:1 (p. 7).

M. Al-Kuwari (✉)
University of Exeter, Exeter, UK
e-mail: ma592@exeter.ac.uk

© The Author(s) 2019
A. Krieg (ed.), *Divided Gulf*, Contemporary Gulf Studies,
https://doi.org/10.1007/978-981-13-6314-6_3

37

modern nation states, and a process that required decades if not centuries in the Gulf in particular, it has been a much more daunting problem.

This paper addresses several serious issues pertaining to the relationship between tribe and state in the Gulf, a region where the tribe is perceived as quasi-sacred and unquestionable. Is the tribe responsible for the failure of national identity projects in the GCC? Are tribal identities and affiliations at conflict with the nation state and its structure? Are the claims in most GCC countries that tribe and state are in harmony with each other realistic, or is the truth that the tribe constitutes a Trojan horse or perhaps an Achilles Heel for state building? Above all, where is this debate placed within the context of the Gulf Crisis between Qatar and its neighbours?

Finally, this paper argues that the revival of tribalism cannot be blamed on the tribes, but rather, on the failure of states to implement viable projects of national identities in addition to pursuing contradictory policies in this respect. Since the weakness of the state creates a power vacuum in society, it is only natural for tribes, tribalism or other source of identity to fill in this vacuum. In this respect, the siege imposed by Saudi Arabia, the UAE and Bahrain on Qatar since the onset of the Gulf Crisis in 2017 seems to be driven by the rationale that weakening and undermining the state in Qatar, combined with the fuelling of tribalism, would eventually result in state collapse and regime change from inside, allowing tribal forces loyal to Saudi Arabia to eventually assume power in Doha.

THE CHALLENGES OF THE NATIONAL IDENTITY PROJECT

Ironically, building a national identity is much more difficult and challenging than building a tribal identity. This is not surprising since the tribe constitutes a basic entity that cannot break down or disintegrate on its own, especially as it does not stand on a political structure.[2] In contrast, as Bodley argues, "*States are especially vulnerable to collapse because they contain social classes based on major inequities in wealth and power.*"[3] The vulnerability of the state to collapse is not limited to small or weak states, but it may plague any large or powerful state that fails to complete

---

[2]Bodley, J. (2017). *Cultural Anthropology: Tribes, States and the Global System.* New York: Rowman & Littlefield (p. 225).

[3]Ibid.

a resilient national identity project as the case is in Spain, which Castells describes as a nation of nationalities, often conflicting nationalities.[4]

According to Lukitz, the process of identity building in nation states depends heavily on a number of components such as the invention of a common historic necessity that transforms into the glue for the idea of the nation.[5] This process is then cemented by cultural, economic and political integration which in turn lays the ground for what becomes a common national identity for the state. Tribal, ethnic and other identities within the state, however, become secondary as the national identity dominates and becomes the leading identity of the group. The problem, however, is that *"national identity is not an irreversible process and that group identities are not unidimensional."*[6]

Moreover, the process of national identity building is in itself unstable, and this is attributed to the inherent instability and fluidity of identities in the first place. In fact, all political processes based on ethnicity and nationality may be cohesive on the one hand, but also disruptive and possibly destabilising on the other.[7] In the Gulf region, the process of building national identities was not fraught with national struggle, bloody civil wars, or other forms of conflicts that often unify groups under a common cause. Rather, it was the result of political and territorial divisions imposed by the British Empire before its withdrawal from the region in the second half of the twentieth century. In this context, building national identities was based on invented histories and traditions that aimed at achieving a unified vision of the nation. The importance of these traditions, according to Hobsbawm is that they *"seek to inculcate certain values and norms of behaviour by repetition, which automatically implies certainty with a historic past. In fact, where possible, they normally attest to establish continuity with a historic past."*[8]

Thus, building national identities in the Gulf was primarily the ability of the state to offer a new form of solidarity and cohesion within the nation state project that could in one way or another replace tribal

[4] Castells, 'Globalization' (p. 11).

[5] Lukitz, L. (1995). *Iraq: The Search for National Identity*. London: Frank Cass (p. 2).

[6] Ibid. (p. 3).

[7] Smith, A. (1996). Culture, Country and Territory: The Politics of Ethnicity and Nationalism. *International Affairs*, 72:3 (pp. 445–446).

[8] Hobsbawm, E. (1997). Introduction: Inventing Traditions. In E. Hobsbawm and T. Ranger (eds.). *The Invention of Tradition*. Cambridge: Cambridge University Press (p. 1).

identities. In a Khaldunian sense, the success of the national project required the successful erosion of tribal *"asabiya"* and its replacement with a national identity.[9] This process was facilitated by several factors such as oil wealth offered the states enormous resources, enabling them to set up social contracts with their subjects, whereby political control was left to the state while citizens enjoyed the benefits of wealth and the rentier state. Secondly, there was no direct conflict with the tribe itself throughout this process. According to Cole, the tribes of Arabia were loosely connected on the political level, using *"the idiom of kinship to explain their solidarity, recognising, however, that they are integrally part of a wider society and culture not based on kinship."*[10] Hence, even as the new states were rapidly formed, their formation did not contradict the existence of the tribes, especially as borders remained open, and tribal chiefs were kept close to the ruling families, even as the tribes gradually lost their political and economic influence throughout the process.

At least in theory, therefore, the circumstances were ideal for smooth processes of national state formation and the building of national identities in the GCC region. In practice, however, this was not the case, and to the contrary, tribalism today may be transforming into a serious threat to the future stability of GCC states.

The Revival of Tribalism in the Gulf Countries

Tribe and tribalism are two different notions. While the tribe as a concept refers to a group associated with social, cultural and other values, tribalism refers to the rise of politics of identities, which in the GCC context, takes on a tribal dimension, in addition to ethnic and sectarian dimensions. Tribalism is a form of mobilisation around a component or several components of identity, which could be kinship, ethnicity, religion, sect, and others. It may or may not be directly related to the existence of the tribe, and it goes far beyond the notion of kinship in bringing people together or separating them from others. According to Al-Ghithami (2009), tribalism is an ethnic or discriminatory notion that is essentially exclusive, thriving on the notion of group unity against

---

[9]Alshawi, A. and Gardner, A. (2013). Tribalism, Identity and Citizenship in Contemporary Qatar. *Anthropology of the Middle East*, 8:2 (p. 52).

[10]Cole, D. (1982). Tribal and Non-tribal Structures Among the Bedouin of Saudi Arabia. *Al-Abhath*, 30 (p. 79).

others, based on identities that are invented in response to new and unprecedented challenges and unknowns.[11]

In the 1960s and 1970s when most GCC states became independent, tribes were an effective component that played a critical role in the process of state formation. It was with their allegiance to the ruling families, their acceptance of the new order under the state, and their support for the national project that GCC states were formed unchallenged, especially in the cases of small entities such as Kuwait, Bahrain, Qatar and the UAE. Moreover, the fluidity and looseness of tribal connections across borders enabled the states to develop their political structures without any real opposition from the tribes.[12] However, this process may not have been as smooth or effective as it may have been previously assumed.

Shortly after the countries of the GCC region had become independent, new serious threats emerged with the end of British protection, specifically from two aggressive neighbours, namely Iraq and Iran. It was within this context that the GCC was formed both as an organisation and as a project for a new regional identity that applied to those countries that were under British protection, and which shared more or less similar social and economic characteristics, most notably tribal associations and rentierism. The so-called *Khaleeji* identity developed at a time when the nations of the region were preoccupied with building their national identities and state institutions. Suddenly, the GCC structure and the regional identity project were introduced, possibly disrupting the national projects and creating an imaginary world in which these nations were all unified as one against the world. Al-Ghithami argues that the invented *Khaleeji* identity was no more than an exaggerated illusion that was born out of oil flux.[13] It seemed, therefore, as if two contradictory projects were at work at the same time in the region in the late 1970s and early 1980s. On the one hand, there was the national state project in which every GCC state sought to invent its national identity and impose its legitimacy over its society and territory, but at the same time, these same states were committed to a regional project in which one *Khaleeji* identity was celebrated and where national borders and differences were

[11] Al-Ghithami, A. (2009). *Tribe and Tribalism or Postmodern Identities* [translated by author]. Casablanca, Morocco: Arab Cultural Center.

[12] Eickelman. D. (2016). Tribes and Tribal Identity in the Arab Gulf States. In J.E. Peterson (ed.). *The Emergence of the Gulf States*. London: Bloomsbury (pp. 223–240).

[13] Al-Ghithami, 'Tribe and Tribalism' (p. 231).

claimed to be meaningless. In this context, Mutairi argues that national identities in the GCC region could not be justified, particularly with the innovation and promotion of the *Khaleeji* identity, and the open border policy among GCC states.[14]

Another factor that further complicated the efforts of the states in the region to build national identities was the timing. The 1980s, just when most of these states were still struggling with nation building, national ideals and values, and the promises of modernisation, the optimism of the middle class was in crisis and decline in many parts of the world.[15] Although the middle class in the Gulf countries was in fact thriving at the time, the loss of optimism and the unprecedented fear of the unknown that accompanied the postmodern world quickly revealed itself in the form of rising tribalism in these countries.[16]

In the 1990s, the revival of tribalism became common across the GCC. Families, for example, started to research their tribal and family trees, and tribal signs became all too common and obvious in schools, at social events, and even on the streets as car owners placed their tribal symbols on their car plates, in a way proclaiming their identities for protection against their fellow citizens who did not share the same tribal affiliation, but at the same time, reviving the ancient tribal practice of branding livestock as a sign of ownership and protection.[17]

Ironically, many of these identities were actually invented rather than revived, and it was not uncommon for individuals and families to associate themselves with a certain tribe or to even invent a tribal affiliation in Gulf countries to avoid being left out. This trend was quickly embraced in the cultural arena with the organisation of poetry contests among tribes as well as camel and horse contests. While these were perceived as some form of cultural revival and richness, they often turned into a source of tensions among contesting tribes and groups.[18] Ironically, Gulf States embraced tribal revival and even encouraged and financed its social

---

[14] Mutairi, H. (2011). Slaves Without Chains. Liberty and Identity Crisis in the Gulf & Arab Peninsula [My Translation]. *Unpublished Manuscript.*

[15] Al-Ghithami, 'Tribe and Tribalism' (p. 225).

[16] Ibid. (p. 213).

[17] Ibid. (p. 226).

[18] Ibid. (p. 230).

and cultural activities.[19] For example, the state in Qatar encouraged the tribes to participate in the National Day celebrations in which the tribes competed to show off their power, difference and identities.[20] While the National Day celebrations intended to commemorate the unification of the country and to fortify national unity, it actually became a source of identity-based tensions and a means of undermining nation building altogether. More dangerously, rather than bring citizens closer to the state away from any other loyalties, the revival of tribalism in Qatar only cemented the idea that

> power in contemporary Qatar comes, in part, from the size and strength of the tribe, for that power yields access to government positions, state-controlled resources, land, both elected and appointed positions, and much more.[21]

RISING TRIBALISM OR WEAKENING STATES?

Whereas scholars may agree that the tribe has lost most of its political and economic relevance during the process of state building, the strong emergence of tribalism seems to imply otherwise. However, it may be misleading to argue that the tribe naturally constitutes a threat to the state or that the tribe is positioned in opposition to the state by default. Peterson, for example, argues that the GCC countries have successfully transformed from a platform of tribe opposed to the state to one in which the tribe coexists successfully within the state.[22] This claim holds true to a great extent, specifically in the sense that since independence, tribes have not openly or seriously challenged the role or legitimacy of the modern state in the GCC region. A few notable exceptions such as al-Ghufran clan of Bani Murra tribe in Qatar who were involved in conspiring for a coup d'état with Saudi involvement in 1996.[23] The state

[19] Khalaf, S. (2000). Politics and Policies of Newly Invented Traditions in the Gulf: Camel Racing in the United Arab Emirates. *Ethnology*, 39:3 (p. 256).

[20] Al-Shawi and Gardner, 'Tribalism, Identity & Citizenship' (p. 56).

[21] Ibid. (pp. 56–57).

[22] Peterson, J. (2018). Tribe and State in the Contemporary Arabian Peninsula. London School of Economics, *MEC Blog*. Available at http://blogs.lse.ac.uk/mec/2018/07/12/tribe-and-state-in-the-contemporary-arabian-peninsula/.

[23] Patrick, N. (2012). Nationalism in the Gulf States. In D. Held and K. Ulrichsen (eds.). *The Transformation of the Gulf: Politics, Economics & the Global Order*. London: Routledge (p. 56).

retaliated against the clan by stripping about 5000 clan members of their nationality, firing them from state jobs, depriving them from state services, and eventually forcing them to take refuge in Saudi Arabia where the bigger extended Bani Murra tribe resides. Although the majority of the clan members eventually regained their citizenship and benefits,[24] this was an example of the threat that the tribe can pose to the state, but also an illustration of the power of the state to impose its sovereignty, will and power over the state.

Overall, however, although the tribe has lost much of its power, the power of tribal identities is relative. Patrick argues that the blame for the strength of tribal identities at the expense of national identities falls squarely on the weakness of the state, not only in the GCC region, but across the Arab world. As a result, members of the elite tend to affiliate themselves with the state whereas most of the population tends to search for alternative affiliations and identities that eventually compete with the national identity. The project for building national identities in the region, moreover, has often depended on the ability of the state to provide, distribute, and share wealth with citizens, thus making the concept of citizenship on accessing wealth and resources.[25]

Hence, the national identity project in the GCC was from the beginning weak and incomplete, relying mostly on the ability of the state to control and distribute wealth, and to provide welfare to its citizens. To a great extent, this constituted the core of the social contract between the state and society after independence. While this social contract may have worked effectively to maintain national identities, this may no longer be sufficient today, especially as the social contract comes under tremendous pressure[26]: population growth, continuous fluctuations in oil revenues, growing demand for development and political participation, and the failure to diversify oil-dependent economies have all contributed to adding pressure on the social contract, thus further straining the ability of

[24] National Human Rights Committee. (2006). Annual Report for Human Rights in Qatar. *National Human Rights Committee.*

[25] Kinninmont, J. (2013). Citizenship in the Gulf. In A. Echague (ed.). *The Gulf States and Arab Uprisings.* Spain: Fride & Gulf Research Centre (pp. 52–54).

[26] Diwan, K. (2016). Gulf Societies in Transition: National Identity and National Projects in the Arab Gulf States. Workshop Report #13. *The Arab Gulf States Institute in Washington* (p. 5).

the state to build a national identity,[27] or as Peterson accurately puts it, "*the fraying of the social contract*" in the Gulf countries.[28]

The traditional response of GCC states in the face of demands for political and other forms of participation has often been to continue bribing their citizens and populations with additional sharing of wealth and other contributions,[29] a policy that is becoming increasingly difficult with declining oil prices. Moreover, as GCC countries have been forced to impose taxes for the first time since independence,[30] this will ultimately undermine the current model on which the social contract has rested for decades, specifically its fundamental pillar that holds "no taxation without representation."[31]

Imposing taxes, a strained social contract, and declining benefits derived from this social contract, are all factors that could likely contribute to further state weakness and a stronger growth of tribalism. Although tribalism cannot and does not present itself as a serious threat to the state in the Gulf at present, this in no way implies that tribalism cannot transform itself into a violent political form of political ethnicity, especially at times of sudden political crises or transformations. Examples of such possibilities were seen to some extent in Yemen, but more evidently in Iraq, Syria and Libya where the sudden challenge or collapse of the national identity and project quickly gave way to the rise of violent and divisive tribalism that eventually led to the complete collapse of the state. In fact, predicting the potential trajectory of tribalism in the Gulf region is simply impossible for two reasons as Tapper points out. First, because tribes have defied the logic that has prevailed for decades, when most scholars from various disciplines discounted tribalism and considered it to be a notion that belongs to the past. Secondly and more importantly perhaps is the fact that tribes are fluid and are not necessarily

[27] Kechichian, J. (2001). Unity on the Arabian Peninsula. In J. Kechichian (ed.). *Iran, Iraq and the Arab Gulf States*. New York: Palgrave (p. 296).

[28] Peterson, J. (2012). *The GCC States: Participation, Opposition, and the Fraying of the Social Contract*. London: Kuwait Programme on Development, Governance and Globalisation in the Gulf States.

[29] Ross, M. (2011). Will Oil Drown the Arab Spring? Democracy and the Resource Curse. *Foreign Affairs*, 90:5 (p. 4).

[30] Osborne, S. (2015). Six Gulf States Will Start Taxing People for the First Time. *The Independent*, 10 December 2015.

[31] Althani, M. (2012). *The Arab Spring and the Gulf States: Time to Embrace Change*. Suffolk: Profile Books (p. 6).

limited to genealogical characteristics, and this is evident from the fact that new tribal identities and alliances can quickly form on political bases.[32]

While it may be easy to point at tribes and tribalism as the danger that lurks within, the fact is that tribalism is simply filling in the vacuum left by states which in many ways have been reduced to bureaucracies that control power in one way or another. Absent any serious attempts to reform the state and to develop real projects for national identities in the region, Gulf States may sooner or later find themselves facing a real threat to their stability as oil prices continue to fluctuate, especially in the event of low oil prices over extended periods of time.[33]

An Enemy Within?

Apart from the challenging realities facing the states in the Gulf, the policies of Gulf States may have also contributed to the strengthening tribalism as a form of socio-political activism and mobilisation on the basis of a modern *asabiya*.[34] This new form of *asabiya* is repeatedly manifested whenever GCC states face a crisis, and it was particularly evident during the crisis between Qatar and its neighbours. With the absence of transparency or knowledge on policy making or decision making, citizens are mobilised through traditional and social media, blindly following trends and making uninformed political expressions. As harmless as such processes may seem to be, they are in fact reinforcing the norms and practices of a tribal form of populism in a region where state stability is at best precarious. Weiner has reflected to the political dimension of kinship, arguing that the boundaries of kinship are fluid and dependent on political and social contexts, further adding that

> Kinship is not merely a historical vestige or catchall for explaining political eccentricities of the Gulf region. Rather, it is an active part of regional

[32]Tapper, R. (2018). Tribalism in Middle Eastern States: A 21st Century Anachronism. *London School of Economics, MEC Blog.* Available at http://blogs.lse.ac.uk/mec/2018/07/11/tribalism-in-middle-eastern-states-a-twenty-first-century-anachronism/.

[33]Vohra, R. (2017). The Impact of Oil Prices on GCC Economies. *International Journal of Business and Social Science,* 8:2 (p. 12).

[34]Al-Khater, A. (2017). Gulf States: Between the Choices of the State, the Tribe or the Band. *Al-Watan Newspaper,* 27 May 2017.

politics that shapes the behaviour of members of Gulf Arab societies, including their leadership.[35]

The real danger posed by tribalism in the Middle East is that the tribe has maintained legitimacy at a time when the state struggles to maintain its legitimacy. As such, tribalism seems to offer the tribe as a viable alternative to the failing state.[36] Ironically, it seems that Gulf States are fully aware of this problem, but instead of exploring ways to reinforce the state and its legitimacy, a few of them have not hesitated to exploit tribalism to attain political gains at the expense of their neighbours, specifically by attempting to take advantage of the fact that identities in the Gulf are not static, but rather, subject to change, transformation and even manipulation. Prior to the Gulf Crisis in 2017, Saudi Arabia has in fact attempted to exploit tribalism to undermine neighbours and attain political influence over them. This was particularly pursued through financial payoffs to tribes that share kinship with Saudi counterparts. Historically, this approach was used with neighbouring countries where Saudi Arabia wished to instigate or exploit tribal tensions against neighbouring governments, especially in Yemen and Jordan.[37] The same tactic was also applied during the Syrian uprising when Saudi Arabia provided both financial and military aid to tribes with kinship ties in Saudi Arabia as part of its efforts to undermine the Syrian regime.[38] Saudi Arabia's attempts to manipulate and exploit tribal relations has also been repeatedly seen in neighbouring Qatar where Saudis have attempted not only to instigate division within the ruling family, but also to turn other tribes against the Qatari state as was the case with al-Ghufran clan in the 1990s and on a number of other occasions.[39]

Since the eruption of the Gulf Crisis in 2017, both Saudi Arabia and the United Arab Emirates have actively organised tribal rallies and

---

[35] Weiner, S. (2016). Kinship Politics in the Gulf Arab States. *The Arab Gulf States Institute*, Issue Paper #7 (pp. 1–2).

[36] Ibid.

[37] Patrick, N. (2016). Saudi Arabia and Jordan. In N. Patrick (ed.). *Saudi Arabian Foreign Policy: Conflict & Cooperation*. New York: I.B. Taurus.

[38] Robertson, N. (2012). Saudi Support for Syrian Rebels Shaped by Tribal, Religious Ties. *CNN*, 20 August 2012.

[39] Dorsey, J. (2017). Saudi–UAE Push to Mobilise Tribes Against Qatari Emir. *International Policy Digest*, 20 November 2017.

conferences involving members of Al-Murra and Al-Hajri, both which are large tribes in Qatar with significant tribal extensions into neighbouring countries. One of the massive rallies was organised in September 2017, was attended by a few Qatari members of al-Murra tribe who were expelled from Qatar in 2017 for expressing support for Saudi Arabia during the crisis. Most of the attendees, however, were Saudi members of the tribe, expressing solidarity for their brethren and tribal cohesion.[40] At the same time, members of al-Murra and other tribes in Qatar quickly responded by reaffirming their loyalty to the state of Qatar and to the Emir.[41]

For decades, the question of al-Murra tribe, the loyalty of its members, and the attempt to exploit it against the state in Qatar have been recurring themes that only emerge whenever tensions break out between Saudi Arabia and Qatar.[42] Such efforts by Saudi Arabia are not surprising, since many members of al-Ghufran clan of al-Murra were in the security and armed forces, and their loyalty were to former Emir Khalifa who lost power in 1995 to his son Emir Hamad bin Khalifa. Their involvement in a failed coup to return Emir Khalifa to power in 1996 was not only driven by their loyalty to the emir, but also by the ability of the Saudi government at the time to mobilise and organise them as part of the failed coup attempt.[43]

The Saudi and Emirati efforts to fuel tribal tensions and divisions, however, seem to have failed with the tribes in Qatar renewing their allegiance to the state. However, the mere attempt to exploit tribalism reveals a more troubling issue. First, it reveals that even at policymaking levels within Gulf States, there are policymakers who believe that tribalism can undermine the state, otherwise, Saudi Arabia and the UAE would not have resorted to such a strategy in the first place. Secondly, it seems to suggest that policymakers at some level, seem to assume that they can freely use and exploit tribalism to their advantage without any consequences.

---

[40] Egypt Today. (2017). Tamim Is Destroying the Qatari Social Fabric: Al-Murrah Tribe. *Egypt Today*, 2 September 2017.

[41] Al-Murra tribe in Qatar Reaffirms Loyalty to Emir. *Qatar Tribune*, 18 June 2017.

[42] Majdi, W. (2017). The Case of Al-Murra Between Qatar and Saudi Arabia. *Masr al-Arabia*, 19 September 2017.

[43] Al-Hakeem, M. (2005). Thousands in Saudi Arabia After Losing Citizenship. *Gulf News*, 1 August 2005.

However, while playing the card of tribalism may be tempting and possibly effective in destabilising neighbouring countries, it can be a dangerous card to play. Tribalism, like any other identity construct, is volatile and cannot be controlled in the long term, and it can easily spill over across borders. In the 1980s for example, Saudi Arabia supported and financed Islamist jihadi groups which eventually formed their own version of tribalism and returned to wreak havoc in Saudi Arabia itself as well as in other Gulf countries.[44] Similarly, as history has shown repeatedly, it may be easy to initiate the manipulation of tribal identities, but the final outcomes are impossible to guarantee[45] After all, tribalism is neither fixed nor static, and it cannot be easily controlled since it is a cognitive way of perceiving the world. When tribalism thrives in weak states, it does so to the extent that it becomes a source of threat to the stability and continuity of the state.[46] By attempting to exploit tribalism to destabilise the political orders of neighbouring nations, a country such Saudi Arabia, which already suffers serious socio-economic challenges as well as domestic divisions and a weak state, can find itself unwittingly importing tribalism to undermine its own political system and possibly its social fabric.

CONCLUSION

Tribes continue to constitute a basic component in GCC countries, and despite the onslaught on their political and economic power and influence since independence, tribes have remained vital and vibrant, especially as they successfully maintained their legitimacy as social actors. Moreover, although the political role of the tribe has been substantially reduced in most GCC countries, this does not in any way imply an end to the political role or involvement of tribes. To the contrary, as events in Libya, Yemen, Iraq and Syria have indicated, tribes can rapidly be mobilised to become active political actors with the capacity to be involved in violent conflict and struggle for power. One advantage that tribes enjoy this respect is their ability to flexibly expand their boundaries of

[44] Hubbard, B. (2016). Saudi Arabia, Blamed for Spawning Jihadists, Is Again Their Target. *The New York Times*, 6 July 2016.

[45] Castells, 'Globalization' (p. 11).

[46] Kao, K. (2015). Do Jordanian Tribes Challenge or Strengthen the State? *Washington Post*, 28 May 2015.

affiliation to include members and allies without being restricted by the limitations of genealogy and kinship. Tribes also seem to have developed the ability to harness and garner power political influence through mobilisation based on identity. Under certain circumstances, it seems that groups such as tribes can generate more legitimacy than states in the eyes of population segments, particularly at times of crisis, when the social contract suffers severe constraints, or when the state is no longer able to deliver its side of the bargain to the population. The combination of such alleged legitimacy and the ability of tribes to mobilise can turn tribes into a real source of threat to the state.[47]

Despite these characteristics and capabilities, this does not warrant branding the tribe as a Trojan horse or as an insidious threat to the integrity, stability and legitimacy of the state, at least not in an absolute sense that pits the tribe against the state in a struggle for power. The involvement of tribes and emergence of tribalism in conflicts in the Middle East has generally been seen in countries where the state has become too weak or has reached the verge of failure. The disintegration of the state or its inability to maintain its legitimacy, and the failure of national identity projects seem to be the precursors to the involvement of tribes in conflict against the state, but it appears that this is only a means by which societies attempt to replace a failed political actor with another. This does not exclude the possibility of a political re-emergence of tribalism in the GCC region. To the contrary, several indicators suggest that this could be the case.

To start with, the state in the GCC region is struggling to develop and implement national identities and state building projects. Add to this, the confusion arising from the invention of the *khaleeji* identity which has undermined national identities but at the same time failed to represent a real alternative, and the emergence of new tribalisms based on ideology as the case is with Islamist and jihadi groups, have also contributed to the stagnation of national identity projects across the Gulf region.

Yet, it has been the weakness of the state itself as an institution and as a political structure that possibly represents the biggest threat for the state in the Gulf. The major weakness of the state has been its failure to

---

[47]This seems to be the case specifically in weak states, failed states, and in states suffering or heading to civil war. For more, see Osaghae (2009), Barfield (2004), Bellina et al. (2009), Duyvesten (2017).

achieve economic diversity and social justice, and this in turn has made it almost impossible for the state to maintain the social contract that was established at independence. The failure of Gulf states to diversify their economies implies that they will remain hostages to oil prices, which makes their promise to share wealth, give handouts maintain a welfare state in return for allegiance and order very unlikely in the long term. The fact that Gulf States have started to introduce taxation to cover their budgetary deficits without offering any opportunities for political participation represents a serious violation of the social contract and is basically a deal that is impossible for Gulf societies to accept in the long term as the state cuts back on the benefits it offers.

With their legitimacy already facing mounting challenges, the fundamental pillars of their social contract undermined, growing pressures for reforms and political participation, and the looming regional chaos that is taking identity-based politics and conflicts to unprecedented levels, the future of the state in the Gulf region is in dire straits. It is under these circumstances and in the face of all these weaknesses that the tribe becomes a potentially threatening challenge for the state as an alternative form of socio-political organisation.

Not so long ago, the states in the GCC deliberately fed and fuelled tribalism in the hope that this could bestow legitimacy on these states. More recently, Saudi Arabia and other GCC States also attempted to manipulate tribes and tribalism in other countries in the region to gain power within ongoing regional conflicts, particularly at present as Saudi Arabia and the UAE have attempted to mobilise and fuel tribalism in Qatar in the hope of undermining the state and toppling the government there. Regardless whether such efforts and involvement achieve their goals, fuelling tribalism in this form is akin to unleashing a genie across a region where states are weak, and their legitimacy is increasingly questioned as the social contracts on which they rest are faltering. This could create a backlash that will not spare any of the states in the Gulf. As such, treating tribalism as an Achilles heel or as a Trojan horse that can be exploited with no consequence is a dangerous strategy, because it is more likely that tribalism is in fact a ticking time bomb which can explode with serious implications for the entire region.

CHAPTER 4

Bitter Brethren: Freud's Narcissism of Minor Differences and the Gulf Divide

Mohammed Hashem Al-Hashemi

INTRODUCTION

I was on a break with a European friend when the news broke that Saudi Arabia had decided to go ahead with its plans to dig a 60-km-long water canal to transform its neighbour Qatar from a peninsula into an island. My European friend's reaction was one of disbelief before he remarked, "No offense to you, but I still cannot understand this, and I cannot even tell a Saudi from a Qatari." Hours later, I was still reflecting on my European friend's remarks, and I could not but agree with him since the countries of the Gulf Cooperation Council (GCC), in general, have so much in common on the ethnic, historic, cultural, and political levels to the point that they are often perceived as one culture in the eyes of outsiders.

Regardless of how serious the Saudi announcement may have been, it was significantly symbolic on two levels. On one level, it reflected the intense nature of the conflict between Saudi Arabia and its allies on the one hand, and Qatar on the other. On a more relevant level, the planned geographic separation aimed at reinforcing the perception that Qatar no longer belonged to the in-group in the GCC, and that it was a different other, perhaps even a physically and geographically separate other.

M. H. Al-Hashemi (✉)
Brunel University, London, UK

© The Author(s) 2019
A. Krieg (ed.), *Divided Gulf*, Contemporary Gulf Studies,
https://doi.org/10.1007/978-981-13-6314-6_4

As surprising as the aggressive nature of the Saudi declared plan may seem to be, especially to observers from outside the Gulf region, the fact is that it may not be too unusual in the context of conflicts among close neighbours and related nations. Civil wars, for example, tend to be extremely and shockingly intense. This seems to sharply contrast with conventional wisdom and the general theory of power and violence which stipulate that conflict is more likely between nations, groups, and cultures that share very little in common. This conventional perspective was perhaps best developed by Samuel Huntington in his book, the *Clash of Civilizations* in which he highlighted the rift in major conflicts along civilizational and cultural lines. On the other hand, while Sigmund Freud never developed a real theory on this type of conflict, he attempted to explain the causes of intensity in conflicts between closely related groups on the basis of what he referred to as the narcissism of minor differences (NMD).

The first section in this chapter will discuss and evaluate Freud's propositions and reflect on the extent to which it may be useful in explaining conflicts among neighbours. The second section discusses the theoretical potentials of this hypothesis and proposes an expanded model that accounts for the rise and role of the narcissistic leader. The last sections of the chapter apply the expanded NMD to the Gulf crisis for an understanding of the crisis.

How Far Can You Hate Your Neighbours?

According to an old Arab idiom, one must pick his neighbours before his home, and in Mark 12:31, the second commandment clearly and emphatically states, "Love your neighbour as yourself." Freud recognized the overpowering nature of such commandments, idioms, and feelings, but he also pointed out in his 1917 work *The Taboo of Virginity* that there exists a force that opposes love and which results in triggering "*the hostility which in every human relation we see fighting successfully against feelings of fellowship and overpowering the commandment that all men should love one another.*" He identified this force as the NMD, a term that he attributed to British anthropologist Ernest Crawley.[1]

---

[1] Freud, S. (1991). 'The Taboo of Virginity' [1917]. The Penguin Freud Library. In Angela Richards (ed.). Trans. James Strachey. *On Sexuality*, vol. 7 (p. 272).

In his 1921 *Group Psychology and the Analysis of the Ego* Freud referred to the behaviours of neighbouring towns and nations:

> Of two neighboring towns each is the other's most jealous rival; every little canton looks down upon the others with contempt. Closely related races keep one another at arm's length; the South German cannot endure the North German, the Englishman casts every kind of aspersion upon the Scot, the Spaniard despises the Portuguese.[2]

In later works, Freud did not add much to this hypothesis, referring to it only briefly in two other works. The first was in his famous 1930 work *Civilization & Its Discontents*:

> I gave this phenomenon the name of 'the narcissism of minor differences', a name which does not do much to explain it. We can now see that it is a convenient and relatively harmless satisfaction of the inclination to aggression, by means of which cohesion between the members of the community is made easier.[3]

Interestingly, Freud saw the NMD to be a harmless means by which individuals expressed and satisfied their inclination to aggression towards others who shared great resemblance with them. His explanation evidently is that this is necessary to keep the cohesion of a community strong vis-à-vis others.

Freud's assessment of this force as harmless may have radically changed by the time the Jews were being persecuted in Germany, and on this he argues in his 1939 work *Moses and Monotheism* that communities cannot feel complete until they have expressed hostility towards "some extraneous minority" and he goes on to explain the roots of anti-Semitism by pointing out that although the Jews seem to fit in well with the general European populations,

[2]Freud, S. (1991). 'Group Psychology and the Analysis of the Ego' [1921]. The Penguin Freud Library. In Albert Dickson (ed.). Trans. James Strachey. *Civilization, Society and Religion*, vol. 12 (pp. 130–131).

[3]Freud, S. (1991). 'Civilization and Its Discontents' [1930]. The Penguin Freud Library. In Albert Dickson (ed.). Trans. James Strachey. *Civilization, Society and Religion*, vol. 12. (pp. 304–305).

they are none the less different, often in an indefinable way different, especially from the Nordic peoples, and the intolerance of groups is often,
strangely enough, exhibited more strongly against small differences than
against fundamental ones.[4]

What Freud suggested was that sameness or the existence of minor differences between two groups may be the cause for tension between
them, the result of which is the expression of aggression that may or may
not be harmless. This force originates from the need for group cohesion,
which only seems possible with the expression of aggression or hostility towards others. Yet, while the NMD may often be harmless as Freud
originally claimed, it may also have "*a malignant potential to erupt in
vast bloodbaths which have even reached the level of genocide.*"[5]

Referring to violent conflicts in Central Asia, Turkish researcher and
political scientist Turkkaya Ataov relies on Freud's hypothesis and even
pushes it to the verge of theory, arguing

> When relations are pleasant, their desirable parts come to the fore. When
> disagreements rise, differences are then magnified. Even if there are no
> minor differences, groups tend to create them.[6]

This drive for groups to differentiate themselves from similar others
was also noted by French anthropologist Levi-Strauss who reflected on
how primitive tribes used different animal totems as symbols "*adopted
as emblems by groups of men in order to do away with their own resem-
blances.*"[7] Likewise, French anthropologist Bourdieu argued that the
NMD is essential for the preservation of group identity against the threat
of resemblance to the identity of the group: "*social identity lies in difference, and difference is asserted against what is closest, which represents the*

[4]Freud, S. (1990). 'Moses and Monotheism' [1939]. The Penguin Freud Library. In
Albert Dickson (ed.). Trans. James Strachey. *The Origins of Religion*, vol. 13 (p. 335).

[5]Werman, D. (1988). Freud's "Narcissism of Minor Differences": A Review and
Reassessment. *Journal of American Academy of Psychoanalysis*, 16 (p. 457).

[6]Quoted in Kolsto, P. (2007). The Narcissism of Minor Differences Theory—Can It
Explain Genocide and Ethnic Conflict? *Filozofija i Drustvo*, 2(33) (pp. 153–171).

[7]Levi-Strauss, C. (1966). *The Savage Mind*. Chicago: University of Chicago Press
(p. 107).

greatest threat."[8] In other words, when a group perceives itself vis-à-vis those who are different, its sense of identity tends to be stable and safe, but it is against those who are similar that identity becomes threatened, eventually leading to violence. According to Dutch anthropologist Blok, famed for studying the society of Sicilian mafia, when a group feels an erosion in its identity as differences with other groups disappear, violence towards those who are similar follows as a result of "*the absence of a stable, impersonal central power that is willing and able to protect minorities and their rights.*"[9]

Ironically, while Freud stands behind the NMD hypothesis, he never actually attempted to elaborate on it or expand it into a theory, nor did he seem to be interested in dwelling onto its assumptions in more depth or detail. Koltso argues that Freud must have realized the numerous inconsistencies of this idea which may be applicable to certain conflicts and particular events but not others, discouraging him from expanding it given the limitations of "*the utility of this idea.*"[10]

NARCISSISM OF MINOR DIFFERENCES, VOLATILE IDENTITIES, AND NARCISSUS

Much of the traditional theoretical work in political science and international relations has focused on power relations and international structures but engaged in "*intermittent episodes of amnesia*"[11] insofar as the critical dimension of the politics of culture and identity is concerned, especially in a globalizing world where differences among cultures, nations, and identities are diminishing. From a psychological perspective, Volkan argues that human groups create minor differences

---

[8] Bourdieu, P. (1984). *Distinction: A Social Critique of the Judgment of Taste.* Trans. Richard Nice. London: Routledge (p. 479).

[9] Blok, A. (1998). The Narcissism of Minor Differences. *European Journal of Social Theory*, 1:1 (p. 43).

[10] Kolsto, 'The Narcissism of Minor Differences Theory' (p. 166).

[11] Kratochwil, F. (1996). Is the Ship of Culture at Sea or Returning? In Y. Lapid and F. Kratochwil (eds.). *The Return of Culture and Identity in International Relations Theory.* Boulder: Lynne Reinner (p. 203).

"in order to strengthen the psychological gap between enemy and our-selves."[12] Figlio also asserted that sameness is more likely to gener-ate conflict than difference, further arguing that when the differences between two groups decrease, this creates a sense of unease as it under-mines the ideal self-perception of the group, an unease that can be elimi-nated *"by violence against the non-ideal, demeaned, other."*[13]

Ignatieff who observed the conflict in the Balkans intimately eventu-ally realized that the civil war among Serbs, Croats, and Bosnians was not much of an ethnic or a religious war in as much as it was a war between volatile identities suffering the dread of sameness. In his attempt to dig deeply into the roots of hatred, Ignatieff eventually found that even the men sacrificing their lives in defence of their national identities against those who to a great extent resembled them.[14] The volatility of identity, perhaps perceived by outsider observers as a problematic factor, is actu-ally what fuels nationalism in a globalizing world. *"Nationalism creates communities of fear, groups held together by the conviction that their secu-rity depends on sticking together."*[15] On the other hand, St. Louis argues that narcissism of small differences is not activated in a vacuum between similar and closely related groups, but rather by status anxiety, economic competition, fear of failure or assimilation, and uncertainty.[16]

It is unlikely that the NMD can be developed into a full-fledged the-ory that can explain why violent conflicts erupt or do not erupt between resembling groups and/or nations,[17] but it is quite evident that violent conflicts have erupted and will continue to erupt in the future among

---

[12]Volkan, V. (1986). The Narcissism of Minor Differences in the Psychological Gap Between Opposing Nations. *Psychoanalytic Inquiry*, 6 (p. 187).

[13]Figlio, K. (2012). The Dread of Sameness: Social Hatred and Freud's Narcissism of Minor Differences. In L. Auestad (ed.). *Psychoanalysis and Politics: Exclusion and the Politics of Representation*. New York: Karnac Books Ltd. (p. 10).

[14]Ignatieff, M. (1998). *The Warriors Honor: Ethnic War and the Modern Conscience*. Toronto: Penguin Books (p. 37).

[15]Ibid. (pp. 44–45).

[16]St. Louis, B. (2005). The Difference Sameness Makes: Racial Recognition and the Narcissism of Minor Differences. *Ethnicities*, 5:3 (p. 348).

[17]The most ambitious attempt to develop narcissism of minor differences into a full the-ory was undertaken by Anton Blok (1998) but it suffered significant theoretical gaps and weakness, see Pal Kolsto (2007).

groups and nations that share geographic spaces or borders[18] and that are distinguished from one another by minor differences. It is worth mentioning, however, that one of the major problems with the attempt to develop this theory lies in developing an accurate and reliable definition of what constitutes a minor difference in the first place, since what may be a minor difference in one region or culture, may not be so minor in another.[19]

In fact, the NMD may simply be, after all, just as Freud had suggested, a harmless means to vent aggression towards a similar other. Yet, at a certain time and point, minor differences suddenly stop being so minor, and this is when the balance is tipped, leading to the eruption of intense violence. According to an old Arab idiom, scarcity begets conflict among brothers, but on the collective levels, the problem of minor differences may go way beyond mere economic scarcity to include other insecurities. In this respect, Volkan (1998) has compellingly suggested that NMD presents its ugly face when the insecurities of the group are triggered

> In times of conflict or stress, often initiated by real-world events such as economic failure, man-made disasters or ill-treatment by another group, minor differences between different groups assume major importance.[20]

The real causes may simply have nothing to do with identities, but as a group or a nation feel the heat under stress and pressure, collective insecurities about the uncertain future start to take over. In such a context, the ability to play on the rich symbolism of identity politics and the ease of mobilizing people and charging emotions around threats to identity, become too irresistible for aspiring and opportunistic leaders.

It is quite intriguing that while Freud used the term "narcissism of minor differences" and while various anthropologists, sociologists, and international relations scholars have followed suit, very little emphasis was given to narcissism itself. What is missing in almost all the analytic perspectives, however, is the origin of the term, namely narcissism itself.

[18] Watts, M. (2001). Violent Geographies: Speaking the Unspeakable and the Politics of Space. *City & Society*, 13:1 (pp. 85–117).

[19] Kolsto, 'The Narcissism of Minor Differences Theory'.

[20] Volkan, V. (1998). Ethnicity and Nationalism: A Psychoanalytic Perspective. *Applied Psychology: An International Review*, 47:1 (p. 50).

It is true that collective identities are "inherently" and naturally unstable as Figlio argues,[21] but this is a constant rather than a variable. Collective identities are unstable at times of peace as well as at times of stress.

From a psychoanalytical perspective, Richards argues that any collective identity such as nationalism "*may function as part of a narcissistic structure wherein it rests heavily on the projection of the ego ideal into an idealized community.*"[22] What if at a time when the collective identity or perhaps the entire narcissistic structure of the group is under stress, and Narcissus himself took the helm of political leadership?

In fact, it is quite interesting that in many of the conflicts attributed to NMD, populist leaders with narcissistic tendencies seem to be in key leadership positions in their communities. This is as true of Hitler in Germany as it was of Radovan Karadzic,[23] Slobodan Milosevic, Ratko Mladic, and Slobodan Praljak in the Balkans and Kosovo just to name a few.[24] These leaders effectively combined their narcissistic and charismatic sides with their populist ideologies, taking advantage of the prevailing sense of insecurity about the future at turbulent times to persuade large numbers of their communities to commit violence and murder against others who resemble them except for minor differences, and who had coexisted with them for centuries.

The ability of the narcissist leader to rise to power is not coincidental, because it is specifically at times of turmoil, instability, and insecurity that narcissists bloom as charismatic polarizing leaders.[25] As uncertainty takes

[21] Figlio, K. (2012). A Psychoanalytic Reflection on Collective Memory as Psychosocial Enclave: Jews, German National Identity and Splitting in the German Psyche. *International Social Science Journal*, 62 (p. 161).

[22] Richards, B. (2012). Collective Identities, Breivik and the National Container. In N. Mircher and R. Hinshelwood (eds.). *The Feeling of Certainty: Psychosocial Perspectives on Identity & Difference*. New York: Palgrave Macmillan (p. 182).

[23] Radovan Karadzic, the psychiatrist/populist leader who became known as the Butcher of Bosnia, revealed strong narcissistic characteristics throughout his life and career. He was also a poet but claimed his ancestry 300 years back to one of the region's most respected linguists bearing the same family name. For more on his narcissism See Donia, Robert. (2014). *Radovan Karadzic: Architect of the Bosnian Genocide*. Cambridge: Cambridge University Press.

[24] Interestingly, Slobodan Praljak, the Croat General committed suicide by drinking poison in courtroom at The Hague. For more see Alasdair Sanford. (2017). Slobodan Praljak: Croatian Theatre Director Turned War Criminal. *Euro News*, 29 November 2017.

[25] Nevicka, B., De Hoog, A., Van Vianen, A., and Ten Velden, F. (2013). Uncertainty Enhances the Preference for Narcissistic Leaders. *European Journal of Social Psychology*, 43:5 (pp. 370–380).

over on the collective level, irrational fears and insecurities prevail in the community, and while rational leaders struggle to search for solutions, the narcissist finds the opportunity to emerge and claim leadership, not necessarily because of an extraordinary capability to find solutions, but simply because he seems himself as capable.[26] This unusual but overinflated self-confidence, coupled with the charismatic nature of most narcissists as a result of *"an exaggerated sense of self-importance, fantasies of unlimited success or power,"*[27] attracts the masses.

On the surface, the narcissistic leader at times of turmoil appears to be a very attractive and charismatic source of a solution, but in reality, to the masses, he himself becomes the solution, a solution to which followers develop a real addiction. In the Chocolate Cake Model of Narcissism, Campbell argues that narcissists are appealing leadings, exciting their followers and keeping them agitated with enthusiasm, but sooner or later, followers begin to realize that they have been dishonestly manipulated, which leaves them with emotions of frustration and depression.[28] In fact, the narcissist, an individual who thrives on favourable self-image, is very likely to revert to aggressive and violent means, especially when he and his capabilities are questioned or doubted, *"When favorable views about oneself are questioned, contradicted, impugned, mocked, challenged or otherwise put in jeopardy, people may aggress."*[29] Worst of all, the narcissist is extremely unlikely to appraise or evaluate himself negatively or to accept a more realistic perception of himself or his deeds,[30] which implies a vicious cycle of escalation, and unlimited aggression and violence.

[26] Brunnell, A., Gentry, W., Campbell, W., Hoffman, B., Kunhert, K., and DeMaree, K. (2008). Leader Emergence: The Case of the Narcissistic Leader. *Personality and Social Psychology Bulletin*, 34:12 (pp. 1663–1676).

[27] Blair, C., Hoffman, B., and Helland, K. (2008). Narcissism in Organizations: A Multisource Appraisal Reflects Different Perspectives. *Human Performance*, 21:3 (p. 255).

[28] Campbell, W., Hoffman, B., Campbell, S., and Marclisio, G. (2011). Narcissism in Organizational Contexts. *Human Resource Management Review*, 21:4 (p. 271). For more on Campbell's Chocolate Cake Model and the dynamics of manipulation by the narcissist in any form of human relations, see Campbell, W. (2005). *When You Love a Man Who Loves Himself: How to Deal with a One-Way Relationship*. Chicago: Sourcebooks Casablanca.

[29] Baumeister, R., Smart, L., and Boden, J. (1996). Relation of Threatened Egoism to Violence and Aggression: The Dark Side of High Self-Esteem. *Psychological Review*, 103 (p. 8).

[30] Ibid.

Therefore, although Freud's NMD was probably never intended to be a full-fledged theory, it may be possible to develop it into a more complex model that takes into consideration the dynamics of collective feelings of insecurity, volatile identities, and opportunistic narcissists who tend to bloom amidst nations or groups facing uncertainty and the risks of the loss of economic opportunities, status, or privilege.

In a Sea of Narcissisms: The Gulf Crisis

Regardless of the diplomatic manoeuvring and the efforts to resolve the Gulf crisis, it all boils down to forcing Qatar to change its foreign policy and its regional strategy. More specifically, the major demands set by the quartet include closing Al-Jazeera, ending Qatar's support to Hamas, ceasing financing to terrorist groups, breaking Qatar's ties with Iran, just to name a few. These conditions, however, are merely excuses and do not justify pushing the crisis to the point that Saudi Arabia and the UAE were actually considering the military invasion of Qatar.[31] Although each and every one of these issues may have been annoying to Qatar's neighbours,[32] these are issues that have persisted for decades, and no new developments can justify triggering a major crisis, imposing an embargo, and even preparing for a military invasion of another state.

The real issue is in fact much simpler and quite straightforward, and it is at core a matter of control and power relations. In the context of the region's tensions, specifically those involving Saudi Arabia's ambition to lead the Arab and Islamic worlds and its ongoing rivalry with Iran, Qatar as a member of the GCC did not only pursue an independent foreign policy, but it has also defied and undermined Saudi Arabia's leadership, not only during the Arab Spring, but also by pursuing friendly relations with Iran and by presenting itself as a power to reckon with in the region. Qatar's growing role, influence, relevance, and image may have all distinguished it from its hegemonic neighbour. It is such distinction that may have led to the fuelling of NMD and to the instigation of Saudi aggression towards Qatar.

[31] Mohyeldin, A. (2017). Qatar and Its Neighbors Have Been at Odds Since the Arab Spring. *NBC News*, 7 June 2017.

[32] Haaretz. (2017). Why Are the Gulf States Turning on Qatar? The Biggest Split in the Middle East Since the Gulf War. *Haaretz*, 5 June 2017.

Identities Engulfed by Instability

The Gulf region, and even the Arab world as a whole, has generally been characterized by instability, at least since the second half of the twentieth century. The region has also been politically, economically, emotionally, and socially divided between two extreme sentiments, namely Arab nationalism that calls for the unity of all Arabs in one nation to bring back the glorious past of the great Arab nation, and the drive for independence within nation states, each with its own political and national identity. Central to the tensions between these two ends of the spectrum is the Palestinian cause which brings all Arabs together, at least rhetorically. In addition to this, the catastrophic defeat of the Arab nations in the Arab-Israeli war in 1967 has dealt a severe blow to Arab nationalism, only to have it replaced by the rise of Islamic fervour which has much stronger appeal on the populist level, and a much more threatening stance towards the national identities of individual Arab nation states.

Amidst this volatile and complex context, it is not surprising that collective identities have been subjected to numerous uncertainties and insecurities, especially with every new crisis that hit the region every few years. This context, however, also represented an ideal environment for the emergence of opportunistic narcissists who confidently flaunted their capabilities, exploited their charisma to manipulate their insecure communities, and to grab power and hold on to it. As the magic of charisma and narcissism wore off, narcissistic Arab leaders have had to engage in new adventures to keep feeding the false hopes and to maintain their legitimacy intact.[33] It is true that most ruled by iron and fire, but it is equally true that most were also charismatic and derived a significant degree of legitimacy by none other than hating and fighting their neighbours, or by pursuing ambitious and costly adventures. The list of such authoritarian narcissists includes Nasser of Egypt, Quaddafi of Libya, Saddam Hussein of Iraq, Saleh of Yemen, Bin Ali of Tunisia, and Assad of Syria, just to name a few.[34]

The Gulf region, on the other hand, may have seemed to be a gulf of stability, even despite the historic rivalries among its leaders, not to

---

[33] Al-Samari, A. (2017). Arab Narcissism: A Disorder or a Trait? [My translation]. *Al-Jazirah Newspaper*, 15 June 2017.

[34] Ibid.

mention their border disputes and grudges over petty differences.[35] This stability may have been attributed to three factors. The first factor is the stability of the hierarchical and tribal structures which in the early years of nation state formation, contributed to the legitimacy of the ruling families and the new states they headed.[36] The second factor was the oil wealth which enabled the rulers of the Gulf to enjoy a significant degree of safety and stability away from the challenges posed by socio-economic suffering in the rest of the region.[37] The third factor was the willingness of the leaders of the Gulf region, to work on developing a shared identity under the umbrella of the GCC which also served as a basic step towards economic integration and regional security for the member nations. This regional structure was formed at a time when the nations of the region sensed real danger from powerful and menacing neighbours, namely Iraq and Iran,[38] consequently contributing to the rise of the shared *khaleeji* identity among the countries of the region. The *Khaleeji* identity was not non-Arab or non-Islamic, but it distinguished the people and nations of Saudi Arabia, Kuwait, United Arab Emirates, Qatar, and Oman from everyone else, not only on the basis of their geographic location, but also on the basis of other attributes such as oil wealth, common tribal ancestry and kinship, and shared traditions and values.[39]

NMD ultimately existed among the Gulf nations, even when they faced the danger of the Islamic Republic of Iran which threatened to export its revolution to the region, or when they faced the wrath and military adventures of Saddam Hussein. To the outside world, however, they constituted one region that to the outside world appeared to be homogeneous and harmonious. In this context, the NMD was of little

---

[35] Sandwick, J. (1987). The Gulf Cooperation Council: Moderation and Stability in an Interdependent World. *Foreign Affairs*. On examples of petty disputes in the Gulf see also Berger, C. (1992). Border Clashes Highlight Power Plays on Persian Gulf. *Christian Science Monitor*, 9 October 1992.

[36] Patrick, N. (2009). Nationalism in the Gulf States. *The Centre for the Study of Global Governance*, No. 9. October 2009.

[37] Champion, D. (1999). The Kingdom of Saudi Arabia: Elements of Stability Within Instability. *Middle East Review of International Affairs*, 3:4 (pp. 49–51).

[38] Wehrey, F. and Sokolsky, R. (2015). Imagining a New Security Order in the Persian Gulf. *Carnegie Institute*. Paper, October 2015.

[39] Abdulla, G. (2016). Khaleeji Identity in Contemporary Gulf Politics. In *Identity and Culture in the 21st Century Gulf*. Oxford: Oxford Gulf and Arabian Peninsula Studies Forum (pp. 2–5).

or no relevance, partly because GCC leaders often found ways to cooperate on matters that mattered, even if by finding the least common
denominator, partly because of the common threats that faced them on
the collective level, but most importantly, because despite all the threats
and instability that surrounded them, they remained stable on the inside.
Even when they engaged in petty politics, spited one another, and
undermined mutual efforts for expanding and deepening the notions of
integrated markets and collective security not to mention the personal
differences and disputes among their leaders, the stability of regimes and
societies remained persistently intact.

Trouble in the paradise of the Gulf nations, however, gradually started
to ferment following the invasion of Iraq, the only Arab country that
was powerful enough to keep Iran's political, ideological, and military
threat in check. A more critical factor was the declining strategic interest
of the US in the security of the region, leaving the security of the Gulf
nations exposed, an exposure that became extremely serious and real
when President Obama signed a nuclear deal with Iran. This awakened
the old fears and anxieties in Saudi Arabia about giving up its regional
leadership to Iran in an era where the US and Iran would be allies at the
expense of Saudi Arabia just as the case was during the Shah era: "*Riyadh
in particular worries that, even if there is a friendly regime in Tehran, the
kingdom will be consigned to the status of junior partner.*"[40] While the
waves of the Arab Spring never hit the shores of the Gulf countries,[41]
Bahrain being the exception, it was a wakeup call as the revolt threatened to trigger the ambitions of the Shiite minority in Saudi Arabia itself.
On the regional and strategic levels,[42] Saudi Arabia's losses as a result of
the Arab Spring were substantial with the collapse of the Tunisian and
Egyptian regimes, while Syria, Lebanon, Iraq, and Yemen fell to Iran's
sphere of influence. To make matters worse, Saudi Arabia's economy
has been strained since the global financial crisis, and with collapsing oil
prices, a booming young population with no real future prospects, and

[40]Al-Saud, F. (2003). *Iran, Saudi Arabia and the Gulf: Power Politics in Transition.*
London: I.B. Taurus (p. 17).

[41]Yom, S. (2016). How Middle East Monarchies Survived the Arab Spring. *The
Washington Post*, 29 July 2016.

[42]Matthiesen, T. (2013). Saudi Royal Family Politics and the Arab Spring. *Foreign Policy*,
14 January 2013.

troubling socio-economic realities, Saudi Arabia found itself in unchartered territory.[43]

The Rise of the Narcissist Saviour

The tremulous world in which Saudi Arabia suddenly found itself in, the unprecedented level of insecurity prevailing at the strategic political and economic levels, the uncertainty about the future, and the fear of the unknown, all created the ideal environment for the rise of the ambitious, narcissist leader, the innovative and self-confident saviour[44]—but also ironically the man that *The Independent* dubbed "*the most dangerous man in the world.*"[45] After successfully eliminating all competition within the ruling family, crown prince Mohammed Bin Salman effectively rules Saudi Arabia although he is just a crown prince. Through plans and actions that reflect grandiose and status rather than real content, policies that primarily aim at attracting positive publicity, and sufficient recklessness to wage wars that cannot be won,[46] he has managed to consolidate his power and to build some temporary and false hopes for the future,[47] specifically with respect to fighting corruption,[48] or winning a quick war in Yemen.[49]

In addition to projecting himself as the confident and capable accomplisher and saviour, even if this means jumping into miscalculated adventures and wars,[50] the narcissistic leader will also thrive and bloom through manipulation, by inventing and overstating new threats, and

[43] Karabell, Z. (2017). Saudi Prince Plans a "City of the Future." Don't Bet on It. *Wired*, 6 December 2017.

[44] Vick, K. (2018). The Saudi Crown Prince Thinks He Can Transform the Middle East. Should We Believe Him? *Time*, 5 April 2018.

[45] Law, B. (2016). The Most Dangerous Man in the World? *The Independent*, 8 January 2016.

[46] Cockburn, P. (2016). Prince Mohammed Bin Salman: Naïve, Arrogant Saudi Prince Is Playing with Fire. *The Independent*, 9 January 2016.

[47] Hubbard, B. and Kirkpatrick, D. (2017). The Upstart Prince Who's Throwing Caution to the Winds. *New York Times*, 14 November 2017.

[48] Ulrichsen, K. (2017). Mohammed Bin Salman Has Unrivaled Authority in Saudi Arabia. Is He Really a Reformist? *World Politics Review*, 29 December 2017.

[49] Lippman, T. (2017). The End of Saudi Style Stability. *New York Times*, 8 November 2017.

[50] Hubbard and Kirkpatrick, 'The Upstart Prince'.

by fuelling the fear of those who are slightly different. Backed and mentored by a more seasoned narcissist, namely MbZ, the crown prince of Abu Dhabi,[51] MbS must have scanned the region for a potential victim to pick on.

Identifying the right candidate was not difficult. Bahrain's leadership owed its survival to Saudi Arabia and was completely dependent on it[52]; the UAE was fully behind in support of the Saudi leadership and willing to jump along into the foray of the Yemeni war; Kuwait was very keen to maintain distance and neutrality by avoiding any tension or upset with the Saudi leadership[53]; and Oman was unlikely to pass as a legitimate threatening target, not to mention that it was significantly different from Saudi Arabia both socially and religiously. Qatar, on the other hand, qualified perfectly as a legitimate target of narcissisms of minor differences.

Qatar became the lurking enemy, the stranger, the outsider. Suddenly, the Qataris were presented as the allies of Iran, the supporters of terrorism, and the "Jews of Arabia" pretending to be Muslims to undermine Islam. Since the outbreak of the crisis in the summer of 2017, Qatar as a state and a nation, Qataris as a group and as individuals, and everything related to Qatar, have been under constant political, diplomatic, economic, and public relations attacks. The most serious of these attacks came in the form of cyberwar and war over narratives, as Krieg writes in Chapter 5, waged by cyber-armies organized in the UAE and Saudi Arabia whose sole purpose was to vilify everything and everyone related to Qatar, to feed bitterness towards Qatar on the mass level, and to picture the Qataris as the villains of Arabia who have betrayed the region and its peoples.[54]

These attacks represent textbook examples of how the NMD can be manipulated to mobilize hatred and direct aggression towards a targeted group or nation. For example, of all the ruling families and societies in

[51] Henderson, S. (2017). Meet the Two Princes Reshaping the Middle East. *Politico Magazine*, 13 June 2017.

[52] Rieger, R. (2013). In Search of Stability: Saudi Arabia and the Arab Spring. In *Gulf Research Meeting Papers*. Cambridge, UK: Gulf Research Centre.

[53] Schanzer, J. and Koduvayor, V. (2018). Kuwait and Oman Are Stuck in Arab No Man's Land. *Foreign Policy*, 14 June 2018.

[54] Al Sharq. (2018). 1.5 Million False Accounts to Attack Qatar. *Al-Sharq Newspaper*, 5 June 2018.

Arabia, Qatar's social structure is the closest to Saudi Arabia. Qatari and Saudi tribes are more closely related and tied than tribes in any two other countries in the Gulf. In fact, even the ruling Qatari family itself traces its origin to extended tribes in Saudi Arabia. Even on the religious and ideological levels, Qatar is the only country in the entire region that embraces Wahhabism as a religious ideology, although its version of Wahhabism is slightly different and more liberal than its Saudi counterpart.[55] Ironically, propagating claims that the ruling family of Qatar is of Jewish descent is not only intended to position Qatar as the most hated enemy, but it is also the easiest and fastest way to invent a fake enemy and make it the target of mass hatred and paranoia. Because within an anti-Semitic environment, nothing seems to scream suspicion, insecurity, fear, and anger than a "lurking Jew" amidst others, an irrational sentiment that Hitler knew too well how to exploit and manipulate.[56]

In a region where Israel has since its formation been used as an excuse for every political, economic, and social ailment in the Arab world, branding Qatar with Judaism and close links to Israel does not only result in targeting waves of hatred towards it, but it also bestows legitimacy and mass support within Saudi Arabia for any action of aggression and violence against it. In this context, the ludicrous and meaningless idea of changing Qatar's geography by digging a 60-km-long canal to turn it into an island may not make sense, except on the symbolic level,[57] reinforcing the narcissist drive for attaining purity by cleansing the perception of the self from any impurity. If Qatar is the source of this impurity, the solution is easy, simply cutting it off from the pure body the Arab Peninsula to ensure that its territories and people do not touch Saudi land.[58]

[55]Dorsey, J. (2017). Qatari Wahhabism vs. Saudi Wahhabism and the Perils of Top-Down Change. *The Huffington Post*, 12 April 2017.

[56]For more on branding Qatar and its ruling family as Jewish, see posts under the Twitter hashtag #Qatrael in 2017 and 2017. Qatrael is the names of Qatar and Israel combined in one word.

[57]Taylor, A. (2018). Saudi Media Says Kingdom Could Turn Qatar—Its Neighbor and Rival—Into an Island. *Washington Post*, 21 June 2018.

[58]Duddley, D. (2018). Saudi Arabia Eyes Up Canal Border Idea, Turning Qatar from a Peninsula into an Island. *Forbes*, 4 June 2018.

Conclusion

NMD seems to have manifested itself in the Gulf Divide between Qatar and its neighbours. This crisis has so far resulted in massive economic costs for all sides,[59] lost opportunities for substantial economic development,[60] and in undermining the future of the GCC as an effective collective organization.[61] As many excuses or rational justifications may be used to explain how this crisis started, its most likely roots can be traced to two important factors; first, the fact that Qatar had become a little too different and distinguished for the comfort of its hegemonic neighbour that expects homogeneity on every level possible; and secondly, the rise of the power-hungry narcissist whose ambitious quest for power requires him to search for a potential symbolic enemy that he can target. Targeting Qatar may or may not be so important on the strategic level, but it is critically relevant from the perspective of Mohammed bin Salman as an ambitious narcissist who can only thrive by turning a neighbour characterized by minor differences into a symbolic evil. Targeting and blaming such a symbolic evil is ultimately the tool of trade that a narcissistic leader needs to overstate his power, to justify his failure, and to keep manipulating the insecurities and fears of his followers to mobilize and rally them behind him.

[59] The Economist. (2017). The Boycott of Qatar Is Hurting Its Enforcers. *The Economist*, 19 October 2017.

[60] Kabbani, N. (2017). The High Cost of High Stakes: Economic Implications of the 2017 Gulf Crisis. *Brookings Institute*, 15 June 2017.

[61] Cafiero, G. and Karasik, T. (2017). Kuwait, Oman and the Qatar Crisis. *Middle East Institute*, 22 June 2017.

CHAPTER 5

The UAE, Qatar, and the Question of Political Islam

Christopher M. Davidson

INTRODUCTION

Gripped since June 2017 by the so-called 'Qatar crisis', the Persian Gulf seems as unstable as ever. Starting out as a putative internecine dispute over the role of political Islam and, by association, Qatar's supposed interference in its neighbors' affairs, it has substantially and perhaps intractably widened existing cleavages between the six Gulf monarchies and has effectively put an end to their longstanding economic and security union—the Gulf Cooperation Council. Led by the self-proclaimed 'Anti-Terror Quartet'—comprising the United Arab Emirates, Saudi Arabia, Bahrain, and Egypt—thirteen demands were made against Qatar, ranging from severing all ties to the Muslim Brotherhood to closing the Al Jazeera broadcasting network, and then submitting to monthly external compliance check.[1] Described as 'not reasonable or actionable'

---

[1]Wintour, P. (2017). Qatar Given 10 Days to Meet 13 Sweeping Demands by Saudi Arabia. *The Guardian*, 23 June 2017; The National. (2017). The 13 Demands on Qatar from Saudi Arabia, Bahrain, the UAE and Egypt. *The National*, 23 June 2017.

C. M. Davidson (✉)
Leiden University College, The Hague, The Netherlands
e-mail: cmd@christopherdavidson.net

© The Author(s) 2019
A. Krieg (ed.), *Divided Gulf*, Contemporary Gulf Studies,
https://doi.org/10.1007/978-981-13-6314-6_5

by Qatari officials,[2] numerous regional analysts pointed out that the demands were impossible for Qatar to accept, at least in their entirety, as doing so would be tantamount to stripping Qatar of its sovereignty and, by extension, irrecoverably delegitimizing the Al-Thani ruling family.[3] Putting it as diplomatically as possible, even the US Secretary of State at the time, Rex Tillerson, lamented that some of the *elements of the demands will be very difficult for Qatar to meet.*[4]

Most provocatively, building on the UAE and Saudi Arabia's earlier, 2014 designations of the Muslim Brotherhood and some of its Gulf-based affiliates as terrorist organizations,[5] the Quartet's allegations that Qatar had also been supporting Al-Qaeda, the Islamic State, and Hezbollah were clearly part of an effort to frame Qatar's supposed sins in the familiar language of the 'War on Terror.'[6] Since 9/11 such discourse has allowed all four of these states, and Saudi Arabia in particular, to curry favor with the US by presenting themselves as the West's premier allies in a dangerous region and by portraying their enemies as enablers and sponsors of anti-Western extremist organizations. This time, however, there are very strong indications that it has primarily been the UAE, and in turn its wealthiest and most dominant constituent federal emirate, Abu Dhabi, that has really been the mover and shaker behind the scenes.[7]

[2] Wintour, P. (2017). Qatar's Neigbours Dismiss Emirate's Response to List of Demands. *The Guardian*, 5 July 2017.

[3] See, for example Hubbard, B. (2017). Arab Nations Demand Qatar Shut Al Jazeera, Cut Islamist Ties and Detail Funding. *The New York Times*, 23 June 2017; Unal, A. (2017). Saudi Demands from Qatar Seen as Breach of Sovereignty. *Daily Sabah*, 23 June 2017.

[4] Carey, G. (2017). Saudi-Led Demands 'Difficult' for Qatar to Meet, Tillerson Says. *The Bloomberg*, 25 June 2017.

[5] In March 2014 Saudi Arabia designated the Muslim Brotherhood a terrorist organization. In November 2014 the UAE designated the Muslim Brotherhood and the UAE-based *Al-Islah* as terrorist organizations. Usher, S. (2014). Saudi Arabia Declares Muslim Brotherhood Terrorist Group. *BBC*, 7 March 2014; The National. (2014). List of Groups Designated Terrorist Organizations by the UAE. *The National*, 16 November 2014; Reuters. (2014). UAE Lists Muslim Brotherhood as Terrorist Group. *Reuters*, 15 November 2014.

[6] Associated Press. (2017). The 13 Demands on Qatar from Saudi Arabia, Bahrain, the UAE and Egypt. *The National*, 23 June 2017.

[7] Henderson, S. (2018). Qatar Diplomacy: Unraveling a Complicated Crisis. *The Washington Institute for Near East Policy*, Policywatch 2941, 8 March 2018; The New

Stepping back, however, from the details of the dispute itself, and putting to one side some of the more lurid finger-pointing about jihadist and Hezbollah funding, at first it seems difficult to comprehend how the UAE and Qatar have managed to reach such contrasting positions on political Islam in general and, more specifically, supposedly moderate groups such as the Muslim Brotherhood. After all, the UAE (or 'Trucial States' as they were previously known) and Qatar experienced fairly similar historical state formation processes, having both emerged from British protection and, as Britain began to withdraw from the region in 1971, both establishing themselves as independent entities—albeit outside of a wider British-sponsored nine-member federation that would have included Qatar and Bahrain alongside Abu Dhabi and the six other eventual UAE emirates.[8] Moreover, notwithstanding the UAE's federal situation, both the UAE and Qatar have since developed extremely similar political systems, most often described as 'traditional monarchies'[9] or, borrowing from Max Weber's classical typology, as some sort of 'patrimonial' (or 'neo-patrimonial') states, in which kinship ties remain paramount and seemingly modern institutions appear grafted onto more traditional sources of authority.[10]

Arab. (2018). MbS and MbZ: Two Princes in a Hurry Shake Up the Gulf. *The New Arab*, 27 April 2018.

[8]Following a series of truces signed with Britain in the early nineteenth century and formalized in 1853 as the 'Perpetual Maritime Truce', most of the sheikhdoms of the lower Persian Gulf or the 'Trucial States' were de facto protectorates of the British Empire. After the Ottoman Empire withdrew its final few troops from Qatar in 1915 the path was clear for the Al-Thani ruling family to also seek British protection, with a treaty signed the following year. Britain had announced its withdrawal from the Persian Gulf in 1968, to be completed within three years. As late as summer 1971 Britain had still hoped that a nine-member federation of sheikhdoms could be formed. See Onley, J. (2005). Britain's Informal Empire in the Gulf: 1820–1971. *Journal of Social Affairs* 22:87 (pp. 30–32); Rahman, H. (2005). *The Emergence of Qatar: The Turbulent Years 1627–1916*. London: Thames and Hudson (pp. 221–225); Lee, J.M. (1970). Unity Eludes Nine Persian Gulf Sheikhdoms. *The New York Times*, 29 November 1970.

[9]Numerous political science texts on the Gulf monarchies have borrowed from and adapted Samuel Huntington's 1966 description of 'traditional monarchies'. See Huntington, S. (1996). The Political Modernization of Traditional Monarchies. *Daedalus* 95:3 (pp. 763–788).

[10]For a discussion on patrimonialism, see Weber, M. (1978). *Economy and Society: An Outline of Interpretive Sociology Part I*. Berkeley: University of California Press (pp. 231–232). For a discussion on patrimonialism in the context of the Middle Eastern monarchies,

On the economic front, there has also been little difference, as both successfully exploited their extraordinary hydrocarbon resources (in the UAE's case oil and in Qatar's case natural gas) to achieve what are now the two highest GDPs per capita in the region, and two of the highest in the world: $37,622 and $59,234 respectively.[11] In turn, this has allowed both sets of ruling families to preside over sophisticated allocative states that, as part of 'social contracts' or 'ruling bargains', have benevolently distributed hydrocarbon rents and lucrative state-funded opportunities to most of their citizens in return for considerable political acquiescence.[12] On the flip side, beyond ruler-citizen social contracts, both monarchies have been able to attract considerable numbers of economic migrants to do the actual heavy lifting, resulting in approximately 89% of the UAE's population and 88% of Qatar's population now being made up of expatriates[13]—again the two highest figures in the region, and very likely the two highest figures in the world.

Given these marked historical, political, economic, and even demographic similarities, how can we begin to account for such

see Achcar, G. (2013). *The People Want: A Radical Exploration of the Arab Uprising.* Berkeley: University of California Press (p. 59). For a discussion on neo-patrimonialism in the context of the UAE, see Davidson, C. (2008). *Dubai: The Vulnerability of Success.* New York: Columbia University Press (pp. 137–138). For a discussion on neo-patrimonialism in the context of Qatar, see Mungiu-Pippidi, A. and Johnston, M. (eds.). (2017). *Transitions to Good Governance: Creating Virtuous Circles of Anti-corruption.* Cheltenham: Edward Elgar (p. 44).

[11] The World Bank GDP data for the UAE and Qatar. Drawn from World Bank national accounts data and OECD National Accounts data files. https://data.worldbank.org/indicator/NY.GDP.PCAP.CD?locations=AE; https://data.worldbank.org/indicator/NY.GDP.PCAP.CD?locations=QA&view=chart (date accessed: 26 June 2018).

[12] For a discussion of 'allocative states' with reference to the Gulf monarchies, see Gray, M. (2011). A Theory of "Late Rentierism" in the Arab States of the Gulf. *Georgetown Qatar, CIRS Occasional Papers*, No. 7, 2011 (p. 8). For a discussion of social contracts or 'ruling bargains' with reference to the Gulf monarchies, see Davidson, C. (2013). *After the Sheikhs.* New York: Oxford University Press (pp. 10–11); Kamrava, M. (ed.). (2014). *Beyond the Arab Spring: The Evolving Ruling Bargain in the Middle East.* New York: Oxford University Press (p. 31).

[13] Global Media Insight data for the UAE and Qatar. The Qatari figures are unofficial, as the Qatari government does not publish data on the population by nationality. https://www.globalmediainsight.com/blog/uae-population-statistics/#expat_population; http://priyadsouza.com/population-of-qatar-by-nationality-in-2017/ (date accessed: 26 June 2018).

remarkable contemporary dissonance on political Islam and the Muslim Brotherhood? By collecting evidence from a range of relevant primary and secondary sources—including archived official documents, records of diplomatic correspondence now in the public domain, and NGO reports—and by investigating a number of possible explanations, including the most popular alongside the more subtle, this chapter aims to move us closer to an empirical understanding of what really underpins the current crisis, and thus seeks to build on some of the most recent, rigorous area studies scholarship on Gulf-Islamist relations.[14] Moreover, supplementing an effort to determine the relative importance of what would seem the most accurate explanations, this chapter also attempts to theorize the situation in an effort to help us not only comprehend how the headline-grabbing standoff has come about, but also how it may help contribute to existing work on international relations theory.

Is It About Religion or Ideology?

An obvious starting point in our search for an explanation is the possibility that despite the considerable common ground shared by the United Arab Emirates and Qatar, there nonetheless exist some deeper and long-standing religious or religio-ideological differences between their ruling families or, more broadly, their political elites, and that these have now boiled over into an international crisis. On paper, such variables do seem important, and—at first glance—would seem to support some of the post-9/11 calls to reemphasize the role of religion in international relations theory, most prominently by Columbia University's Jack Snyder, and most systematically by Ohio University's Nukhet Sandal and Bar-Ilan University's Jonathan Fox.[15]

---

[14] Recent work on Gulf-Islamist relations includes Roberts, D. (2017). Qatar and the Arab Spring: Exploring Divergent Responses to the Arab Spring. *Middle East Journal*, 71:4; Hedges, M. and Cafiero, G. (2017). The GCC and the Muslim Brotherhood: What Does the Future Hold? *Middle East Policy*, 24:1; Freer, C. (2017). Rentier Islam in the Absence of Elections: The Political Role of the Muslim Brotherhood Affiliates in Qatar and the United Arab Emirates. *International Journal of Middle East Studies*, 49:3.

[15] Snyder, J. (2011). Introduction. In Jack Snyder (ed.), *Religion and International Relations Theory*. New York: Columbia University Press (pp. 1–3); Sandal, N. and Fox, J. (2013). *Religion in International Relations Theory: Interactions and Possibilities*. Abingdon: Routledge (p. 6).

After all, although unlike in Saudi Arabia where it is effectively part-and-parcel of the establishment, 'Wahhabism' is nonetheless the predominant religious school in Qatar. Derived from the ultraconservative teachings of the prominent eighteenth-century preacher Muhammad ibn Abd Al-Wahhab, it has called for the restoration of *tawhid* or absolute monotheism by force if necessary, and has also been heavily influenced by the contentious medieval scholar Ibn Taymiyyah.[16] In a recent 2011 reaffirmation of Qatar's Wahhabi credentials, its newly built state mosque was named the Sheikh Muhammed ibn Abd Al-Wahhab Mosque, with the Qatari ruler at the time, Sheikh Hamad bin Khalifa Al-Thani, even claiming that he was one of Al-Wahhab's great-grandsons.[17] In contrast, most of the UAE's emirates, or rather the Trucial States before 1971, historically resisted Wahabbi incursions into their territory, both militarily and ideologically, with Abu Dhabi and Dubai's interrelated elites having followed the considerably less puritanical Maliki school of Islam,[18] which derives its rulings from *istislah* or the 'principle of public interest' in those areas which the Qur'an or the *hadith* do not provide explicit guidance.[19]

Although attractively straightforward, any religiously grounded explanation nonetheless runs aground, as until relatively recently the UAE's rulers enjoyed a longstanding and fairly warm relationship with many of the same sort of conservative religio-political organizations that Qatar is now accused of sponsoring. As a function of the so-called 'Arab Cold War', in which the Western-backed traditional monarchies, including Abu Dhabi and Dubai, had viewed the ostensibly secular Gamal Abdel

---

[16] Juergensmeyer, M. and Roof, W.C. (eds.). (2011). *Encyclopaedia of Global Religion.* Thousand Oaks: Sage (p. 1369); Glasse, C. (ed.). (2001). *The New Encyclopaedia of Islam.* Lanham: Rowman & Littlefield (pp. 469–472); Esposito, J. (2003). *The Oxford Dictionary of Islam.* New York: Oxford University Press (p. 333).

[17] Reuters. (2017). Descendants of Saudi Wahhabism Founder Distance Themselves from Qatar. *Reuters*, 28 May 2017.

[18] Abu Dhabi's Al-Nahyan rulers and their tribal allies repelled numerous Wahhabi incursions into their territory. In contrast, Ra's al-Khaimah's Al-Qasimi ruling family followed the stricter Hanbali school of Islam and was more open to reaching an understanding with Al-Wahhab's followers. See US Department of State. (2009). A Long Hot Summer for UAE-Saudi Relations (cable: 09ABUDHABI981_a)', 15 October 2009; Davidson, C. (2009). *Abu Dhabi: Oil and Beyond.* New York: Columbia University Press (pp. 8–9).

[19] Nasir, J. (1990). *The Islamic Law of Personal Status.* Leiden: Brill Academic (pp. 16–17).

Nasser-led Arab nationalist movement as the most potent threat to their regimes,[20] it is unsurprising that numerous Egyptian Brotherhood exiles were granted refuge in what was to become the UAE.[21] Many went on to become teachers and academics—a not unwelcome development for the UAE's rulers, given that they blamed an earlier influx of pro-Arab nationalist expatriate teachers in the 1950s for having indoctrinated their youth and having given rise to an indigenous anti-Western nationalist movement.[22]

By the 1970s, the UAE's rulers' willingness to integrate with the Brotherhood was even more explicit, with the newly founded Dubai Islamic Bank and Emirates Islamic Bank both being stocked with Brotherhood-leaning executives.[23] Again a function of the Arab Cold War, as Tufts University's Ibrahim Warde has explained, by the time that these sort of banks were establishing themselves, 'ideologically both liberalism and economic Islam were being driven by their common opposition to socialism and economic dirigisme.'[24] Clearly blessed by the Western powers, others have described how major figures in the new Islamic banking sector were often non-Muslim Westerners, 'many of whom were readily able to quote narrowly Qur'anic interpretations supporting the view that Islam was essentially a free market-supporting religion.'[25]

In parallel to such Brotherhood and Cold War alignments, for many years the UAE's most prominent domestic Islamist organization, *Al-Islah* or 'Reform', had not only been tolerated but in some cases actually supported by various ruling family members, with a ruler of Dubai

---

[20] For a full discussion of the Arab Cold War, see Kerr, M. (1975). *The Arab Cold War: Gamal 'Abd al-Nasir and His Rivals, 1958–1970.* Oxford: Oxford University Press.

[21] Bloghardt, L.P. (2013). The Muslim Brotherhood on Trial in the UAE. The Washington Institute for Near East Policy. *Policywatch* 2064, 12 April 2013.

[22] Davidson, C. (2007). Arab Nationalism and British Opposition in Dubai, 1920–1966. *Middle Eastern Studies*, 43:6 (pp. 884–885).

[23] Ehrenfeld, R. (1992). *Evil Money: Encounters Along the Money Trail.* London: HarperCollins (p. 196).

[24] Warde, I. (2010). *Islamic Finance and the Global Economy.* Edinburgh: Edinburgh University Press (p. 84).

[25] Dreyfuss, R. (2006). *Devil's Game: How the United States Helped Unleash Fundamentalist Islam.* New York: Metropolitan (p. 180).

having played a role in its 1974 foundation,[26] and, as part of an apparent deal with Abu Dhabi ruler Sheikh Zayed bin Sultan Al-Nahyan, with some *Al-Islah* members even assuming key positions in the UAE's education and justice ministries. Although officially dissolved in 1994, *Al-Islah* remained influential in schools, universities, and cultural clubs, with its leader being a nephew of the ruler of Ra's al-Khaimah.[27]

IS IT ABOUT PERSONALITIES?

Given the manifold shortcomings behind any religious/ideological explanation, a more credible explanation for the United Arab Emirates—Qatar dissonance might be the personal politics of the man who, according to most regional analysts, now seems to be at the center of everything: the UAE's Sheikh Muhammad bin Zayed Al-Nahyan—known in Western policy circles as 'MbZ.' Since becoming crown prince in late 2004 after his father Sheikh Zayed bin Sultan Al-Nahyan's death, and then having key executive powers transferred to his court in early 2007, he has emerged as not only Abu Dhabi's de facto ruler, but also as the UAE's de facto president and, in many ways, as one of the Arab world's most powerful figures. Although still constitutionally below his older half-brother, Sheikh Khalifa bin Zayed Al-Nahyan, who is officially Abu Dhabi's ruler and the UAE's president, MbZ has spent the past decade steadily taking over almost all the UAE's key institutions, including the military,[28] and as such currently controls almost every aspect of UAE policymaking. As *Bloomberg* put it in November 2015, the UAE's 'military power rises in the Middle East, courtesy of one man', and as the *Financial Times* described in October 2017, MbZ is the 'man driving change' and the 'chief executive' of the UAE.[29]

---

[26] It was approved by the ruler of Dubai, Sheikh Rashid bin Said Al-Maktoum. See Bayoumy, Y. (2013). UAE Islamist Group Had No Desire to Topple Government: Families. *Reuters*, 2 July 2013.

[27] Referring to Sheikh Sultan bin Kayed Al-Qasimi. See Bloghardt, 'The Muslim Brotherhood on Trial'.

[28] Davidson, *Abu Dhabi* (pp. 79, 102–103).

[29] Syeed, N. (2015). A Military Power Rises in the Mideast, Courtesy of One Man. *Bloomberg*, 24 November 2015; Kerr, S. (2017). UAE: the Middle East's Power Broker Flexes Its Muscles. *The Financial Times*, 24 October 2017.

In this context, the international relations subfield of personality studies, combined with some elements of political psychology—a relationship clearly defined by Brown University's Rose McDermott—might provide us with a better way of understanding the crisis.[30] After all, although no dedicated, detailed biographic study yet exists of MBZ (or indeed of any of his contemporary Gulf leader peers), and although he has usually shied away from giving interviews, making public speeches, or providing us with the sort of 'spontaneous material' usually relied upon in leadership trait analysis,[31] there are nonetheless numerous indications and a growing body of evidence that suggest he has held very strong views on political Islam for most of his political life and, for at least the past fifteen years, has had a correspondingly very low tolerance level for Qatar's perceived support for Islamist organizations.

In early 2007, for example, and within weeks or possibly days after the transfer of powers to MBZ's court, it emerged that numerous UAE schoolteachers and university academics who were believed to be members of *Al-Islah* or to have Islamist sympathies were either put on gardening leave or made redundant. Witnessed by the author, some of the men took part in a rare public protest in Abu Dhabi, holding small placards addressing their plight. Although surrounded by a small number of supporters, including some of their students, the event received no local media coverage, and it would seem most were not allowed to return to work.[32]

Dating from both before and after this episode, a string of recently leaked US diplomatic cables, most of which are summaries of conversations between MbZ and US officials, give us perhaps the best insight into MbZ's evolving political thought. In 2003 for example, the author of one such cable revealed that MbZ had previously asked the commander of US Central Command to 'bomb Al Jazeera', and confirmed that MbZ's preference for 'reining in the Doha-based Al Jazeera satellite network prior to any military action' remained a 'common theme in his

---

[30] See McDermott, R. (2004). *Political Psychology in International Relations*. Ann Arbor: University of Michigan Press.

[31] For a discussion on the use of spontaneous material in leadership trait analysis, see Hermann, M. (2003). Assessing Leadership Style: Trait Analsysis. In Jerrold Post (ed.). *The Psychological Assessment of Political Leaders*. Ann Arbor: University of Michigan Press (pp. 179–181).

[32] Author's personal research diaries: UAE 2000–2010 (unpublished).

discussions with visiting US officials.'[33] In 2004, another cable recorded MbZ stating that Al Jazeera was the 'mouthpiece of Al-Qaeda' and, in something of a personal admission, revealing that one of his own sons had been 'influenced by the misinformation on Al Jazeera.' According to MbZ his son was a 'straight A student' but had begun to voice anti-Western opinions as a result of watching too much Al Jazeera. As he put it, "if [Al Jazeera] can affect the grandson of a moderate leader like Sheikh Zayed this way, imagine what it can do to the uneducated or the lower classes.'[34]

Recounting a meeting between MbZ and Nicholas Burns, the US undersecretary of state for political affairs, a 2007 cable focused instead on MbZ's fear of Islamists taking advantage of future democratic openings in the Middle East. Clearly upset by Hamas' victory in the 2006 Palestinian legislative elections, MBZ remarked to Burns that he did not agree with the US' promotion of elections on the basis that 'the Middle East... is not California' and that 'in the post 9/11 world in any Muslim country you will see the same result.' He further explained that 'while members of the US Congress and Senate are loyal to their states and their constituencies, the masses in the Middle East would tend to go with their hearts and vote overwhelmingly for the Muslim Brotherhood and the jihadists represented by Hamas and Hizballah.' Referring to the Egyptian president, who the cable's author noted was considered a 'family friend of the Al-Nahyan', MBZ remarked 'Thank God for Hosni Mubarak. If Egypt has free elections, they will elect the Muslim Brothers.' Looking ahead, he also made the point that significant educational reform had to come before democracy, but that this would be a 'process that will take 25 to 50 years of focused effort to turn around deeply-rooted cultural phenomena.' He also provided more detail on the UAE's education sector crackdown, stating that 'in the western part of Abu Dhabi emirate alone... the [UAE government] has closed down 80% of 262 so-called "talebani Qur'an schools," to which no Emirati household would refuse to send its sons', and that 'the UAE is addressing the educational aspect of the problem by privatizing government

[33] US Department of State. (2003). Director Haass and Chief of Staff Muhammad bin Zayid Discuss Iraq, Iran and Saudi-U.S. Relations (cable: 03ABUDHABI237_a)', 15 January 2003.

[34] US Department of State. (2004). UAE Officials Query Deputy Secretary Armitage on Arab Media, Iraq, and Israel (cable: 04ABUDHABI1344_a)', 28 April 2004.

schools with the aim of privatizing 25% in 5 years so that there will eventually be 0% "talebani Qur'an schools".' Nonetheless, despite these efforts he confessed to Burns his fear that that 'of the 60,000 soldier UAE armed forces and its loyalties, some 50 to 80% would respond to a call of "some holy man in Mekkah,"' and, as the cable's author noted, 'he repeatedly alluded to being stoned by his own citizens if he pushed some subjects too openly.'[35]

In a follow-up 2007 cable, based on a discussion between MbZ and the commander of US Special Operations Command about the Afghanistan conflict, MbZ seemed especially keen to conflate 'Islamists' with 'jihadists' and Al-Qaeda, stressing the dangers of radicalization to UAE society and revealing that the UAE had already 'lost' some of its 'own young men... to the Islamists', and that they were 'recruited for jihad in Afghanistan without their even knowing what was happening.' He further argued that 'this recruitment is a greater threat than most people think' and, in apparent reference to the UAE and the other Gulf monarchies, warned that there are 'smart, intelligent, and well-spoken mullahs and Imams who are successfully recruiting everywhere.' With regard to strategy, he said that the focus of nonmilitary actions needed to be 'the Imam in the mosque, and the teacher in the madrassa' and, seeming to confirm his preference for secular leadership, he praised the Afghani president Hamid Karzai as being 'perfect for this' on the basis that 'a secular leader can see and understand things that religious leaders and anyone with a ribbon on his head simply cannot.'[36]

In a lengthy cable from 2009 summarizing the UAE's relations with its neighbors and written by the US ambassador to the UAE, it was reiterated that 'senior Abu Dhabi ruling family members have made clear their concern about extremism and have taken concrete actions to minimize both the presence and influence of extremist Islam in the Emirates.' Alluding to the education crackdown, it was also noted that 'although part of controlling terrorist incitement falls to the security services, perhaps nowhere are [the UAE government's] efforts more recognizable

---

[35] US Department of State. (2007). U/S Burns' January 22 Meeting with Abu Dhabi Crown Prince and UAE Foreign Minister (cable: 07ABUDHABI97_a)', 24 January 2007.

[36] US Department of State. (2007). Abu Dhabi Crown Prince Presses SOCOM Commander for Assistance (cable: 07ABUDHABI304_a)', 22 February 2007.

that in the sphere of educational reform.'[37] In a follow-up cable the same year, noting MbZ's comments to US officials attending an Abu Dhabi military conference, MbZ had reportedly claimed that Qatar 'is part of the Muslim Brotherhood,' had then made 'strident remarks about 'Qatar's dangerous ties to extremist elements,' and had warned that the Brotherhood was the UAE's 'mortal enemy.' He was also understood to have stated his 'desire to defend his country as a counterpoint to extremists' loyalty to [the Brotherhoods's] movement' and had then encouraged 'the US to review the employees of Al Jazeera', predicting that '90% of the staff [would be] affiliated with the Brotherhood.' Revealingly, the cable's author reflected that 'being labelled a Muslim Brother is about the worst epithet possible in MbZ vocabulary' and, seeming to corroborate the 2004 cable's reference to one of MbZ's sons, the author recounted how MbZ 'told a story of his son who was becoming interested in the teaching of Muslim fundamentalists' and that 'his son had only heard the stories of the West through the lens of Al Jazeera and others similarly aligned.'[38]

Taken together, these conversations and statements strongly suggest there has been a fundamental, longstanding, and MBZ-led commitment to a secular UAE foreign policy. With reference to the UAE's more recent anti-Islamist messaging, David Roberts has even suggested that the UAE is now pursuing a 'Jeffersonian' foreign policy,[39] in reference to US founding father Thomas Jefferson's calls for a 'wall of separation between Church and state.'[40] This does seem to be true, and certainly makes sense given MBZ's repeatedly expressed concerns over Al Jazeera being able to indoctrinate even members of his own family, let alone the UAE's armed forces. Nonetheless, it is possible—although most likely as something of an ancillary strategy—that MbZ's unwaveringly anti-Islamist position has also been part of an effort to reduce the influence of *Al-Islah* on the basis that it was one of the few remaining influential UAE organizations outside his immediate control, and that it

[37] US Department of State. (2009). A Long Hot Summer for UAE-Saudi Relations (cable: 09ABUDHABI981_a)', 29 October 2009.

[38] US Department of State. (2009). Strong Words in Private from MBZ at IDEX—Bashes Iran, Qatar, Russia (cable: 09ABUDHABI193_a)', 25 February 2009.

[39] Roberts, 'Qatar and the Arab Spring' (pp. 557, 561); Roberts, B. (2016). Mosque and State: The United Arab Emirates' Secular Foreign Policy. *Foreign Affairs*, 18 March 2016.

[40] US Library of Congress, 'Jefferson's Letter to the Danbury Baptists', 1 January 1802.

was continuing to provide members of other UAE ruling families—most notably Ra's al-Khaimah's Al-Qasimi dynasty—with potentially powerful patronage networks beyond Abu Dhabi's reach. After all, when the UAE authorities eventually moved to put on trial 94 political activists in summer 2013—the 'UAE 94'—it transpired that among their number was Sheikh Sultan bin Kayed Al-Qasimi, who had originally been arrested and placed under house arrest the previous year.[41] Described as the chairman of *Al-Islah*, which at the time was claiming it had 20,000 members,[42] Sultan is a cousin of Ra's al-Khaimah's ruler, Sheikh Saud bin Saqr Al-Qasimi. Moreover, his brothers have served in key positions in Ra's al-Khaimah's government and have previously represented Ra's al-Khaimah in the UAE's Federal National Council. His father, the late Sheikh Kayed bin Muhammad Al-Qasimi, even has one of the main commercial streets in the center of Ra's al-Khaimah named after him.

WHAT ABOUT THE ARAB SPRING?

As significant as Sheikh Muhammad bin Zayed Al-Nahyan's anti-Islamist leanings and any domestic power centralizing machinations within the United Arab Emirates may be, the dramatically escalatory nature of the most recent bout of anti-Muslim Brotherhood and anti-Qatar actions nonetheless do seem to have another, more international dimension. Certainly, the UAE's current stance would appear at least in part to be a product of the so-called 'Arab Spring' uprisings that swept through much of the rest of the Arab world in late 2010 and early 2011. These were clearly seen by the UAE, and at least a majority of the other Gulf monarchies, as not only threatening to reduce their influence in the Arab and Islamic worlds, but also raising the prospect of 'demonstration effect' protests spilling over into their own backyards or, more likely, indigenous Islamist groups in the Gulf such as *Al-Islah* taking advantage of the situation and emerging as either domestic opposition forces or as potential 'fifth columns' on behalf of the Muslim Brotherhood which,

[41] Salem, O. (2013). 94 Emiratis Charged with Compromising UAE Security. *The National* 28 January 2013.

[42] Kerr, S. (2012). UAE Islamist Detained in Ruler's Palace. *Financial Times*, 25 April 2012; The Guardian. (2013). UAE Sentences "Coup Plotters" to Jail. *The Guardian*, 2 July 2013.

in June 2012, had gained control over the Egyptian presidency,[43] before being ousted a year later by the *Tamarod* or 'Rebellion' campaign. Although described by the BBC and other international media at the time as a 'grassroots protest movement', it later emerged that *Tamarod* been orchestrated by the Egyptian military and partly financed by the UAE.[44]

In this context, in early 2013 several of the pretrial UAE 94 detainees had been described by the Abu Dhabi state-owned media as having 'confessed to setting up a secret organisation with an armed wing with the aim of seizing power and establishing an Islamist state in the UAE.' They were also accused of having 'communicated with the international Muslim Brotherhood organisation… and [having] asked them for help, expertise and financial support to serve their undeclared goal of seizing power.'[45] In parallel, and seemingly also part of the effort to link *Al-Islah* to foreign entities, at least twenty Egyptian expatriates in the UAE were charged with 'setting up an international branch of the Muslim Brotherhood and stealing secret information from the [UAE] security services.'[46]

For Saudi Arabia's rulers the concerns were much the same, as notwithstanding their well-established relations with the Muslim Brotherhood, they had long been aware that the greatest historical threat to their regime had never been the 1979 seizure of the grand mosque seizure by fanatics,[47] nor the short-lived 2003 Al-Qaeda campaign targeting the kingdom's oil infrastructure.[48] Rather, they recognized that it had been the *Sahwa al-Islamiyya* or 'Islamic Awakening' movement, which had reached its peak during the 1990s and had seen numerous religiously conservative Saudis—many of whom had been taught by

[43] Kirkpatrick, D. (2012). Named Egypt's Winner, Islamist Makes History. *New York Times*, 24 June 2012.

[44] BBC. (2013). Profile: Egypt's Tamarod Protest Movement. *BBC*, 1 July 2013; Kirckpatrick, D. (2015). Recordings Suggest Emirates and Egyptian Military Pushed Ousting of Morsi. *New York Times*, 1 March 2015.

[45] The National, '94 Emiratis Charged with Compromising UAE Security'.

[46] BBC. (2014). UAE Jails 30 Over Muslim Brotherhood Ties. *BBC News*, 21 January 2014.

[47] For an account of the Grand Mosque seizure, see Hegghammer, T. and Lacroix, S. (2011). *The Meccan Rebellion: The Story of Juhayman al-Utaybi Revisited*. Beirut: Amal.

[48] Hegghammer, T. (2010). The Failure of Jihad in Saudi Arabia, Combating Terrorism Centre at West Point. *Occasional Paper Series*, 25 February 2010.

or were in sympathy with Brotherhood-aligned scholars—begin to press for significant reforms in favor of the clergy and question the ruling family's close relationship with the Western powers.[49] As such, the February 2011 announcement that a new, seemingly Brotherhood and Arab Spring-inspired organization—the *Hizb al-Ummah al-Islamiyya* or 'Islamic Nation Party'—had submitted a request to be approved as Saudi Arabia's first ever political party was a particularly unwelcome development, with the authorities moving almost immediately to arrest all of its founding members.[50]

Less tangibly, another, longer-term danger to the UAE and Saudi Arabia was that the 2011 uprisings—which had effectively prized open enough space for the Muslim Brotherhood and its affiliates to either dominate or even win power outright in hitherto secular authoritarian states—would allow new Arab regimes to emerge that might soon represent an alternative blueprint for conservative and religiously legitimated governance over Sunni Muslim majority populations. Moreover, with at least some sort of democratic processes being followed—of the type clearly predicted and feared by MBZ in 2007—there was not only the prospect that such states might be more appealing to young conservative Muslims than hereditary unelected monarchies, but that the Western powers too—in theory at least—might also jump on the Islamist-democrat bandwagon. After all, in April 2012 a Muslim Brotherhood delegation to the US was invited to meet with senior White House officials and, as the Council on Foreign Relations' Steven Cook describes, 'from the perspective of the leaders of Saudi Arabia, the UAE... it [became] an article of faith that [Secretary of State] Clinton enabled the rise of the Muslim Brotherhood in 2011 and 2012.' As he put it, such leaders saw 'losing' Egypt to the Brotherhood as a 'major geopolitical blow.'[51]

[49] Lacroix, S. (2011). Saudi Islamists and the Potential for Protest. *Foreign Policy*, 2 June 2011; For a more general discussion, see Lacroix, S. (2011). *Awakening Islam: The Politics of Religious Dissent in Saudi Arabi*. New Haven: Harvard University Press.

[50] HRW. (2011). Saudi Arabia: Free Political Activists. *Human Rights Watch*, 19 February 2011; Laessing, U. (2011). Pro-Reform Saudi Activists Launch Political Party. *Reuters*, 10 February 2011.

[51] Tau, B. (2012). Muslim Brotherhood Delegation Meets with White House Officials. *Politico*, 4 April 2012; Cook, S. (2018). Riyalpolitik and the Art of Influence in Trump's Washington. *Foreign Policy*, 28 May 2018.

QATAR'S GREAT GAMBLE

Qatar's evidently deep level of involvement and significant contributions to this fast-developing, unsettling situation understandably infuriated the UAE and Saudi Arabia. Despite being a fellow Gulf monarchy, and regardless of its status as a member of the Gulf Cooperation Council, there is little doubt that by 2011 both Abu Dhabi and Riyadh viewed Qatar as not only a full member of the enemy camp, but also the state that was doing the most to elevate any previously existential threat to their regimes posed by political Islam into a veritable, more imminent threat. In particular, Qatar's state-funded Al Jazeera network, and especially its Arabic news channel, was—as anticipated by Sheikh Muhammad bin Zayed Al-Nahyan—in a position to provide enormously strong media support for the Muslim Brotherhood. Having mushroomed in the 2000s, with more and more Brotherhood-linked members joining its staff, by the time of the Arab Spring Al Jazeera's weekly *Shari'a and Life* show—hosted by Yusuf al-Qaradawi—was by far the channel's main event, with viewing figures of more than sixty million.[52] Abandoning impartiality, especially when it came to covering Egypt, Al Jazeera was soon described as 'breathlessly pro-Brotherhood' with 'obvious bias.'[53] Also alarming for the UAE and Saudi Arabia, especially given the emerging Islamist-democrat dynamic, much of the Western media seemed keen to portray Al Jazeera—and by extension Qatar—as progressive. In June 2013, for example, Britain's widely read *Daily Telegraph* even called Al Jazeera the 'revolutionary force' that was allowing Qatar to 'buck the hierarchical conservatism that has dominated the Arab heartland.'[54]

Exacerbating the situation further, Qatar had also been willing to bankroll the Brotherhood, or more specifically the short-lived Muhammad Morsi government in Egypt, including promises of $18 billion spread over five years and 'no limits' on future support.[55] Meanwhile over in Tunisia—arguably the birthplace of the Arab Spring—Qatar

[52] Smoltczyk, A. (2011). Islam's Spiritual Dear Abby: The Voice of Egypt's Muslim Brotherhood. *SPON*, 15 February 2011.

[53] Goldberg, J. (2014). Why Does Al-Jazeera Love a Hateful Islamic Extremist? *Bloomberg*, 10 July 2013; Ulrichsen, 'Qatar and the Arab Spring' (p. 50).

[54] McElroy, D. (2013). Qatar: New Emir, New Broom? *Daily Telegraph*, 25 June 2013.

[55] The $18 billion was to be divided between power plants, gas, steel, and tourism projects. Awad, M. (2012). Qatar Says to Invest $18 Billion in Egypt Economy. *Reuters*, 6 September 2012.

seemed equally willing to bolster the Brotherhood-inspired *Ennahda* or 'Renaissance' party, which, especially after electoral successes in October 2011, seemed poised to become the country's dominant political force. A $2 billion Qatar-funded new oil refinery was duly announced, along with promises of assistance for the Tunisian central bank to help ameliorate its worsening balance of payments.[56] In return, as Columbia University's Alfred Stepan and Yale University's Juan Linz observed, the new Tunisian government seemed willing to leave the country's mosques open to foreign funding, with 'a vacuum that Gulf-financed theocratic extremists rushed to fill amid the new conditions of greater religious liberty.'[57]

Given the current 'Anti-Terror Quartet' pressure and what Qatar's leaders undoubtedly knew of MBZ's earlier suspicions and accusations, the post-2011 intensification of Doha's pro-Brotherhood strategy retrospectively seems to have been based on poor judgement, as it was inevitably going to lead to some sort of conflict with its closest neighbors. But from Qatar's perspective, especially during the heady days of the Arab Spring when it seemed anything was possible, such wrath was clearly worth risking, as above and beyond any historical ideological affinity its rulers and elites may have had with the Brotherhood, Qatar had evidently identified a golden opportunity to create a network of alliances with potentially powerful new revolutionary Arab states. Perhaps best viewed through the lens of 'realist' international relations scholarship—which usually emphasizes the anarchic nature of the international system and states' corresponding efforts to ensure their own survival—these alliances were unquestionably seen by Qatar's leaders as a means to counter the influence and might of their larger and militarily more powerful monarchical neighbors, which they had long distrusted and with which they had a long history of troubled relations.

Certainly, despite the comfort Qatar began to enjoy after signing a defense cooperation agreement with the US in 1992 and then hosting major US military facilities on its territory, including since 2002 the

[56]Reuters. (2012). Qatar to Proceed with $2 bln Refinery in Tunisia. *Reuters*, 15 May 2012; Al-Arabiya. (2013). Qatar Bank Gives Tunisia $500m Deposit, Says Source. *Al Arabiya*, 23 November 2013.

[57]Stepan, A. and Linz, J. (2013). Democratization Theory and the Arab Spring. *Journal of Democracy*, 24:2 (p. 25).

de facto forward headquarters for US Central Command,[58] there is little doubt that the Al-Thani family has continued to fear UAE and Saudi-sponsored attempts to undermine Qatari sovereignty and even topple their regime. In 1995 for example, Abu Dhabi and Riyadh were widely accused of trying to reinstall Sheikh Khalifa bin Hamad Al-Thani, who had been ousted from power by his ostensibly more popular son, Sheikh Hamad bin Khalifa Al-Thani. Although the counter-coup was unsuccessful, the following year some six thousand Qatari tribesmen were disenfranchised, and several ruling family members were arrested after being linked to another Saudi-backed plot.[59]

CONCLUSION

Damaging to all involved, both economically and reputationally, at the time of writing there is no end in sight to the Qatar crisis. With little apparent middle ground between the two camps, and with efforts thus far by outside mediators—including the US—having led to nothing or, in some cases, even inflaming the situation, there is every indication that it will become yet another long-running, intractable Middle Eastern dispute with negative international ramifications.[60] As is now clear, Qatar's support for the Muslim Brotherhood and other such organizations has very much been at the heart of the dispute. In many ways, this has been puzzling given that Qatar's chief antagonist—the United Arab Emirates—has, on top of its marked structural similarities with Qatar, historically enjoyed warm and cordial relations with many of the same groups. The UAE's earlier, well-documented connections to the Brotherhood and its fellow travelers certainly undermine any attempt to explain the crisis on the basis that there are deep-rooted religious or religio-ideological differences between the Qatari and UAE ruling families and political elites.

[58] US Congressional Research Service. (2012). *Qatar: Background and U.S. Relations*. Washington, DC: CRS. The Washington Post. (2012). At Qatar Base, a Test Run for War. *The Washington Post*, 10 December 2012.

[59] Kamrava, M. (2009). Royal Factionalism and Political Liberalization in Qatar. *Middle East Journal*, 63:3 (p. 415).

[60] For examples of failed mediations, see Bloomberg. (2017). Qatar Crisis Mediation Is Deadlocked. *Bloomberg*, 26 July 2017; Bakir, A. (2017). GCC Crisis: Why Is Kuwaiti Mediation Not Working? *Al Jazeera*, 11 August 2017.

More compelling, it would seem, is an explanation that combines the personal politics of the most influential figure in the crisis—the UAE's Sheikh Muhammad bin Zayed Al-Nahyan—and the catalytic effect of the 2011 Arab uprisings on UAE policymaking. As this chapter has demonstrated, for many years MBZ had been pushing for a much harder line against the Brotherhood and Qatar than any of the UAE's other leaders, frequently using high level discussions with visiting diplomats as an opportunity to warn them of the potential for Al Jazeera to indoctrinate UAE citizens (including his own close relatives) and the likelihood that any future democratic openings in the Arab world were likely to be seized upon by Islamists and, by extension, Qatar. As something of a wake-up call for the UAE (and allies such as Saudi Arabia), especially after the 'loss' of Egypt to the Brotherhood and of Tunisia to *Ennahda*, the uprisings clearly propelled the UAE into taking much firmer action, concerned over the intentions of their own indigenous Islamist sympathizers and, more generally, worried that across the Arab world new Islamist dominated democracies were forming that would ultimately offer an alternative form of conservative Sunni Muslim governance to their own unelected, monarchical system. To make matters worse, at one point it even seemed that their mutual superpower protector, the US, was willing to endorse these new states.

On a theoretical level, MBZ's evidently unwavering, personalized stance on the Brotherhood and Qatar, which has translated into contemporary UAE policy, certainly supports the calls of Rose McDermott and others to promote a greater understanding of personalities in international relations and, more generally, of the need for more detailed biographic studies. Although in this case data was hard to come by, there is now enough material in the public domain to perform at least a basic leadership analysis, especially with regard to key influences and kinship factors. Meanwhile, viewed through a state-to-state lens, the evidence would seem to support something of a realist interpretation of the crisis, especially after the Arab uprisings began to flush out into the open the UAE and Saudi Arabia's shared fears, along with Qatar's motives for getting so heavily involved in the first place. After all, all three monarchies were conspicuously aware they were operating in an increasingly turbulent and, after 2011, potentially anarchic environment. In this context all saw a range of elevated threats to their states and respective regimes: either from each other (from Qatar's perspective), or from new alliances comprising hostile revolutionary states linked to potential 'fifth columns' in their own territories (from the UAE and Saudi Arabia's perspective). Thus, although the Qatar crisis has very clearly revolved around the perceived influence of an organization that openly fuses politics with religion, the dispute is actually less about the role of religion in international relations—at least in the sense envisaged by Jack Snyder and others—and much more about the survival of three competing, wary monarchical states, all of which have been willing to co-opt political Islam at different stages in their histories, and two of which have already dispensed with it.

CHAPTER 6

The Weaponization of Narratives Amid the Gulf Crisis

Andreas Krieg

INTRODUCTION

The 2017 Crisis commenced with a cyberattack on the Qatar News Agency (QNA) and was preceded by weeks of bad press against Qatar predominately in the United States. According to joint Qatari-US investigations, the cyberattack emanated from the United Arab Emirates and directly targeted the reputation and legitimacy of the Qatari ruling family.[1] The reasons behind this cyberattack attributing false statements to the Qatari Emir remain hidden. Speculations from individuals involved in the investigation, suggest that these fabricated statements were meant to incite the Qatari public to raise up against the ruling family amid mounting international pressure—a scenario that never materialized.

Moving beyond the immediate context of the 2017 Gulf Crisis and looking at the Gulf divide as a development that unfolded over the past two decades, the information domain has played an increasingly

---

[1] Finn, T. (2017). Qatar Says Media Report Reveals UAE Role in Hack That Sparked Crisis. *Reuters*, 17 July 2017.

A. Krieg (✉)
Defence Studies Department, King's College London, London, UK
e-mail: andreas.krieg@kcl.ac.uk

A. Krieg (ed.), *Divided Gulf*, Contemporary Gulf Studies,
https://doi.org/10.1007/978-981-13-6314-6_6

important part in splitting Gulf unity—not least because of the controversial role of Al Jazeera. Apart from the obvious feuds over interests, influence and power, the emancipation of the smaller Gulf States from the long shadow of Saudi Arabia brought with it an ideological clash over narratives. More precisely, as particularly Doha and Abu Dhabi realized in the early 1990s that development and modernization would require an alternative grand strategy to that of a widely paralyzed Saudi kingdom, both states created two almost diametrically opposed visions of how to move into the twenty-first century. The two visions were tied to two narratives that were conceived by the two rulers that would shape the outlook and appearance of their respective countries for the decades to come: Hamad bin Khalifa al Thani (HbK), the now Father Emir of Qatar, and Mohamad bin Zayed al Nahyan, the Crown Prince of Abu Dhabi.

As this chapter will argue, the Gulf rift dates to the rise of power of the two individuals HbK and MbZ whose visions for their countries and the region at large, would come head to head as the Arab Spring erupted. This chapter will demonstrate how the ideological feud between the two neighbours eventually escalated into a soft power war in the public sphere after the Arab Spring. While cyberattacks had been relatively rare in the Gulf, the hack on the QNA comes after years of information and disinformation warfare mostly directed by the United Arab Emirates against Qatar and its policies during the Arab Spring. The clash over narratives between the two ambitious small states has not only split the Gulf but created ripple effects that were felt across the Arab World.

The chapter commences by outlining the roots of the two opposite narratives in Doha and Abu Dhabi before explaining how these narratives were securitized during the Arab Spring. While Qatar used its narratives of social justice and inclusive governance to propel the people's revolutions, the Emirates used their narrative about authoritarian stability to legitimize the counterrevolutions. The chapter continues by showing how the counterrevolutions on the ground in Egypt, Libya and Yemen were supported by a communication strategy that would not only provide legitimacy to the Emirati cause but undermine the Qatari cause. The chapter concludes by outlining how the UAE eventually activated its extensive PR machine, particularly in the United States, in an attempt to isolate Qatar in the Gulf and the West.

Two Opposing Worldviews

As Jervis once said 'it is often impossible to explain crucial decisions and policies without reference to the decision-makers beliefs about the world and their images of others'[2]—nowhere does this seem to be more accurate than in the tribal monarchies of the Gulf where individuals often matter more than formal institutions. As the two architects of the contemporary appearance of their respective countries, HbK and MbZ have shaped the *raison d'état* of Qatar and the UAE in the twenty-first century more than anyone else.

A state's *raison d'état* is a narrative that combines historical experience, geography, political tradition and norms to illustrate the self-perception of a nation's character vis-à-vis partners, allies and adversaries within a geo-strategic and regional environment. This self-image of the state and the nation as a socio-political entity is shaped by historical experiences of foreign and security policy, its geographic location vis-à-vis other states and communities, its socio-political tradition as an open or closed society, and societal moral norms.[3]

Hamad and the Creation of a Soft Power

Hamad bin Khalifa started to conduct state affairs in the early 1990s already before officially taking power from his father in a bloodless coup in 1995. A rebel and revolutionary at heart, Hamad was eager to redevelop not just Qatar's image but more importantly its place in the region. As a small state without considerable wealth, sandwiched between Iran and Saudi Arabia as the region's great powers, Qatar had long been haunted by structural insecurities—insecurities that Riyadh as the traditional protector was not only unable to protect against but more importantly actively contributing to. Hamad's vision for securing a city-state was founded on societal, intellectual and economic liberalization that would set the emirate free from the extended reach of the Saudi state and its *Wahhabi* clergy. Although adhering to a more liberal form of Salafi Islam, the people of the Qatari Peninsula had traditionally looked

---

[2] Jervis, R. (1976). *Perception and Misperception in International Politics*. Princeton, NJ: Princeton University Press (p. 28).

[3] Drew, D.M. (2002). *Making Strategy: An Introduction to National Security Processes and Problems*. Maxwell, AL: Air University Press (p. 57).

to the *ulama* of the kingdom for spiritual guidance[4]—a considerable instrument of soft power that Saudis had often used as a political tool against the Al Thani rulers of Doha. Yet, for Hamad leaving the Saudi orbit was not just about power and influence but equally about emancipating Qatar's ultraconservative society from the shackles of Wahhabist norms and traditions that would constrain individual liberties and the ability of societies to inclusively excel into the post-hydrocarbon era.

Hence, for Hamad sustainable economic and societal growth in the era of globalization meant liberalizing society, providing inclusive access to the country's wealth, opening liberal education for all and cultivating a sense of liberal public discourse.[5] While it is too far-fetched to define Hamad as a democrat, he nonetheless believed that an open society should have relative freedom of speech and thought to help build an economy that could eventually exist without the rentier state. Attracting Western universities and creating Al Jazeera as a revolutionary, relatively independent, pan-Arab international broadcaster, was as much about exposing the ultraconservative Qatari public to new ideas as it was about building a soft power hub in Qatar that would differentiate the emirate from its neighbours. Undermining the Arab regimes' monopoly over information, Qatar's investment into liberal access to information, whether via universities, think tanks or media outlets, would constitute a challenge to the regional status quo.

Al Jazeera's leading motto 'providing a voice to the voiceless' was thereby an extension of a Qatari tradition that dates back further than the era Hamad: Qatar as the *Kaaba al Madiyoun*, the Kaaba of the dispossessed. The Qatari peninsula had long been a place to which exiles gravitated—pirates, outlawed sheikhs, persecuted Islamists and exiled dissidents.[6] As the home of the exiled, Qatar under Hamad was supposed to become a hub for alternative thought, new ideas and unconventional approaches to solving conflict. Sometimes hailed as the 'Switzerland of the Middle East', Qatar began promoting itself as an international meeting hub where any party to a conflict, whether state or non-state, Islamist or secular autocrat, Sunni or Shia, was welcome. As such, Qatar has often been criticized as pursuing a strategy of duality—one where

---

[4]Fromherz, A.J. (2012). *Qatar: A Modern History.* London: I.B. Tauris (p. 91).

[5]CBS. (2003). Qatar: Embracing Democracy. *CBS 60 Minutes,* 25 July 2003.

[6]Roberts, D. (2016). *Qatar—Securing the Global Ambitions of a City State.* London: Hurst (p. 33).

Israel could open a trade office between 1996 and 2009 while Hamas leader Khalid Mashal would frequently fly in and out of Doha. Hamad was not uneasy about Muslim Brotherhood clerics and followers to come into Qatari exile. The United States were welcome to plan and execute their regional military strategy from Al Udeid base near Doha, while Washington asked Hamad to host a Taliban office in the Qatari capital. As an internationally recognized mediator, Qatar was able to broker deals between Hezbollah and the Lebanese government, between Khartoum and the most powerful rebel group in Darfur, and between Yemen and the Houthis.[7]

Qatar's resource abundance, its small indigenous population with direct tribal ties to the emir, provided Hamad with an opportunity to host a diverse range of protagonists and ideas without having to fear that it might undermine his legitimacy or authority domestically. Hamad's strategic narrative of openness promoting human development through social justice and civil liberties, as well as promoting individual self-determination, was meant to solidify Qatar's role as a regional soft power. Following the Islamic socio-political maxim of *Al Adla wa al'amen*, social justice and security, Qatar's soft power strategy was as much about interests as it was about values that Qatar would not only try to promote domestically but increasingly across the region, causing friction particularly with the rulers in Riyadh and Abu Dhabi.

MbZ and the Birth of a Fierce State

In parallel to the rise of power of Hamad bin Khalifa in Doha in the early 1990s, Mohamad bin Zayed al Nahyan rose through the ranks of the Emirati military to become their chief of staff. Unlike Hamad, the son of Zayed was not in a position to become an influential political player although the country's federal power politics would eventually be decided in favour of the Al Nahyans of Abu Dhabi. MbZ approached development and growth through the lens of security.[8] While Hamad was eager to deal with dissidence through engagement, MbZ approached any form of dissidence through securitization—most importantly the

---

[7] Kamrava, M. (2011). Mediation and Qatari Foreign Policy. *The Middle East Journal*, 65:4.

[8] Young, K. (2014). *The Political Economy of Energy, Finance and Security in the United Arab Emirates.* London: Palgrave (pp. 102–130).

issue of Islamist dissidence. Consequently, the Emirates' path to sovereignty and social as well as political emancipation from Saudi Arabia was a fundamentally different one to that of Qatar.

While Qatar under Hamad had betted on soft power diversification, securing the UAE would be achieved through an investment into its security sector and an alignment with the United States both in terms of interests and values. MbZ envisaged the creation of a new Middle Eastern state, one that would overcome both the shackles of Arab Nationalism and political Islam to embrace modernity by clearly separating religion from statecraft.[9] Statecraft would be the prerogative of the autocratic, centralized ruler whose transactional relationship with his subordinates was supposed to be governed by both means of accommodation and repression. The ideal strongman, from MbZ's point of view, was in control of the security sector, both military and law enforcement, and governed over a society emancipated from religious conservatism and empowered by capitalist market structures.[10] Thus, social and economic liberalism was never to be confused with political liberalism. Paradoxically, MbZ's model of the Jeffersonian state was based on an absolute monarchy dominating a centralized state bureaucracy.

Often coined the Gulf's 'Little Sparta',[11] MbZ's obsession with security and securitization transformed the country from a mediocre military force to a regional military powerhouse, willing to use all instruments available to secure the state both internally and externally.[12] Advised by Egyptian security officials and intelligence officers, the UAE imported much of the security narratives of Mubarak's Egypt: a paranoia about Islamist opposition and dissidence.[13] Like Egypt, the UAE developed increasingly into a *mukhaberat* state, a police state obsessed with the threat of terrorism, political dissidence and Islamist activism—an

[9] Roberts, D. (2016). Mosque and State: The United Arab Emirate's Secular Foreign Policy. *Foreign Affairs*, 18 March 2016.

[10] Young, K. (2014). *The Political Economy of Energy, Finance and Security in the United Arab Emirates*. London: Palgrave (pp. 102–130).

[11] Economist. (2017). The Gulf's Little Sparta. *The Economist*, 6 April 2017.

[12] Roberts, D. (2017). Qatar and the UAE: Exploring Divergent Approaches to the Arab Spring. *Middle East Journal*, 71:3 (p. 557).

[13] Fanack. (2017). UAE and the Muslim Brotherhood: A Story of Rivalry and Hatred. *Fanack Chronicle*, 16 July 2017. https://chronicle.fanack.com/united-arab-emirates/history-past-to-present/uae-muslim-brotherhood/.

obsession that would witness a relentless crack down on Islamist opposition in the Emirates, particularly after 9/11. Following America's War
on Terror, MbZ, meanwhile promoted to Crown Prince of Abu Dhabi,
was eager to demonstrate to Washington that the UAE were different
from all other Middle Eastern states in that it would determinedly move
against any form of political Islam.

Similar to Qatar and the other Arab States in the Gulf, the UAE had
witnessed the arrival of Islamists as early as the 1950s and 1960s who
came as educators and judges. Particularly the Muslim Brotherhood's
Emirati franchise of al-Islah came to dominate both the education sector and judicial system. The disproportionate influence of al-Islah in
the UAE had drawn in locals from the less wealthy northern emirates
and even members of their royal families.[14] MbZ conceived the politicization of Islam and the consequent Islamization of politics as a fundamental threat to his Jeffersonian vision of the strong state. In Abu Dhabi
the Muslim Brotherhood appeared increasingly as the antithesis to the
Emirati state-building project and its narrative of a secular nation state
in the Middle East. Multiple attacks against high profile targets in the
1990s had already triggered a purge of Muslim Brothers in the country.[15] But it was not until after 9/11 that MbZ was taking a hard-line
approach based on neo-conservative narratives of zero tolerance towards
Islamism, that scores of individuals believed to be affiliated with al-Islah
were either removed from their posts, stripped of their nationality, exiled
or arrested.[16]

Instead of addressing potential grievances that might have facilitated the appeal of *al-Islah* in parts of the Emirates, MbZ's state looked
increasingly like a fierce state, i.e. a state that Ayubi defines as dealing
with societal demands through repression and force rather than engagement.[17] Abu Dhabi's paranoia over political dissidence was further

[14] Bayoumi, Y. (2013). UAE Islamist Group Had No Desire to Topple Government:
Families. *Reuters*, 2 July 2013.

[15] AlSharq AlAwsat. (2013). الإخوان المسلمون في الإمارات. القصة الكاملة. *AlSharq AlAwsat*,
19 February 2013.

[16] Herb, M. (2010). Kuwait and the United Arab Emirates. In Michele Penner Angrist
(ed.). *Politics and Society in the Contemporary Middle East*. Boulder, CL: Lynne Rienner
Publishers (p. 359).

[17] Ayubi, N. (1995). *Overstating the Arab State: Politics and Society in the Middle East*.
London: I.B. Tauris (p. 449).

fuelled by the developments of the Arab Spring to which MbZ internally reacted by further curtailing the freedom of speech, thought and assembly in the country.[18]

THE ARAB SPRING: REVOLUTION VS. COUNTERREVOLUTION

Qatar: Action Against Authoritarianism

When protests broke out in Tunisia, closely followed by Egypt, Libya and other Arab countries, Hamad saw an opportunity to put narrative to practise in an effort to appeal to the West as a partner in liberalizing the region, to expand his country's influence and provide access to new markets across the region. Unlike other Arab states, Qatar could look at the socio-political upheavals on the way in the region from a place of relative comfort as Qatari citizens remained protected from the individual insecurities that had inspired the Arab Spring elsewhere. With unprecedented levels of individual wealth, a relative freedom of speech and assembly, Qataris were widely apathetic to the developments in the region.

Consequently, Hamad had the luxury of experimenting with his country's soft power to amplify the diverse range of dissident voices in the region. For the Father Emir, the protests that started in Tunisia were an expression of an Arab yearning for more socio-political pluralism, more social justice and freedom from oppression—demands that resonated well with Qatar's strategic narrative. It suddenly felt as if Qatar's *raison d'état* fell on fertile ground as the Arab youth broke the barrier of fear to confront the authoritarians that had dominated the Arab World since Nasser's time. Defying Keohane's definition of a small power,[19] Hamad was determined to seize the opportunity of taking ownership of what looked like a watershed moment in the history of the Arab World, to help shape the future of the Arab people. Through financial and soft power, Qatar was to transform from an arbitrator to an activist using all instruments to its availability to oust the *ancien régimes* of the region.

---

[18] Roberts, D. (2016). Mosque and State: The United Arab Emirate's Secular Foreign Policy. *Foreign Affairs*, 18 March 2016.

[19] Keohane, K. (1969). Lilliputians' Dilemmas: Small States in International Politics. *International Organization*, 23:2 (p. 296).

At a time when the international community stood by passively as millions took to the streets pushing regimes into a state of uncertainty and countries into civil war, Qatar offered a simple, albeit naïve, strategy: 'support the people against oppression'. In pursuit of this objective, Doha repeatedly neglected due diligence and scrutiny over whom to support. The fact that the pool of revolutionaries eager to topple the regimes was as diverse as their often contradictory agendas, was often disregarded in Doha.

As the traditional opposition to the Arab nationalist regime, the Muslim Brotherhood (*Ikhwan*) and its many local affiliates appeared to provide Qatar with a network and local institutions to channel support to the masses. While secular liberals were lacking platforms or numerical superiority, the moderate Islamists of the Brotherhood such as Ghanouchi in Tunisia, Al Sallabi in Libya, Mashal in Gaza or Riad al-Shaqfa in Syria, were not only able to tap into local networks but had direct personal links with Brotherhood exiles living in Doha. Hence, not ideological preference but pragmatism prompted Hamad to cultivate a rapport with the *Ikhwan* as the most extensive informal institution of the Arab world. Spiritual leaders of the Brotherhood, such as Qaradawi had lived in Qatar already for decades and enjoyed Hamad's protection from persecution.[20] Qatar's exposed role as the *Kaaba al Madiyoom* had provided Hamad with avenues into dissident communities across the region that would all participate in revolutionary activity once people had taken to the street.

Al Jazeera jumped on the revolutionary bandwagon providing protestors with a voice by bundling social and new media coverage of the revolution to broadcast calls for social justice and inclusive governance. While Al Jazeera's transformative impact on the revolutions of the Arab Spring is well documented, the 'Al Jazeera effect' appears to be often overrated. After all, the broadcaster did little more than amplify an already existing voice for change, providing an inclusive platform to liberal, secular and Islamist voices alike.[21] Nonetheless, Al Jazeera developed into a soft power tool working in parallel to the government's foreign and security policy helping to transport Qatar's narrative into the epicentres

[20] Roberts, D. (2014). Qatar and the Muslim Brotherhood: Pragmatism or Preference? *Middle East Policy*, 21:3, 3 September 2014.

[21] Seib, P. (2008). *The Al Jazeera Effect. How the New Global Media Are Reshaping World Politics*. Lincoln, NE: Potomac Books.

of the people's protests from Tunisia and Libya over Egypt to Syria and Bahrain.

While Doha had approached the revolutions initially through soft power engagement and financial support, Qatar's approach become increasingly hard-power focused in face of regimes using violent repression against mostly unarmed protestors. When in Libya and Syria regimes started to crack down heavy-handedly against dissidents, Hamad did not shy away from providing first material and then armed support to emerging rebel groups in the countries—all that while sanctioned by the US government or NATO partners. Qatar commenced by supporting groups that would be able to display operational effectiveness, a clear commitment to *Al Adla wa al'amen* and a form of inclusive governance. However, as the Civil War in Syria turned sour, the desperation of many moderates over the lack of international community support witnessed a visible radicalization of the revolutionary environment. It was the appearance of Al Qaeda and later the Islamic State on the battlefields of Syria and Libya that would undermine Qatari efforts to unite the rebellions under one banner—the jihadists were no longer just focusing on the Assad regime but increasingly on the moderate opposition. As global public opinion diverted its attention away from the revolutions to the rise of jihadism, Qatar's moment to reshape the region appeared to be over.

UAE: The Myth of Authoritarian Stability

From the onset, Qatar's expansive foreign and security policy was a thorn in the side of Emirati regional policy as it directly undermined MbZ's narrative of authoritarian stability. With political Islam having been widely securitized in the Emirates, Qatar's support for dissident non-state actors with Islamist affiliations was a security nightmare for the Crown Prince of Abu Dhabi. While Hamad's agenda can be described as revolutionary, MbZ became increasingly the counterrevolutionary, taking action where possible to reverse the effects of the Arab Spring.

For 'Little Sparta' Qatar's proliferation of its revolutionary ideology about socio-political change and reform was empowering non-state actors that neither Doha nor any other regional player could really control. The UAE's response to the people's call for more social justice and freedom from oppression was cautious to begin with and revisionary later on. From MbZ's statist point of view, internal stability had to take precedence over individual liberty, regime security over public security and sectarian autocracy over pluralism. Effectively, the UAE tried to revive the age-old neo-conservative myth that the Arab World would be best governed by authoritarian autocrats rather than by pluralistic or democratic governance systems. The myth of authoritarian stability stood in stark contrast to Qatar's belief that only inclusive governance could eventually bring about stability to the Arab World.[22] For Abu Dhabi dissidence and uncontrolled civil society were potentially disruptive forces that could easily spin out of control into insurgency and terrorism, which would undermine the security and stability of the region.

The 'terrorism label' has since been the centrepiece of Emirati narratives in response to the Arab Spring. Based on the neo-conservative 'conveyer belt theory' that any form of Islamism, or politicized religion, gradually turns followers into jihadists, the UAE have approached Islamist organizations domestically and regionally with suspicion. Moderate Islamist groups such as the charitable branches of the Muslim Brotherhood have been labelled as an 'entry drug to jihadism'.[23] Abu Dhabi reacted to the growing influence of Islamism during the revolutions of the Arab Spring with a crack-down on any form of Islamist organization outside of state control. Since 2011 a range of Islamist charities and groups have been banned in the Emirates as 'terrorist organizations'. Under the cover of counterterrorism, MbZ's fierce state has moved against any civil society activism in the country outside state control. At the heart of the Emirati crackdown on political Islam is a securitization effort framing both Islamists and their supporters as existential enemies of the state. The post-revolutionary chaos in Libya, Egypt, Syria and Yemen has been used by Abu Dhabi as evidence that the old authoritarian order must be restored.

Whereas Qatar has provided material and armed support for revolutionary groups, the UAE found themselves supporting the counterrevolutionaries such as Hafter in Libya, El Sisi in Egypt or the now assassinated former Yemeni President Saleh. The Emirati connection consists of like-minded strongmen who prioritize security over liberalism and fierce centralized governance over inclusive socio-politics.

---

[22]Gause, G. (2011). Why Middle East Studies Missed the Arab Spring—The Myth of Authoritarian Stability. *Foreign Affairs*, 90:4 (p. 81).

[23]Trager, E. (2017). The Muslim Brotherhood Is the Root of the Qatar Crisis. *The Atlantic*, 2 July 2017.

More recently Mohammad bin Salman al Saud, the overambitious Saudi Crown Prince, has joined MbZ's cause using authoritarian liberalization as a tool to bring the ultraconservative kingdom into the twenty-first century. Following the Emirati model, MbS seems to hope that Saudi Arabia can eventually become an economically and socio-politically resilient state. An unlikely ally to MbZ's revisionary policy to restore the old order lost in the Arab Spring, has become Israel's Prime Minister Netanyahu whose zero tolerance towards political Islam overlaps with the security paranoia in Abu Dhabi.

Bolstered by change of White House tenancy in 2017 and a range of powerful allies in the Arab World, the UAE today lead an international struggle to reverse the achievements of the Arab Spring as local communities and the international community seemingly have grown tired of uncertainty and instability in the region. The Emirati effort to weaponize its narrative in the West has become a critically important component in its strategy to counter the Qatari narrative.

From Soft Power Clashes to Offensive Information Warfare

The story of Emirati information warfare commenced in 2006, when the UAE found itself on the receiving end of a disinformation campaign amid a potential takeover of the British company P&O by the Dubai Ports World (DPW). As this takeover would have seen DPW controlling six US American ports, a bipartisan campaign in Congress commenced that vehemently objected to relinquishing control over US port facilities to a company based in the Middle East—Dubai Ports World was stigmatized as a Middle Eastern entity amid a still polarized and emotional post-9/11 environment.[24] As one security official was quoted by the Washington Post saying in 2006, '*letting a Middle Eastern company to manage key ports would be like putting the fox in charge of the henhouse*'.[25] Labelling the UAE a sponsor of terrorism, US policy makers on both sides of the aisle created a hostile environment that eventually triggered DPW to give up on their commercial ambitions. The Emirates'

---

[24]Qassemi, S. (2017). U.A.E's Reformed Foreign Ministry a Pioneer in the Region. *The Middle East Institute*, 11 April 2017. http://www.mei.edu/content/article/uae-s-reformed-foreign-ministry-pioneer-region.

[25]Gertz, B. (2016). Security Fears About Infiltration by Terrorists. *The Washington Post*, 22 February 2006.

undifferentiated reputation as 'another Islamic country in the Middle East' had undermined its freedom to do business and manoeuvre. The UAE realized that they had to invest in changing their branding by investing proactively in a global outreach program, particularly focusing on Washington, DC.

The DPW controversy had demonstrated to leaders in Abu Dhabi how effective messaging in the United States could shape policy discourse and eventually policy making. The lessons learned for MbZ were that a carefully implanted narrative into the discourse on Capitol Hill sustained and amplified by a nexus of think tanks, experts and media could make or break a country in the bipolar partisan atmosphere in DC. The Emirates had to change its image from being 'another Islamic country in the Middle East' to a 'progressive Middle Eastern partner for the United States'. Based on the UAE's narrative demonizing political Islam, MbZ's new ambassador in Washington, Yussuf al Otaiba, a socialite with impeccable American accent and Western lifestyle, identified the neo-conservative circles in Washington as the most receptive to the Emirati message.[26] Tapping into the neo-conservative fears of political Islam, the UAE's narrative in America would help conservative policy makers, think tankers and journalists to securitize Islamism as radicalized religion used by its proponents to Islamize the Middle East. The Emirates would appear as the alternative, secular Middle Eastern state— one that would work together with the United States to counter Islamic terrorism. The country that in 2006 was demonized as a terrorist sponsor by security officials from the Bush administration was now to be framed and marketed as a champion of countering terrorism in partnership with the US government.

Thereby, Otaiba was able to exploit the overly simplified nature of conservative discourse on terrorism. The fact that individuals with conservative worldviews tend to perceive the world through a lens of fear,[27] makes them particularly susceptible to securitization efforts, particularly on matters of complex nature such as terrorism or Middle Eastern affairs. Abu Dhabi's willingness to support its outreach campaign with tens of millions of dollars allowed Otaiba to not only fund luncheons, galas and events, but more importantly provided the funds to invest into

---

[26] Grim, R. (2017). Gulf Government Gave Secret $20 Million Gift to D.C. Think Tank. *The Intercept*, 10 August 2017.

[27] Castells, M. (2013). *Communication Power*. Oxford: Oxford University Press (p. 169).

the powerful neo-conservative nexus of Washington's think tank world and the political establishment.[28] Since 2007 the UAE have invested into think tanks such as the Centre for Strategic and International Studies, the Atlantic Council and the Middle East Institute[29] to support Emirati messaging with authority and legitimacy provided by allegedly independent experts.[30] The revolving door between Republican policy makers and Washington think tanks meant that Emirati funding would reach deep into the heart of US policy making—something that Abu Dhabi was increasingly trying to exploit offensively as the Arab Spring was perceived as a direct threat to the Emirati project.

By the end of the decade at the eve of the Arab Spring the Emirates had positioned themselves strategically within the United States, clearly demarcating their narrative and vision from its neighbours.[31] Socialite Otaiba had become the posterchild of a Middle Eastern country that set itself apart from its peers—at least in the eyes of conservative elites in Washington. The protests turning revolutions took the West and the Middle East alike by surprise creating further uncertainty about the future of an already unstable region. While liberals in the West were quick to embrace the revolutions as liberal expressions of people's strife for self-determination, conservatives were in fear that the toppling of the old mostly secular, authoritarian order, could be exploited by the Islamist opposition movements from Northern Africa over the Levant to the Gulf—a fear that was as prevalent in conservative circles in Washington as it was in Abu Dhabi.[32] MbZ's domestic crackdown on Islamist groups

---

[28] Lipton, E., Williams, B., and Confessore, M. (2014). Foreign Powers Buy Influence at Think Tanks. *The New York Times*, 6 September 2014.

[29] Krieg, A. (2018). Never Mind Russia, the UAE Has United with AIPAC to Capture Washington. *Middle East Eye*, 13 March 2018.

[30] Jilani, Z. and Emmons, A. (2017). Hacked Emails Show UAE Building Close Relationship with D.C. Think Tanks That Push Its Agenda. *The Intercept*, 30 July 2017.

[31] Qassemi, S. (2017). U.A.E's Reformed Foreign Ministry a Pioneer in the Region. *The Middle East Institute*, 11 April 2017. http://www.mei.edu/content/article/uae-s-reformed-foreign-ministry-pioneer-region.

[32] Bradley, J.R. (2012). *After the Arab Spring: How Islamists Hijacked The Middle East Revolts*. New York: St. Martin's Press; Gerges, F. (2011). The Irresistible Rise of the Muslim Brothers. *NewStatesman*, 28 November 2011; Joscelyn, T. (2015). Osama Bin Laden's Files: The Arab Revolutions. *The Long War Journal*, 3 March 2015. https://www. longwarjournal.org/archives/2015/03/osama-bin-ladens-files-the-arab-revolutions.php; Rosen, J. (2011). Arab Spring Optimism Gives Way to Fear of Islamic Rise. *FoxNews*, 28

and dissidents in 2011 was matched by an international outreach effort to rally support for a reactionary Middle East policy in the West. Amid the initial Western enthusiasm about liberalization and democratization in the Arab World, the pessimistic paranoia-driven approach of the Emirates took a back seat.

While Qatar naively jumped onto the liberal bandwagon of supporting the 'people's revolutions', the Emirates activated its powerful communication nexus in Washington to offensively push its neo-conservative agenda. The objective was no longer to establish the UAE's brand in America through positive messaging but to use its PR machine to advance its narrative by undermining both the agenda of Arab opposition movements and their sponsors—most notably Qatar and Turkey. When by 2012 the Muslim Brotherhood was elected into power in Egypt, the Ennahda Party established in post-revolutionary Tunisia, *al Islah* on the rise in Yemen, Islamists in control of key cities in Libya and Islamist opposition groups in sight of Assad's palace, Abu Dhabi's narrative required a substantial boost. The policy debate about the future of the Arab Spring, which was increasingly labelled as the 'Arab Winter' by neo-cons and pro-Israel lobby groups,[33] was approached by a three-tier messaging process.[34] First, amid a climate of uncertainty and unpredictability, the narrative of liberalization through regime change was challenged by Otaiba himself 'robo-emailing' DC influencers,[35] by prominent former policy makers absorbed by think tanks funded by the UAE, and by media outlets based in the UAE, most notably the daily *National* and the broadcaster *Al Arabiya*. Second, experts working for UAE-funded projects would amplify the securitization of political Islam. Here, the existent demonization of Hamas as an extension of the Muslim

October 2011. http://www.foxnews.com/politics/2011/10/28/arab-spring-optimism-gives-way-to-fear-islamic-rise.html.

[33] Haaretz. (2011). The Arab Spring Turned into Arab Winter. *Haaretz*, 19 December 2011; Smith, L. (2014). A Coming Arab Winter? *The Hudson Institute, Weekly Standard*, 6 June 2011. https://www.hudson.org/research/8054-a-coming-arab-winter-.

[34] Brüggemann, M. (2017). Die Medien und die Klimalüge. In Volker Lilienthal and Irene Nervala (ed.). *Lügenpresse – Anatomie eines politischen Kampfbegriffs*. Cologne: Kiepenheuer (p. 150).

[35] Grim, R. and Ahmed, A.S. (2015). His Town. *The Huffington Post Highline*, 2 September 2015.

Brotherhood among pro-Israeli think tanks helped putting into question the 'moderateness' of the *Ikhwan*. Third, particularly after the last Gulf Crisis in 2014, the Emirati neo-conservative nexus spread allegations that Qatar and Turkey were sponsoring terrorism by supporting armed and unarmed non-state actors in Libya, Egypt and Syria. Thereby, Qatar's discretion and lack of proactive communication strategy created a void that was filled with neo-conservative conspiracy theories and widely unsubstantiated allegations. The absence of a Qatari narrative explaining its foreign and security policy objectives, meant that direct attacks on Qatari and Turkish policies in the region remained widely unchallenged until 2017. Consequently, the Emirati narrative, although simplistic and underdeveloped, could dominate the policy discourse in Washington laying the groundwork for an Emirati advance on the Trump campaign in 2016.

While Otaiba had long campaigned against the Obama administration and its policy towards the Middle East, the 2016 Presidential campaign promised to be a close call between two worldviews, the liberal Hillary campaign against the neo-conservative Trump campaign. Trump's anti-Iran and anti-Islam rhetoric resonated well with conservative circles in Washington and beyond. His closest advisors appeared to be highly receptive to Otaiba's narratives, supporting regional strongmen to fight 'terrorism', a label generously put upon any form of Islamic dissidence and those supporting it. In particular Kushner, Trump's son-in-law and designated Middle East advisor with close ties to America's pro-Israel lobby AIPAC, was singled out as someone whose predispositions against Islamism and Qatar, as well as his private financial troubles, made him vulnerable to manipulation. After reaching out personally to Kushner and close advisors in November 2016, MbZ tried to establish a direct communication link to the White House after the new president's inauguration.[36] Brody, a prominent Republican businessman with commercial links to Abu Dhabi and deep ties into AIPAC, volunteered to help Abu Dhabi's Crown Prince to further his anti-Qatar narratives in Washington. More importantly, Brody was able to arrange a direct meeting between MbZ and the President,[37] who had been already briefed by

[36] Krieg, A. (2018). Never Mind Russia, the UAE Has United with AIPAC to Capture Washington. *Middle East Eye*, 9 March 2018.

[37] Mazzetti, M., Kirkpatrick, D., and Haberman, M. (2018). Mueller's Focus on Adviser to Emirates Suggests Broader Investigation. *The New York Times*, 3 March 2018.

a cohort of conservative advisors exposed to UAE-sponsored messaging for years. In parallel to Brody's direct lobbying work with the new White House, the anti-Qatar advocate had reached out to two conservative think tanks, the Foundation for the Defence of Democracy and the Hudson Institute, conveying financial support from Abu Dhabi to host conferences that would portray Qatar as a terrorist sponsor.[38] Amid this climate and an increasingly polarized Gulf discourse in Washington, the UAE-linked hack on the QNA took place—the false statements of Qatar's Emir, released to the public sphere, were merely meant to escalate tension beyond a point of no return for joint UAE-Saudi action against Qatar under tacit approval by the Trump administration.

CONCLUSION

As this chapter illustrates, the Gulf divide is as much about values, ideologies and worldviews as it is about interests. More accurately, values and interests wrapped in strategic narratives have torn apart the Middle East more widely and the Gulf in particular. At the heart of this divide stands the question of whether authoritarian state-centrism should prevail over the socio-political self-determination of individuals, communities and nations in the Arab World. Should the fragile short-termism of authoritarian stability take precedence over sustainable, inclusive governance arising from the ashes of revolt, revolution and conflict? The polarization of this debate after the Arab Spring is thereby not unique to the Gulf or the Arab world but is a question that has caused a heated discourse among intellectuals and policy makers in the West as well.

Qatar and the United Arab Emirates are the two most prominent poles in that debate—two small states that since 2010 have played a role in the region that might be greater than their size. While Qatar idealistically invested efforts and money into supporting dissident movements in their struggle against authoritarians, the Emirates have invested into counterrevolutionaries reversing the humble achievements of the Arab Spring. As much as these policies of Doha and Abu Dhabi respectively, were about taking action on the ground, they were dominated by an extensive strategy to sell a narrative. While Qatar could rely on Al Jazeera

---

[38] Butler, D., Lobianco, T., and Klapper, B. (2018). A Witness in the Mueller Probe Allegedly Sent Millions to a Trump Fundraiser to Push a UAE Agenda. *TIME*, 26 March 2018.

as the government's indirect force multiplier, the UAE went about implanting its narrative more directly and strategically.

Unlike Qatar, the Emirates have weaponized its narrative by exploiting an extensive communication network it had built over many years in conservative circles particularly in Washington. Instead of merely proactively implanting its narrative in close proximity to key policy makers, Abu Dhabi has used its nexus of conservative think tanks, experts, media and policy makers since 2014 to directly attack Qatar's reputation and legitimacy. The soft power war between Doha and Abu Dhabi had been simmering in the background while GCC collaboration, integration and summits suggested business as usual. Although Qatar had been warned in 2014 that the Emirates were ready to take more decisive action to roll back the revolutions and punish Qatar for its support for both secular and Islamist dissidents in the region, Doha remained oblivious to how dangerous this feud was becoming.

In parallel to the UAE's increased leverage over the post-revolutionary landscape of Libya, Egypt and Yemen, the Emirati fear-based and security-obsessed narrative was exported to the region and the West. In an uncompromising manner, partners and friends were pressured to take a side: with or against the UAE. The regional alliance of Egypt, Saudi Arabia and Bahrain would provide the UAE with backing regionally, while the neo-conservative nexus in Washington and Jerusalem empowered the Emirates internationally. By late 2016 with Trump being elected US President, MbZ saw himself in a position powerful enough to translate his narrative into geopolitical action. Instead of undermining Qatar's position and narrative rhetorically, the UAE felt that Qatar could be muted once and for all.

CHAPTER 7

The Saudi Dimension: Understanding the Kingdom's Position in the Gulf Crisis

Neil Quilliam

INTRODUCTION

This chapter will question whether Saudi Arabia's role in the blockade against Qatar has been motivated by Crown Prince Mohammed bin Salman's personal ambitions, the primacy of national interests or a wider clash over values. The chapter will argue that the kingdom's decision to implement the blockade against Qatar was based upon four factors: primacy of national interest; personality of MbS; influence of Abu Dhabi Crown Prince Mohammed bin Zayed; and MbS and MbZ's vision for the regional order.

Whilst much analysis has focused on the historical nature of the struggle between Saudi Arabia and Qatar, and the Al Saud and the Al Thani families, this chapter will mostly focus upon contemporary events, starting with succession of Salman in January 2015. However, it does not discount history; indeed, it is informed by history. But, given the constraints on space, it takes a contemporary and forward look.

It should be noted that is not the author's intention to evaluate the merit of the accusations that Saudi Arabia (Egypt, Bahrain and the UAE)

N. Quilliam (✉)
Chatham House, London, UK
e-mail: nquilliam@chathamhouse.org

© The Author(s) 2019
A. Krieg (ed.), *Divided Gulf*, Contemporary Gulf Studies,
https://doi.org/10.1007/978-981-13-6314-6_7

have levelled at Qatar nor Doha's counterpoints. The author is interested only in evaluating the reasons behind the accusations and the outcomes that followed.

Deteriorating Saudi-Qatari Relations: From Local Tremor to Regional Earthquake

The Saudi-Qatari relationship has been well-documented; and, in most cases, analyses point to the uneasy relationship between the two states and, indeed, their ruling families.[1] The tension between Saudi Arabia and Qatar became notably strained during the Arab Spring, when Qatar lent political, financial and military support to groups, mostly Islamist groups, including the Muslim Brotherhood and Salafi Jihadi groups intent on overthrowing their governments, namely, in Egypt, Libya, Tunisia and Syria.[2]

It was clear from the outset of the Arab Spring that Saudi Arabia and Qatar viewed the protests differently. Qatar saw it as an opportunity to project its power throughout the region and be at the forefront of profound political change from which it could benefit. Cultivating and deepening relations with political actors that looked likely to govern their respective countries, such as Morocco, Tunisia, Libya, Syria and Egypt, offered Qatar the chance to extend its influence throughout the region and, by doing so, acquire strategic depth to balance the long-term threat its leadership felt from Saudi Arabia.[3] Qatar did see an opportunity to promote political Islam and arguably further democratic change, but national interest was at the heart of its policy. The Arab Spring provided the Qatari leadership with the chance to increase its presence in the region, deepen ties with key countries, especially Egypt, with the goal of counterbalancing Saudi hegemony.[4]

Saudi Arabia—at the time, a status quo power—viewed the protests with deep suspicion and saw in them a deep challenge to their leadership

---

[1] Zahlan, R.S. (2017). *The Creation of Qatar*. London: Routledge.

[2] Coates Ulrichsen, K. (2014). *Qatar and the Arab Spring*. Oxford: Oxford University Press.

[3] Khatib, L. (2013). Qatar's Foreign Policy: The Limits of Pragmatism. *International Affairs*, 89:2, 11 March 2013 (pp. 417–431).

[4] Ibid.

of the Islamic world. The fact that the Qataris were supporting mostly Islamist groups during the Arab Spring made the threat seem more pernicious: first, the emergence of new Islamist regimes with radical agendas could come to challenge one of the Al Saud's cornerstones of legitimacy, the Saudi king's role as Custodian of the Two Holy Mosques; second, it could foment dissatisfaction and unrest in the kingdom and give rise to a new generation of radical clerics able to tap into discontent amongst youth and come to threaten stability. Although the Saudi leadership's fears appear at first sight exaggerated, the same set of fears had been commonplace amongst successive leaders who saw perennial threats over the decades from the Arab Cold War,[5] Iranian Revolution, Iran–Iraq War, US-led invasion of Iraq and the Arab Spring. Those fears were symptomatic of several factors, including Riyadh's dependence upon the US security umbrella, suspicions of its own security establishment and the resulting position of the kingdom being a status quo power in a region full of activist powers.[6]

Like all states in the region, Saudi Arabia has had to adapt to a changing regional dynamic. In essence, the Saudi leadership has had to manage two major challenges. First, it has come to realise that whilst the US remains a key partner, it is disengaging from the region, at least, politically. The vacuum left behind is already manifest in Syria, and it has allowed Iran to extend its influence further into the Gulf and the Levant. This has heightened the kingdom's sense of insecurity, especially at a time when former US President Barack Obama signed the Joint Comprehensive Plan of Action (JCPOA) with Iran and criticised the Gulf Arab states for being 'free-riders'.[7]

Second, the Saudi leadership has long known that it must address two long-term, but looming, domestic issues. In the first instance, the country's demographics require a major economic transformation to meet the needs of a youthful population. The current economic model, which is

[5] Kerr, M. (1971). *The Arab Cold War: Gamal 'Abd al-Nasir and His Rivals, 1958–1970.* Oxford: Oxford University Press.

[6] Roberts, D. (2018). The Gulf Monarchies' Armed Forces at the Crossroads. *Focus Stratégique*, No. 80, May 2018 (p. 14). https://www.ifri.org/sites/default/files/atoms/files/roberts_gulf_monarchies_forces_2018.pdf, accessed 22 July 2018.

[7] Goldberg, J. (2016). The Obama Doctrine. *The Atlantic*, April 2016.

based on rent, patronage and buoyed by a parasitic business community is no longer sustainable. In the second instance, the kingdom's dependence upon oil will come to end and it needs to diversify now.[8]

Given these two major challenges—both of which are pressing matters and require immediate action, Saudi Arabia's national interest has arguably changed since MbS became defence minister in January 2015.[9] Saudi Arabia can no longer be a status quo power: in modern parlance, it can no longer be a rule taker. In the Gulf, it had to be a rule maker. To this end, since MbS emerged, the kingdom's national interest has changed. It can now be defined by the country's ability to manage US political disengagement and push back against Iranian influence in the region, and transform the kingdom's economic model to preserve the rule of the Al Saud.

The move against Qatar, therefore, fits with the Saudi leadership's new definition of national interest viz regional dynamics. In one fell swoop, MbS turned Saudi Arabia's tradition of sustaining the status quo and pursuing a cautious foreign policy into a policy of adventurism and intervention. MbS was persuaded that Qatar's policy in the region was inimical to Saudi interests because it supported groups opposed to the kingdom, maintained close relations with Iran, owned news channel Al Jazeera, which he deemed anti-Saudi and pro-Muslim Brotherhood and sponsored groups that Saudi Arabia considered to be terrorist groups.[10] Although Saudi Arabia had long complained about Qatar's foreign policy, which had resulted in an earlier diplomatic spat in 2014, the emergence of MbS as de facto leader brought with it a desire for action, rather than diplomacy.

Clash of Values or Interests?

Although Saudi Arabia did not always oppose Qatari support to Islamist armed groups and, in many cases, notably in Syria, sponsored similar

---

[8] Coates Ulrichsen, K. (2015). *Insecure Gulf: The End of Certainty and the Transition to the Post-oil Era*. Revised, Updated Edition. Oxford: Oxford University Press.

[9] Al Arabiya. (2015). Saudi Prince Mohammad bin Salman Named Defense Minister. *Al Arabiya News*, 23 January 2015.

[10] Roberts, D. (2017). *Qatar: Securing the Global Ambitions of a City-State*. London: Hurst.

armed groups, such as the Nusra Front and Ahrar al-Sham[11] some of which were closely allied al-Qaida linked groups and Islamic State in Iraq and Sham (ISIS),[12] it came to strongly object to Doha's broader support for Islamist armed groups across the region. The Saudi leadership believed that Doha aimed at not only subverting domestic political orders but was also supporting the creation of a new regional order based on an alignment of Islamist governments. As such, this amounted to more than Qatar punching above its weight. It now posed a direct threat to Saudi Arabia's ability to influence events in the region and, at a particularly sensitive time; Iran's intervention in Syria had cost Saudi Arabia dearly.[13]

Qatar's effort, therefore, to be at the forefront of the Arab Spring supporting 'revolution' and overthrowing discredited dictatorships—reinforced with the populist narrative of its Arabic language news network Al Jazeera—posed a direct challenge to the status quo powers of the prevailing order, namely, Saudi Arabia and the UAE. Qatar had seemingly positioned itself as the doyen of democracy, the handmaiden of Islamist democracy and the trumpet major of the new order.[14] Qatar appeared to be challenging the legitimacy of leaders right across the region; unsurprisingly, it caused deep anger amongst Saudi and Emirati leaders and others.

Adding insult to injury, Western government support of Islamist parties, either vying for power or already governing, added to Saudi Arabia and the UAE's sense of vulnerability. Against the backdrop of the Arab Spring, Saudi and Emirati leaders viewed transnational organisations, notably, the Muslim Brotherhood, as not only a threat to the regional order but also a direct threat to their rule. Until this point in history, their main ally the US had largely stood against political Islam, particularly after the Iranian Revolution in 1979, the seizure of the Grand Mosque in Mecca, during the same year and the attacks against the Twin

[11] Blair, D. (2014). How Qatar Is Funding the Rise of Islamist Extremists. *The Telegraph*, 20 September 2014.

[12] Phillips, C. (2016). *The Battle for Syria: International Rivalry in the New Middle East.* London: Yale University Press (p. 122).

[13] Terrill, W.A. (2015). *The Saudi-Iranian Rivalry and the Future of Middle East Security.* Carlisle: Strategic Studies Institute.

[14] Roberts, D. (2017). *Qatar: Securing the Global Ambitions of a City-State.* London: Hurst.

Towers and Pentagon on US soil in September 2001.[15] Of course, it has been well documented how the US funded and helped equip Saudi-backed Islamist groups resist the Soviets in Afghanistan.[16] Nevertheless, these efforts were aimed at undermining Soviet expansion in central Asia and undertaken with Saudi co-operation and coordination,[17] rather than furthering the spread of political Islam or the promotion of democracy.

It, therefore, came as a major surprise to the Saudis and Emiratis that the US—and more broadly, the West—would lend political support to Islamist parties, especially the Muslim Brotherhood competing in democratic elections following the fall of Tunisia's Ben Ali and Egypt's Mubarak. After all, the experiments with democracy in Algeria in the 1990s had ended in civil war,[18] and the elections in Gaza in 2006 had produced the 'wrong' results—a Hamas majority.[19]

As mentioned elsewhere, then US President Obama's decision to withhold support for long-time US ally Egyptian President Hosni Mubarak shocked the Saudi leadership.[20] It should not be underestimated just how this rocked the foundations of the Saudi–US and UAE–US relationships as Cafiero demonstrates in Chapter 8. At the time, it made the Saudi King Abdullah bin Abdul Aziz Al Saud question the very essence of the relationship, which had been founded on the US providing security to the Gulf Arab states for the free flow of oil. Moreover, the Saudi leadership, especially the then-National Security Adviser Prince Bandar bin Sultan, came to realise that the superpower's willingness to project military power into the region was in irreversible retreat and the kingdom would need to work towards guaranteeing its own security.

[15] Wright, L. (2006). *The Looming Tower: Al-Qaeda and the Road to 9/11*. New York: Knopf Publishing Group.

[16] Coll, S. (2004). *Ghost Wars: The Secret History of the CIA, Afghanistan, and Bin Laden, from the Soviet Invasion to September 10, 2001*. London: Penguin Books.

[17] Riedel, B. (2014). *What We Won: America's Secret War in Afghanistan, 1979–1989*. Washington, DC: Brookings Institution Press.

[18] McDougall, J. (2017). *A History of Algeria*. Cambridge: Cambridge University Press.

[19] Brenner, B. (2017). *Gaza Under Hamas: From Islamic Democracy to Islamist Governance*. London: I.B. Tauris.

[20] Quilliam, N. (2017). Saudi Arabia's Syria Policy. In I. Galariotis and K. Ifantis (eds.). *The Syrian Imbroglio: International and Regional Strategies*. Florence: European University Institute, Robert Schuman Centre for Advanced Studies (p. 24).

Although Obama had made clear in 2011 that the US would pivot towards Asia,[21] few believed that it would result in a military drawdown in the Middle East. Whilst his policy, which set in train a new direction in policy towards the region, has not yet led to a military drawdown, it has already set in motion a process of political disengagement. Whereas MbZ had already recognised that the era of pax-Americana would come to an end during his lifetime, the Saudi leadership was caught unawares.

Obama's active pursuit of a nuclear deal with Iran, which appeared as a legacy project to most Saudi leaders, signalled strongly that the US no longer considered the kingdom a priority partner. Although the Saudis welcomed the goal of curtailing Iran's nuclear ambitions, they considered the expansion of Iranian influence throughout the region to be the more pernicious and immediate threat to their interests. Saudi officials including late foreign minister Saud al-Faisal and former ambassador to the US and General Intelligence Department Director Prince Turki al-Faisal argued both publicly and privately that any deal with Iran should be comprehensive and include provisions to roll back its influence in the region and stop its ballistic missile programme. The signing of the JCPOA in April 2015, therefore, was seen as another betrayal of Saudi interests by the US.[22]

Whereas Qatar was promoting the Arab Spring both materially and via the Al Jazeera network, Iran also looked to be benefiting from the ensuing unrest and conflict in the region. Despite its initial reluctance to either endorse or oppose the protests, Iran was able to extend its influence throughout the region either by supporting states, such as the Assad regime in Syria,[23] non-state actors, including the Popular Mobilisation Forces (PMFs) in Iraq, Hezbollah in Syria[24] and the Houthis in Yemen.[25] The Bahraini government and its Gulf Arab allies largely attributed the large-scale protests in Pearl Roundabout in

---

[21]Wang, C. (2015). *Obama's Challenge to China: The Pivot to Asia.* London: Routledge.

[22]Borger, J. (2015). Iran Nuclear Deal Reached in Vienna. *The Guardian*, 14 July 2015.

[23]Khatib, L., Eaton, T., Haid, H., et al. (2017). Western Policy Towards Syria: Applying Lessons Learned. Chatham House, March 2017 (p. 4).

[24]Akbarzadeh, S. (2017). Iran's Uncertain Standing in the Middle East. *The Washington Quarterly*, 40:3, Fall 2017.

[25]Saul, J., Hafezi, P., and Georgy, M. (2017). Exclusive: Iran Steps Up Support for Houthis in Yemen's War—Sources. *Reuters*, 21 March 2017.

Manama in 2012 to Iranian interference.[26] As such, the Saudis found themselves almost under siege from Doha and Tehran and their security partner looked to be missing in action.

The combination of Qatar's leading role in undergirding the Arab Spring, apparent US pivot away from the region, withdrawal of US support for Mubarak, advent of civil wars in Syria, Libya and later Yemen, success of Islamist parties in Tunisia, Morocco and Egypt and sustained protests in neighbouring Bahrain heightened Saudi and Emiratis own sense of vulnerability. As a consequence, MbZ, who had already begun a process of diversifying key partnerships away from the US and EU towards Asia, used his leverage—a combination of financial muscle, political capital (secular) and military strategy—to persuade both the Saudi leadership and his erstwhile allies to redesign the regional order—with the UAE at the centre of it.

Personality Politics

Against this background, MbS became defence minister in 2015 when his father King Salman succeeded late king Abdullah and then replaced Muhammed bin Nayef (MbN) as Crown Prince in June 2017.[27] The combination of the historical struggle between Saudi Arabia and Qatar, Doha's hearty embrace and sponsorship of the Arab Spring, Saudi and Emirati growing sense of vulnerability, MbZ's vision for the new regional order and the new Saudi Crown Prince's youth set the kingdom on a direct collision course with its small neighbour.

MbS rose to power at a time when the kingdom had felt challenged on many fronts, especially from Doha and Tehran and from Washington's recalibration of interests in the region. Although late King Abdullah and his Gulf Arab partners had already used diplomatic isolation and a series of economic measures to censure Doha's behaviour in 2014,[28]

---

[26]Coates Ulrichsen, K. (2013). Bahrain's Uprising: Regional Dimensions and International Consequences. *Stability: International Journal of Security and Development,* 2:1.

[27]Al Arabyia. (2017). Saudi Arabia Declares Mohammed bin Salman as Crown Prince. *Al Arabiya News,* 21 June 2017.

[28]The National. (2017). Revealed: The Secret Pledges Qatar Made—And Then Broke. *The National,* 11 July 2017.

it soon became clear that the newly appointed crown prince was in no mood to countenance Qatar's 'bad' behaviour.

Typically, Western policymakers, academics and analysts have described the Al Saud's style of governance as slow and consensual.[29] The Saudi leadership would rarely make major decisions without reaching consensus amongst the kingdom's most senior princes and, by doing so, it would nearly always sacrifice urgency for finding a common position. It meant that Saudi decision-making, therefore, appeared slow, sometimes inert, deliberate and was based on the exercise of strategic patience. For example, King Abdullah afforded Syrian President Bashar al-Assad in 2012 three separate opportunities to desist crushing the Syrian uprising in return for Saudi diplomatic, political and economic support; Abdullah made this offer despite Assad having called him a 'half-man' following the Israel–Hizbullah conflict in 2006.[30] Similarly, Abdullah had given the new Qatari Emir Tamim a number of opportunities to realign Doha's foreign policy, amongst other issues, before withdrawing its ambassador in coordination with UAE and Bahrain in March 2014.[31] MbS has broken this mould; so far, he has proven to be an impulsive, dynamic, self-assured and retributive leader.[32]

The decision to place the blockade upon Qatar in June 2017 was one made in haste by MbS and apparently with little thought of the consequences not only upon intra-GCC relations to which he seems to have given scant regard, but also upon his population and its familial relations with Qataris.[33]

[29] Niblock, T. (2006). *Saudi Arabia: Power, Legitimacy and Survival.* London: Routledge; Madawi, R. (2010). *A History of Saudi Arabia.* 2nd Edition. Cambridge: Cambridge University Press; Thompson, M. (2014). *Saudi Arabia and the Path to Political Change: National Dialogue and Civil Society.* London: I.B. Tauris.

[30] Quilliam, N. (2017). Saudi Arabia's Syria Policy. In I. Galariotis and K. Ifantis (eds.). *The Syrian Imbroglio: International and Regional Strategies.* Florence: European University Institute, Robert Schuman Centre for Advanced Studies (p. 21).

[31] Black, I. (2014). Arab States Withdraw Ambassadors from Qatar in Protest at 'Interference'. *The Guardian,* 5 March 2014.

[32] Younes, A. (2017). Bin Salman and the End of Saudi's Consensus Rule. *Al Jazeera News,* 7 November 2017.

[33] Bianco, C. and Stansfield G. (2018). The Intra-GCC Crises: Mapping GCC Fragmentation After 2011. *International Affairs,* 94:3, 4 May 2018 (pp. 613–635).

Influence of MbZ

Since MbS' rise to power, the relationship between Saudi Arabia and UAE has gone from strength to strength. Whilst the relationship had been strong generally, a number of issues separated them, including long-running border disputes and territorial claims[34] and most recently, the UAE's frustration that the GCC Central Bank would be located in Riyadh instead of Abu Dhabi.[35]

On a personal level, whilst MbZ was known to respect Salman, he did not share the same sentiment with his contemporary MbN. Although the US and other international partners had invested considerable political capital cultivating close relations with MbN, especially as he was the prime candidate of the next generation princes to govern the kingdom, MbZ held reservations.

MbZ has developed a long strategic vision for the UAE and, in his estimation, MbN did not have the will, capacity or foresight to share that vision, let alone implement it. As such, MbN represented more of the same—a slow, consensual decision-maker, whilst the world around them was changing fast. Salman's decision, therefore, to appoint his preferred son to the post of defence minister and then ultimately to replace MbN as crown prince with MbS in 2017 was of major interest to MbZ.

MbZ had already begun to develop a close working relationship with MbS and impressed upon him the need for rapid change in both the domestic and regional environments. By doing so, MbZ, in effect, became a close confidante and adviser to MbS or perhaps more accurately, their relationship can be described as a tutor–tutee partnership.[36]

The influence of MbZ on MbS is manifest in many ways. First, MbS has learned from MbZ's Washington playbook. The appointment of his

---

[34] Saudi Arabia and the UAE signed the Treaty of Jeddah in 1974 to end forty years of territorial dispute. Saudi Arabia ratified the treaty in 1993, but it was not formalised until 2004. Al-Mazrouei, N.S. (2016). *The UAE and Saudi Arabia: Border Disputes and International Relations in the Middle East*. London: I.B. Tauris; Habeeb, W.M. (2012). *The Middle East in Turmoil: Conflict, Revolution and Change*. Westport: Greenwood Press.

[35] Morris, M. (2009). Riyadh Named as HQ for GCC Joint Central Bank. *Arabian Business*, 6 May 2009.

[36] Henderson, S. (2017). Meet the Two Princes Reshaping the Middle East, But for Good or Ill? *Politico*, 13 June 2017.

full-brother Khaled bin Salman to the post of ambassador[37] to the US and the direct access he now enjoys to key figures around the president echoes the UAE model. In the meantime, the Qatari ambassador, Sheikh Meshal bin Hamad Al Thani, is compelled to follow the formal diplomatic channels through the State Department. Second, MbZ has not only persuaded MbS that Iran poses a major threat to the region (pushing on an open door to use the vernacular), but also that the Muslim Brotherhood—in all its forms—does too. This amounts to a substantial leap of faith given that political Islam is an essential component of the Al Saud's legitimacy. Whilst the Al Saud saw Qatar's promotion of the Muslim Brotherhood during the Arab Spring as a threat, it was more that Doha was pulling the strings than the parties themselves.

MbS' introduction of social reforms in the kingdom, which have included curtailing the authority of the religious police (*mutawaeen*),[38] detention of dozens of clerics, including leading figures, such as Salman al-Auda, Awad al-Qarni, Ali al-Omari[39] and Safar al-Hawali[40] and opening up of social spaces for men and women to meet,[41] has the hallmarks of UAE-style development. Saudi Arabia is opening up the social agenda to help drive the economy, whilst further closing down the space for political opposition.

Of course, MbZ's influence on MbS is most obvious in Saudi Arabia's policy towards Qatar. As noted above, Saudi Arabia's decision to impose the blockade, alongside the UAE, Bahrain and Egypt, was determined by a number of factors, including structural factors, such as the US signalling its imminent withdrawal from the prevailing security arrangement and inter-state competition, as well as the catalytic component of MbS' promotion to crown prince. However, MbZ also seems to have played an instrumental role in persuading MbS to enforce the blockade.

[37] McKernan, B. (2017). Fighter Pilot Prince Named New Saudi Ambassador to US. *The Independent*, 24 April 2017.

[38] Worley, W. (2016). Saudi Arabia Strips Religious Police of Powers of Arrest and Says They Must Be 'Kind and Gentle'. *The Independent*, 14 April 2016.

[39] Reuters. (2017). Saudi Clerics Detained in Apparent Bid to Silence Dissent. *Reuters*, 11 September 2017.

[40] Reuters. (2018). Saudi Arabia Arrests Prominent Cleric Safar al-Hawali: Activists. *Reuters*, 12 July 2018.

[41] AFP. (2018). Saudi Arabia's First Cinema in Over 35 Years Opens with Black Panther. *The Guardian*, 20 April 2018.

MbZ's Regional Order

The move against Qatar, however, differs from previous spats amongst the Gulf Arab states. It will have a profound and long-term impact upon the region. Saudi Arabia has signed up to a decision that will cleave the region into two distinct alliances, as envisioned by MbZ.

The core of one alliance is Saudi Arabia, UAE and Egypt, and the common factor that draws it together is strong, autocratic, military and secular leadership. The alliance is opposed to Iran, political Islam and political reform, but in favour of economic diversification, social reform and new partnerships.

This alliance also stretches to include Bahrain, Hafter in Libya, and enjoys good relations with Israel. In the Quartet's move against Qatar, Doha was basically given a stark choice—which was no real choice—you are either with us or against us. MbS and MbZ decided that Tamim was against them and therefore in the counter alliance, including Turkey and Iran.

The Quartet's move against Qatar was a defining moment in the shaping of the new regional order. It signalled the UAE and Saudi Arabia's intent to transform themselves from status quo powers into active participants in the regional security architecture. They would no longer wait for the US green light before pursuing their interests. Instead, they would act and then seek permission, retroactively, through direct channels to the White House and President Trump. MbS had already taken the lead in declaring war against the Houthis in Yemen and deploying forces—along with the UAE—against the Houthi-Saleh alliance.[42] However, the blockade against Qatar was different. The small archipelago off Saudi Arabia is a key US ally and houses al-Udaid airbase—a significant military installation that has allowed the US to prosecute wars against Saddam Hussein in Iraq, Taliban in Afghanistan and ISIS in Iraq and Syria.[43]

MbS and MbZ took a calculated risk that President Trump would not oppose the blockade; and, indeed, that has been the case between

---

[42] Roberts, D. (2018). The Gulf Monarchies' Armed Forces at the Crossroads. *Focus Stratégique*, No. 80, May 2018 (pp. 15–17).

[43] Des Roches, D. (2017). A Base Is More Than Buildings: The Military Implications of the Qatar Crisis. *War on the Rocks*, 8 June 2017.

presidential tweets that both criticise[44] and praise Doha's efforts at combatting terrorism.[45]

They did, however, miscalculate Doha's resilience in the face of such a move and had expected the country to capitulate within a matter of days. After a shaky start, Doha has, by and large, weathered the storm and in the words of Qatari foreign minister Sheikh Mohammed bin Abdulrahman bin Jassim Al Thani, at the United Kingdom's Royal Institute of International Affairs (Chatham House) in July 2017 'turned crisis into opportunity'.[46] The increase in trade and diplomatic traffic between Doha and Tehran, and Doha and Ankara, and the very presence of a new large-scale dairy farm that meets the milk needs of Qatar's population, are cited as successes.[47]

The squeeze on Qatar was also intended to send a strong message to other states within the GCC and the wider region. Although Oman and Kuwait have not joined the blockade, when succession takes place in either state, they will expect to come under pressure to choose sides between the Saudi–UAE alliance or the Iran–Qatari alliance. To date, they have navigated the choice well; but next generation leaders will face a stark and far-reaching choice.

There is little doubt that MbZ sees Saudi Arabia as critical to his vision of a new regional order based on two alliances. The UAE started its own orientation away from the West or at least reorientation towards Asia over a decade ago and its efforts at acquiring strategic depth, a critical resource Qatar overlooked, is clear to see in its ports and naval bases across the Horn of Africa.[48]

The succession of Salman to the throne and the consequent moves that led to MbS becoming crown prince provided MbZ with the perfect opportunity to work with the young Saudi and persuade him that the

[44]Wintour, P. (2017). Donald Trump Tweets Support for Blockade Imposed on Qatar. *The Guardian*, 6 June 2017.

[45]BBC. (2018). Trump Praises Qatar's Efforts on Combating Terrorist Financing. *BBC*, 11 April 2018.

[46]HE Sheikh Mohammed bin Abdulrahman bin Jassim Al-Thani, Minister of Foreign Affairs. (2017). The Crisis in the Gulf: Qatar Responds. Chatham House, 5 July 2017, https://www.chathamhouse.org/file/crisis-gulf-qatar-responds, accessed 22 July 2018.

[47]Economist. (2018). Milk Sheikhs: Why Qatar Is Raising Cows in the Desert. *The Economist*, 17 May 2018.

[48]Brennan, A. (2018). The UAE Weaves a Regional 'String of Pearls'. *Asia Times*, 26 May 2018.

regional security architecture is changing and that both countries need to be much more active, diversify key partnerships, including with China and Russia and undertake change at home, not just attending to economic reforms, but also curtailing the influence of religion over policy. To that end, MbZ was able to capitalise upon the challenges that MbS faces within the kingdom and present him with a blueprint that appears to have appealed to his personality.

What's Driving Domestic Change?

Although Saudi Arabia's leaders have known for decades that the kingdom has to diversify its economy and move away from its dependency upon oil and, at best, have made half-hearted efforts to do so, MbS seems intent to make it happen in double-quick time and with little consideration of the risks. In his landmark interviews with the Economist[49] and Bloomberg,[50] he made clear that he wanted to bring about a transformation of the kingdom's economy in order to prepare for the post-oil era.

Although his predecessors understood the need for reform, they moved at a snail's pace arguing that society was not ready for a rapid change. Given the country's demographics, however, with almost 50% of Saudi population under the age of 25,[51] it was clear that its septuagenarian and octogenarian leaders were out of touch with the kingdom's youthful and highly-connected population; most of whom were impatient for change.[52]

MbS recognised the pressing risks that the country would face if it continuously fails to diversify the economy; more importantly, it would come to pose a threat to the ruling family's ability to govern. Therefore,

[49] Economist. (2016). Transcript: Interview with Muhammad bin Salman. *The Economist*, 6 January 2016.

[50] Nereim, V. and Shahine, A. (2017). Saudi Arabia Crown Prince Details Plans for New City: Transcript. *Bloomberg*, 26 October 2017.

[51] General Authority for Statistics. (2016). https://www.stats.gov.sa/en/5305, accessed 10 July 2018.

[52] Internet users reached 91% (i.e. 30 million out of population of 33 million), with active social media account 75% (25 million) and active mobile social accounts 54% (18 million). Global Media Insights, Saudi Arabia Social Media Statistics. (2018). https://www.globalmediainsight.com/blog/saudi-arabia-social-media-statistics/, accessed 10 July 2018.

Salman's elevation of his son from Royal Court gate-keeper to defence minister in 2015 and then crown prince in 2017, empowered the latter to fast-track the transformation project in part via Vision 2030[53] and by pushing aside potential opposition figures within the kingdom's power centres, including the ruling family.

There are two main factors, therefore, driving domestic change in Saudi Arabia. First, an urgency to transform the economy away from rentierism and more towards a diversified and knowledge-based economy and, by doing so, better prepare and equip the Saudi workforce before the world moves irreversibly into a post-oil era; second, and most importantly, to ensure that the ruling Al Saud family undergoes its own process of reform, so that it is fit for purpose and continues to govern Saudi Arabia indefinitely.

MbS not only wants to push Saudi Arabia firmly into the twenty-first century, but he also wants to lead the country into his old age. This requires a major economic and social transformation; and in order to achieve it, he has sought to mobilise popular support behind him. As such, MbS has cultivated a much stronger sense of Saudi nationalism, especially amongst the kingdom's youthful population, most notably by developing new narrative of Saudi exceptionalism; and foreign policy adventures are in part intended to stoke national pride.

This section argues that the emphasis on shaping a new Saudi identity—counterpoised to a wider Gulf or GCC identity—has played a large part in determining recent foreign policy decisions, in particular, the blockade against Qatar. In other words, MbS has used the Qatar crisis to further the following aims: strengthen Saudi national identity; limit the role of the clerical establishment in defining the business environment; and portray the Al Thani as a threat to peace and stability in the region with the wider goal of attracting investment into the kingdom.

MbS has had to overcome a number of domestic peculiarities that have in the past frustrated efforts at deepening what it means to be 'Saudi' given the strong regional identities within the kingdom and the clerical establishment's belief that national identity is irrelevant vis-a-vis the *umma*. For example, it has only been in recent years that Saudi National Day has been celebrated widely inside and outside the kingdom despite late King Abdullah raising its profile in the late 1990s. At the

---

[53] Kinninmont, J. (2017). *Vision 2030 and Saudi Arabia's Social Contract: Austerity and Transformation*. London: Chatham House.

same time, the GCC has played a role in promoting a Gulf Arab identity amongst the populations of the six states; and its goal of further integrating the social and economic aspects of Gulf nationals seemingly obscured national differences, though more in theory than practice.

It soon became clear after MbS had become Minister of Defence that he would employ a more muscular approach to domestic and foreign policy. His leadership style differed drastically from his predecessors, and it was clear that he had a mission to make policy much punchier than passive. As a young dynamic leader with popular appeal in the kingdom, MbS has sought to transform self-identity amongst young Saudis from passive observers to active nationalists. Despite the apparent failures of his foreign policy initiatives to date, he has used his management style effectively to help forge a more assertive nationalism amongst Saudi youth and counterpoised to it Iranian nationalism and Qatar-driven pan-Islamism. By doing so, MbS—with the aid of strategic communications experts—has helped develop a new sense of national pride, which was previously missing—and his interventions in regional crises and tours of the US and European states have strengthened it further. To that end, a motivation for instituting the blockade against Qatar was to forge further a distinct national identity and mobilise widespread support behind it, thus, giving him political capital to implement changes at home. It set a direct challenge to not only Qatar, but also the relevance of the GCC and has since undermined its integrity as an organisation. Consequently, the 'Gulf Arab' identity is basically over.

It appears that MbS drew heavily upon MbZ's playbook in sidelining the clerical establishment, attributing the ills of society to the role played by the Muslim Brotherhood, and ultimately placing full responsibility for the actions of the transnational Islamist organisation upon Qatar. The blockade against Qatar, therefore, played an important role in justifying MbS' stringent actions taken against some members of the clerical establishment, reinforcing Saudi identity against a pan-Islamic identity emanating from Doha.

As noted above, MbZ has been influential in helping shape MbS' worldview. The emerging personal relationship between MbS and MbZ has created an alliance based on mutual interests, ideologies and values. This is manifest in MbS' domestic and foreign policies. It is clear that MbS has turned to Abu Dhabi as a role model for reforming the kingdom's conservative society. Again, the goal of doing so is to transform Saudi Arabia's economic model, so that the Al Saud can continue to govern in perpetuity. The domestic changes that MbS has introduced echo some of the reforms that MbZ has introduced since becoming crown prince in 2004. This has included centralising powers in the hands of a few: in the case of the UAE, the Bani Fatima and a close circle of trusted advisers[54]; in Saudi Arabia, the Bani Salman and a close circle of technocrats.

Reforms also included a series of measures that appear intended to limit the role of clerics in determining or shaping the business environment. MbS has accelerated a pushback against the religious establishment's influence first started under late King Abdullah. Over the past few years, its activities have been curtailed, which have included a new regulation, passed in April 2016, restricting the powers of the Committee for the Promotion of Virtue and Prevention of Vice. The new regulation required them to report any suspected crimes witnessed to the relevant authorities who can then take the necessary action whether 'pursuit of suspect, capture, interrogation and detainment'.[55] The move has been instrumental in curtailing the activities of the Committee, but more importantly, changing the image of the country and arguably making it more welcoming of international investment.

These measures have also been followed by the arrest of popular clerics Salman al-Auda, Awad al-Qarni, Ali al-Omari and Safar al-Hawali and other high-profile social media activists, who have challenged current policies. Significantly, al-Auda's arrest followed his tweet welcoming a resolution of the Qatar crisis[56] and has given a strong indication that MbS will brook no public criticism of the government's domestic or foreign policy positions. MbS' objective in doing so is to promote an environment that is an attractive international investment, emulates the UAE business climate and stands in contrast to Qatar.

Saudi Arabia has long viewed Qatar's business environment with a mix of suspicion and envy. Former Emir Hamad was able to capitalise upon Qatar's North Field—the world's largest non-associated gas field and transform the country from a sleepy backwater into an active business hub and more significantly a global player. Whilst the kingdom sits on

[54] Gulf States News. (2014). Mohammed Bin Zayed—a President-in-Waiting. *Gulf States News*, Issue 963, 7 February 2014.

[55] Arab News. (2016). Haia Can't Chase, Arrest Suspects. *Arab News*, 14 April 2016.

[56] Al Jazeera. (2018). Cleric Salman al-Awda 'Held Over Qatar Tweet'. *Al Jazeera News*, 7 January 2018.

25% of the world's proven oil reserves, it faces a number of structural challenges that have continuously discouraged international investors from considering it outside of the energy sector. Neighbouring Qatar and the UAE have looked to be more promising centres for investment and neither country faces the same structural constraints as Saudi Arabia.

Given this environment, MbS views Qatar as a regional competitor for foreign direct investment (FDI), as well as a global player and one which could undermine the fulfilment of Vision 2030. Until the blockade in 2017, Qatar's sovereign wealth fund Qatar Investment Authority (QIA) continuously outperformed Saudi Arabia's hamstrung sovereign wealth fund the Public Investment Fund (PIF) and enjoyed multiple high-profile and strategic international investments. PIF, on the other hand, has been playing catch up and waiting for the Aramco IPO to generate funds.

Although not a primary factor, Saudi Arabia's move against Qatar, which has not only blockaded the country but also sought to portray it as a sponsor of Islamist terrorism, has served to undermine the small state's integrity as a centre for investment and a global actor committed to international peace. Furthermore, it has given a boon to MbS' goal of cultivating a strident Saudi nationalism and helped justify his curtailing of the clerical establishment. As such, MbS has sought to reposition Saudi Arabia's image amongst the international community in a much more favourable and investment-friendly light and, at the same time, darken the image of Doha.

CONCLUSION

This chapter has argued that Saudi Arabia's decision to implement the blockade against Qatar was based upon four factors: primacy of national interest; personality of MbS; influence of MbZ; and MbS and MbZ's vision for the regional order. Although the ruling families of Saudi Arabia and Qatar have long since quarrelled, the nature of the dispute in June 2017 was less personal and more structural owing to the political vacuum left by the US. Nevertheless, the combination of MbZ' strategic vision for the region and the strong personality of Saudi Arabia's new crown prince—and their shared common interests—have made sure that the conflict with Qatar cannot be resolved through diplomatic means, but submission to the new regional order.

CHAPTER 8

The "Trump Factor" in the Gulf Divide

Giorgio Cafiero

Introduction

Donald Trump's victory in America's 2016 presidential election surprised government officials worldwide. Across the Middle East and North Africa (MENA), countless statesmen scratched their heads and asked endless questions. How would a Trump presidency change US foreign policy in the Arab world? What vision would the new White House have for America in the MENA region? In the wealthy states of the Arabian Peninsula, which have relied on Washington as a security guarantor for decades, regime officials had major concerns about uncertainties in US-Gulf Cooperation Council relations in the post-Barack Obama period.

Nonetheless, while extremely alienated by the Obama administration's approach to the MENA region, the leadership in the Kingdom of Saudi Arabia and the United Arab Emirates welcomed, and quickly adapted to, the Trump presidency. Riyadh and Abu Dhabi saw Trump's entry into the Oval Office as an invaluable opportunity to shift Washington's foreign policy in a new direction that could serve Riyadh and Abu Dhabi's perceived national interests. The inexperience of Trump and many of those in his inner circle, coupled with Trump's anti-Iranian and anti-Muslim Brotherhood stances laid out on the campaign trail,

G. Cafiero (✉)
Gulf State Analytics, Washington, DC, USA

© The Author(s) 2019
A. Krieg (ed.), *Divided Gulf*, Contemporary Gulf Studies,
https://doi.org/10.1007/978-981-13-6314-6_8

127

left the Kingdom and Abu Dhabi convinced that they had a chance to settle scores with Qatar in ways that would have been far less realistic with either Obama or Hillary Clinton in the Oval Office. Indeed, leaked emails have illustrated how Saudi and Emirati interests influenced Trump, both as a president-elect and as commander-in-chief.[1]

This chapter analyses the Trump factor in both the GCC crisis' eruption and the dispute's unfolding since May/June 2017. This chapter argues that although it is nearly impossible to prove that the so-called "Anti-Terror Quartet"—Bahrain, Egypt, Saudi Arabia, and the UAE—would not have blockaded Qatar had Trump lost the 2016 election, there is solid reason to conclude that the Trump presidency was likely the most important game-changing variable that led to Riyadh and Abu Dhabi's decision to blockade a fellow and founding GCC member. As Andreas Krieg argues, the US has been the Qatar *"crisis' centre of gravity from the beginning."*[2]

US-GCC TENSIONS UNDER OBAMA

During Obama's presidency, Washington's alliances with Riyadh, Abu Dhabi, and Manama suffered significantly from numerous points of contest amid the Arab Spring's tumultuous fallout. Egypt was the first major source of tension. Most Arab Gulf rulers viewed Obama as willing to embrace a grassroots-driven revolution that led to the ascendancy of a Muslim Brotherhood-led government in 2012 and 2013, unsettling the Saudi and Emirati leadership which began questioning Washington's commitment to the survival of regimes in the Gulf that enjoyed strong alliances with the US as did the Hosni Mubarak regime. Angry at Obama, Saudi officials accused the former US president of discarding Mubarak like a "used Kleenex".[3] The last administration's meetings with members of Bahrain's now-dissolved Shia opposition faction, *al-Wefaq* National Islamic Society, fuelled more friction between

---

[1] Ulrichsen, K. (2018). The Needless Crisis in the Arabian Gulf. *Arab Center Washington DC*, 5 June 2018. http://arabcenterdc.org/policy_analyses/the-needless-crisis-in-the-arabian-gulf/.

[2] Krieg, A. (2018). One Year on, Trump Remains the Cause of—And Solution to—The Qatar Crisis. *Middle East Eye*, 23 May 2018.

[3] Lynch, M. (2013). *The Arab Uprising: The Unfinished Revolutions of the New Middle East*. New York: Public Affairs.

Washington and Manama, along with Bahrain's Arab Gulf allies, which saw America under Obama's leadership as failing to comprehend the nature of the perceived Iranian menace not only within the greater MENA region, but also within the GCC. Despite the UAE's military joining both the US and Qatar during the NATO-led military campaign against the Libyan regime in 2011, the Libyan Civil War that erupted in mid-2014 quickly become a point of contest between the Obama administration and Abu Dhabi, as El Gomati will further illustrate in Chapter 11. The US backed Libya's internationally-recognized Tripoli-based Government of National Accord (GNA). Yet the UAE's Libya policy rested on working with Egypt to support the Tobruk-based secular-leaning House of Representatives (HoR) and Field Marshal Khalifa Hafter's Operation Dignity campaign against Islamist militias operating under the GNA umbrella, namely the Doha- and Ankara-backed Muslim Brotherhood-linked Misratan fighters.[4]

Unquestionably, the Obama administration's diplomatic overtures to Iran made the Saudis, Emiratis, and Bahrainis most nervous about the future of Washington's role in the region. The watershed Iranian nuclear accord of 2015 left these Arab Gulf officials believing that Washington was set on restoring Washington and Tehran's pre-1979 alliance with negative implications for Riyadh and Abu Dhabi in terms of their importance and relevance to US interests in the Gulf. Another key factor in play were Saudi/Emirati expectations that the lifting of sanctions on the Islamic Republic would embolden Iran's confident foreign policy in the Arab world's hotspots from Syria to Yemen and Iraq to Lebanon.

In Iraq, the meteoric rise of Islamic State (ISIS) in 2014 provided Iran an invaluable opportunity to earn more goodwill from the West as the Islamic Republic's interests in fighting the extremist force overlapped with Washington and European capitals. From the perspective of Saudi Arabia and other Arab Gulf states, the Obama administration's tacit alliance with Iran in the fight against ISIS only reinforced their belief that the White House failed to take sufficient consideration of GCC concerns over Tehran's regional conduct into account.[5]

[4]Sheiko, Y. (2018). The United Arab Emirates: Turkey's New Rival. *The Washington Institute for Near East Policy*, 16 February 2018. www.washingtoninstitute.org/fikraforum/view/the-united-arab-emirates-turkeys-new-rival.

[5]Younis, N. (2017). ISIS: The Rise of ISIS: Iraq and Persian Gulf Security. In K. Ulrichsen (ed.). *The Changing Security Dynamics of the Persian Gulf*. London: Hurst.

Within this context, the Crown Princes of Saudi Arabia and Abu Dhabi—Mohammed bin Salman and Mohammed bin Zayed—initiated more muscular foreign policies to address the destabilizing impacts of the MENA region's 2011 revolutions and uprisings against the backdrop of Tehran's perceived regional ascendancy and the rise of ISIS in the Levant, Libya, and Yemen. With MbS and MbZ at the helm, both Saudi Arabia and the UAE's regimes have further concentrated power within the hands of their de facto rulers and waged increasingly hawkish and more security-oriented foreign policy agendas.

In Saudi Arabia, power is far less diffused among members of the Al Saud family with MbS and King Salman driving the Kingdom's foreign and domestic policies. Adel Abdel Ghafar explained:

> MBS is signalling to the House of Saud and its estimated 15,000 princes that the old, consensus-based order and previous power-sharing arrangements amongst the various branches of the ruling family is effectively over. In the new political order, power is to be consolidated in the office of the king and the crown prince. MBS has established control over all coercive arms of the state apparatus: the army, the police, and now the national guard. The message is clear: Kinship does not guarantee safety; fall in line or be purged.[6]

In the UAE, political clout has been increasingly placed into MbZ's hands with Abu Dhabi growing increasingly influence at the expense of Dubai and the other emirates, largely because of the financial crash of 2008 which resulted in Abu Dhabi bailing out Dubai.[7]

Within this context of Saudi and Emirati foreign policy becoming increasingly shaped by MbS and MbZ, the two leaders' perceptions of dangers in the Middle East have driven both to seize any chance to position their countries as geopolitical drivers in the MENA region to fend off security threats. MbS and MbZ both saw the relative decline of US hegemony coupled with the inability of the Arab world's traditional heavyweights—Egypt, Iraq, and Syria—to lead the regional transitions of

---

[6]Ghafar, A. (2017). Muhammed bin Salman and the Push to Establish a New Saudi Political Order. *The Brookings Institution*, 9 November 2017. www.brookings.edu/blog/markaz/2017/11/09/muhammed-bin-salman-and-the-push-to-establish-a-new-saudi-political-order/.

[7]Ulrichsen, K. (2017). *The United Arab Emirates: Power, Politics and Policy-Making*. New York: Routledge.

the post-2011 period, given their internal conflicts and sources of instability, as an opportunity to assert Arab Gulf hegemony in a rapidly evolving region.

MbS and MbZ's visions for the future of the MENA region are extremely similar and based on many of the same fundamental understandings of the perceived threats posed by Iran, Tehran's regional Shia proxies, such as Lebanese Hezbollah and Iraq's Popular Mobilization Units, among others, and Sunni Islamist actors, namely the Muslim Brotherhood.[8] Seeking to become a regional hegemon that continues serving a leadership role in the Islamic world, as the home two Islam's two holiest sites—Mecca and Medina, Saudi Arabia is determined to have the smaller GCC states operating within Riyadh's geopolitical sphere of influence with the Council being understood as a Saudi-led institution. Although the UAE's concerns about Saudi Arabia's hegemonic aspirations in the Arabian Peninsula have prompted officials in Abu Dhabi to worry about Emirati sovereignty, with MbS and MbZ both at the helm, the two states' alliance has grown closer albeit with certain points of friction in bilateral affairs.

One issue which the Kingdom and the UAE currently see eye to eye on is Qatar's role in the MENA region. As the world witnessed in 2014, and much more so in 2017, Saudi Arabia and the UAE have shared perception of Qatar as a "squeaky wheel" within the GCC as Bernard Haykel put it.[9] Basically, Doha's foreign policy throughout the past 23 years (2019–1996) has frequently undermined the sub-regional organization's collective security interests, according to Riyadh and Abu Dhabi's perspectives. A geopolitical ambition shared by Saudi Arabia and the UAE is to reign in Qatar, limit Doha's regional autonomy, and bring the Arabian Peninsula's geopolitical order back to the pre-1996 period in which Qatar, much like Bahrain in the current era, joined the "Riyadh consensus" and acted somewhat as a vessel state, never veering too far from the "Saudi shadow."

Saudi Arabia has had major problems with Qatari foreign policy since Emir Hamad bin Khalifa Al Thani's ascendancy in 1995, which led to

---

[8] Gadel, A. and El-Bouanani, M. (2018). MbS and MbZ: Two Princes in a Hurry Shake Up the Gulf. *The New Arab*, 27 April 2018.

[9] Al Jazeera. (2017). What's Next for Qatar and the GCC? *Al Jazeera UpFront*, 7 July 2017. www.aljazeera.com/programmes/upfront/2017/07/qatar-gcc-170707094554748.html.

Doha playing an "oversized" role in regional geopolitics and broadcasting media networks—namely Al Jazeera—that criticized Saudi Arabia's rulers and other autocratic regimes in the GCC and greater Arab world.[10] MbZ, who has been the Crown Prince of Abu Dhabi since 2004, has long seen Qatar as a destabilizing force in the region that has undermined the GCC's collective security interests. Equating virtually all forms of political Islam with terrorism, Abu Dhabi has been extremely angry at Doha over the years because of Qatar's support for Muslim Brotherhood offshoots and figures. When the 2011 Arab uprisings erupted, Qatar saw the political openings as an opportunity to extend Doha's clout throughout the MENA region via Qatari-backed Islamist factions in Egypt, Libya, Syria, and elsewhere. From Abu Dhabi's vantage point, however, Doha's pro-Muslim Brotherhood orientation constituted an unacceptable flaw in the GCC as Davidson argues in Chapter 5. It required the Council's other members to act against Doha in order to pressure Qatar into realigning more closely with its Arab Gulf neighbours.

It is these tensions that have widened the Gulf Divide not least since the last diplomatic crisis in the Gulf in 2014. In contrast to Riyadh and Abu Dhabi's diplomatic moves against Doha in March 2014, the Saudi and Emirati actions in the current GCC dispute—imposing a land, sea, and air blockade, publishing inflammatory articles calling for regime change in Doha in state-owned media networks, etc.—underscore not only how internal dynamics changed in Riyadh and Abu Dhabi between 2014 and 2017, but also how the Trump presidency encouraged MbS and MbZ to use their countries' leverage over Doha in an effort to pressure the emirate into capitulating to a set of 13 demands which, in practice, would have required Qatar to relinquish its sovereignty.[11]

[10] Mangan, D. (2018). Tiny Qatar Plays a Big, Complicated Role in Trump's World. *CNBC*, 10 September 2018. www.cnbc.com/2018/09/10/qatar-plays-a-big-complicated-role-in-trump-world.html.

[11] Hennessey-Fiske, M. (2017). Will Qatar Agree to Arab Countries' New List of Demands? Unlikely. *Los Angeles Times*, 24 June 2017.

Target: Qatar

Saudi and Emirati anger towards Qatar's post-Arab Spring foreign policy and media culture first culminated in the Gulf crisis of 2014. In March of that year, Saudi Arabia, the UAE, and Bahrain withdrew their envoys from Doha until November. During that spat the Obama administration maintained neutrality and believed that picking sides in the *Khaleeji* dispute would undermine US national interests in preserving Washington's close alliances with all six GCC members. Rather than egging on either Qatar or its Arab Gulf neighbours, the White House pushed both sides to reach the November 2014 Riyadh agreement, which, at least on paper, resolved the spat. According to one interlocutor in Qatar, amid the Gulf crisis of 2014 the Obama administration conveyed to Saudi Arabia and the UAE that any military action against Doha would meet a firm response from the US, which has its largest military installation in the Middle East—US CENTCOM's forward headquarters—based in al-Udeid, Qatar.[12]

According to Kristian Coates Ulrichsen, there were strong signs that Abu Dhabi sought to pressure Doha into changing its foreign policy during 2016. Yet the Obama administration rebuffed such Emirati efforts, only to exacerbate friction between the previous White House and the UAE.[13] In January 2018, Ben Rhodes, Obama's deputy national security advisor for strategic communications and speechwriting, stated that during "*the break with Qatar, we basically had to spend a lot of time trying to prevent that from happening.*"[14] Rhodes affirmed that the Qatar crisis' eruption in June 2017 was a development which the Obama administration had invested energy into forestalling in the interest of preserving the GCC's institutional relevance.[15]

---

[12] Interview with interlocutor in Doha, Qatar (May 2016).

[13] Ulrichsen, K. (2018). Fire and Fury in the Gulf. *Gulf State Analytics*, 31 January 2018. https://gulfstateanalytics.com/fire-fury-gulf/.

[14] Glasser, S. (2018). The Full Transcript: Ben Rhodes and Samantha Power. *Politico*, 15 January 2018.

[15] Ibid.

THE TRUMP FACTOR

MbS and MbZ quickly saw Trump's 2016 victory as a special opportunity to settle scores with Qatar given that the new US leadership had indicated that its preference was for discarding traditional and conventional decision-making that for decades had shaped Washington's foreign policy in the MENA region. In Ulrichsen's words, *"To the rulers of Saudi Arabia and the UAE, the Trump White House appeared to be operating in the same personalized top-down manner as their own royal courts in Riyadh or Abu Dhabi."*[16]

Moreover, after Trump won the presidential election and began forming his cabinet, anti-Islamist regimes and administrations in MENA states—chiefly the UAE, Egypt, and Libya's HoR—were optimistic about the incoming White House reversing policies of the Obama administration in Egypt, Libya, and elsewhere, which the UAE and some of its regional allies saw as being pro- Muslim Brotherhood. Officials in Libya's UAE- and Egypt-backed HoR, which has aligned with the quartet against Qatar since June 2017, quickly expressed optimism about the incoming Trump administration following Clinton's defeat. In November 2016, one parliamentarian in Tobruk, Tarek al-Jaroushi, announced:

> I strongly support Trump because of his and the Republicans' resolute and decisive attitudes… The Republican Party, which understands the truth about [ISIS] and the positions and the victories of the Libyan army, will support us.[17]

Indeed, rhetoric and legislative action from the new administration's officials served as the basis for this optimism on the part of Saudi, Emirati, Bahraini, and Egyptian officials that Trump's White House would remove pressure on Qatar's Arab neighbours to avoid confronting Doha. While campaigning for the presidency, Trump identified the Muslim Brotherhood as a "radical" group and joined officials in Riyadh and Abu Dhabi in criticizing Obama's response to Egypt's Arab Spring revolution

[16] Ulrichsen, K. (2018). The Needless Crisis in the Arabian Gulf. *Arab Center Washington DC,* 5 June 2018. http://arabcenterdc.org/policy_analyses/the-needless-crisis-in-the-arabian-gulf/.

[17] Lewis, A. (2016). East Libyan Factions See Possible Boost in Trump Victory. *Reuters,* 10 November 2016.

of 2011.[18] Secretary of State Mike Pompeo, who previously served as CIA director, co-sponsored legislation to ban the Muslim Brotherhood in his capacity as a Republican Congressman during the Obama presidency.[19] During his confirmation hearings as a nominee for Secretary State, Rex Tillerson accused the Muslim Brotherhood of being "an agent of radical Islam".[20] Frank Gaffney, who served Trump's team as an advisor, stated that the Sunni Islamist movement is set on *"destroying Western civilization from within"* and *"its penetration and manipulation of the Republican Party and the conservative movement in America"* was one of its *"most successful influence operations."*[21]

Shortly after Trump defeated Clinton, Saudi and Emirati officials initiated contact with their counterparts in the incoming administration. In the month following Trump's victory, MbZ quietly travelled to New York for a three-hour meeting in Trump Tower, which escaped the media's radar at the time. The Crown Prince of Abu Dhabi met with Jared Kushner, Steve Bannon, and Michael Flynn. MbZ's visit created a degree of controversy given that officials in Abu Dhabi did not notify the outgoing administration that the UAE's de facto ruler was present in the US, which is customary for any leader of a foreign country visiting the US.[22]

Kushner, the Trump administration official responsible for devising much of the White House's MENA foreign policy, developed particularly close relations with the UAE's ambassador to Washington, Yousef al-Otaiba. An old confidante of Trump, Thomas Barrack Jr., facilitated Kushner and Otaiba's meeting.[23] Annie Karni wrote in a *Politico* piece that early on in Trump's term, Kushner and the UAE's ambassador to

[18] Beckwith, R. (2016). Read Donald Trump's Speech Criticizing Hillary Clinton on Foreign Policy. *Time*, 22 June 2016.

[19] Beinart, P. (2018). Mike Pompeo's Allies on the Anti-Muslim Right. *The Atlantic*, 15 March 2018.

[20] Hosenball, M. (2017). Trump Administration Debates Designating Muslim Brotherhood as Terrorist Group. *Reuters*, 9 January 2017.

[21] Cafiero, G. (2016). Donald Trump: A Win for the UAE? *LobeLog*, 28 November 2016. https://lobelog.com/donald-trump-a-win-for-the-uae/.

[22] Kumar, A. and Wieder, B. (2017). Steve Bannon's Already Murky Middle East Ties Deepen. *McClatchy Washington Bureau*, 23 October 2017. www.mcclatchydc.com/news/politics-government/white-house/article180111646.html.

[23] Kirkpatrick, D. (2018). Who Is Behind Trump's Links to Arab Princes? A Billionaire Friend. *New York Times*, 13 June 2018.

the US were *"in almost constant phone and email contact."*[24] According to Karni's article, Otaiba said that in his conversations with Kushner, *"he did all the asking, and I did all the talking."*[25]

During the transition from Obama to Trump's administration, one of Trump's key fundraisers, Elliot Broidy, who worked in tandem with Lebanese business tycoon George Nader, pressed the incoming White House to adopt an anti-Qatar agenda. Reportedly, both Broidy and Nader were acting on behalf of MbZ *"in exchange for the promise of lucrative contacts in the UAE, some of which materialized."*[26]

UAE-based Erik Prince, who was a strong Trump supporter during the 2016 election, brother of the Trump administration's Secretary of Education Betsy DeVos, and former head of Blackwater, played a role in shaping the incoming White House's special relationship with Abu Dhabi. Having been hired by the UAE to form a new private security force in the aftermath of Blackwater shutting down in 2009, Prince *"presented himself as an unofficial envoy for Trump to high-ranking Emiratis."*[27] Additionally, he met with a member of Russian President Vladimir Putin's inner circle in the Seychelles for a UAE-organized meeting in January 2017, shortly before the Trump administration entered the White House.[28] Reportedly, the meeting in the East African archipelago state was aimed at creating a solid backchannel between the Trump administration and the Kremlin on the Iranian and Syrian files.[29]

After Trump's first term began, ambassador Otaiba deepened his relationship with Kushner who, at that time, also began consulting more frequently with Saudi officials, including his fellow millennial MbS. Kushner and MbS' closeness was such that by October 2017, when Trump's advisor and son-in-law made an unannounced visit to the

---

[24] Karni, A. (2017). Jared Kushner's Mission Impossible. *Politico*, 11 February 2017.

[25] Ibid.

[26] Ulrichsen, 'The Needless Crisis in the Arabian Gulf'.

[27] Entous A., Miller, G., Sieff, K., and DeYoung, K. (2017). Blackwater Founder Held Secret Seychelles Meeting to Establish Trump-Putin Back Channel. *Washington Post*, 3 April 2017.

[28] Ibid.

[29] Ibid.

Kingdom, the two allegedly stayed up until the early hours each morning *"swapping stories and planning strategy."*[30]

By the time of Trump's historic visit to Riyadh in May 2017, which was his first overseas trip as president, it appeared that Saudi and Emirati efforts to influence the White House to adopt a harsh stance against Qatar had proven successful. As one analyst contended, *"the blockading countries wanted the Riyadh summit and their relationships with the Trump administration to be a bridge to isolate Qatar and possibly invade it."*[31] Despite the US President's speech in Riyadh including praise for Qatar as a "crucial strategic partner" and a host of US CENTCOM, his reaction on Twitter to the blockade one day after its implementation led to officials in Doha interpreting his tweets to signal the White House's green light for a Saudi/UAE-led military campaign against Doha, aimed at changing the regime in Doha.[32]

According to Bannon, Trump's visit to Riyadh was the catalyst for the siege on Qatar. Speaking at a Hudson Institute conference in October 2017, titled "Facing Violent Extremism: Qatar, Iran and the Muslim Brotherhood," the former White House strategist stated that the summit created a "fundamental change" in Saudi Arabia, the UAE, and Egypt's approach to combatting terrorism with Qatar becoming their renewed target.[33] Bannon asserted:

> I do not think it is just a coincidence that two weeks after this summit, you saw the blockade imposed by the UAE, Bahrain, Egypt, and Saudi Arabia on Qatar… We went to the summit with the UAE, Saudi Arabia and others. The first thing is that we have to pay attention to this funding for radical Islam, and there cannot be more [funding]… You cannot be on two roads. On the one hand, you cannot say you are a friend and an ally, and on the other hand you fund the Muslim Brotherhood or Hamas.[34]

[30] Emmons, A., Grim, R., and Swisher, C. (2018). Saudi Crown Prince Boasted That Jared Kushner Was "In His pocket". *The Intercept*, 21 March 2018. https://theintercept.com/2018/03/21/jared-kushner-saudi-crown-prince-mohammed-bin-salman/.

[31] Qatar Tribune. (2018). A Year After Riyadh Summit, Unity and Stability Elude the Region. *Qatar Tribune*, 22 May 2018.

[32] Ulrichsen, 'The Needless Crisis in the Arabian Gulf'.

[33] MEMO. (2017). Former Adviser to Trump: Riyadh Summit Triggered Siege on Qatar. *Middle East Monitor*, 25 October 2017. www.middleeastmonitor.com/20171025-former-adviser-to-trump-riyadh-summit-triggered-siege-on-qatar/.

[34] Ibid.

Kushner provided the blockading states assurances that the White House would not defend a blockaded Qatar under siege or counter any of the quartet's actions against Doha.[35] Writing for *The Intercept*, Clayton Swisher and Ryan Grim reported that Kushner Companies—the real estate firm headed by Kushner's father Charles—turned to Qatar's Minister of Finance in an effort to receive investment for the firm's property at 666 Fifth Avenue in a brief meeting held at the St. Regis Hotel in New York during the final week of April 2017.[36] The following day there was a follow-up meeting at the Kushner property, which the Qatari Minister of Finance did not attend. The failure of both sides to reach a deal might have motivated Kushner to make moves which "*undermined efforts by Secretary of State Rex Tillerson to bring an end to the [Gulf] standoff,*" according to Swisher and Grim.[37]

Upheaval in the Trump Administration

One day after the ATQ blockaded Qatar, Trump took to Twitter to express his initial support for the bloc's unprecedented action against Doha. The American commander-in-chief tweeted:

> During my recent trip to the Middle East I stated that there can no longer be funding of Radical Ideology. Leaders pointed to Qatar... So good to see the Saudi Arabia visit with the King and 50 countries already paying off. They said they would take a hard line on funding extremism, and all reference was pointing to Qatar. Perhaps this will be the beginning of the end to the horror of terrorism![38]

Shortly after the diplomatic row broke out in the Gulf and just before Trump's perceived endorsement of the quartet's siege of Qatar on Twitter, Tillerson stressed the importance of GCC members remaining

---

[35] Qatar Tribune, 'A Year After Riyadh Summit'.

[36] Swisher, C. and Grim, R. (2018). Jared Kushner's Real-Estate Firm Sought Money Directly from Qatar Government Weeks Before Blockade. *The Intercept*, 2 March 2018. https://theintercept.com/2018/03/02/jared-kushner-real-estate-qatar-blockade/.

[37] Ibid.

[38] Rampton, R. (2017). Trump Takes Sides in Arab Rift, Suggests Support for Isolation of Qatar. *Reuters*, 6 June 2017.

"unified."[39] Of course, Trump's tweets severely undermined Tillerson's statement and highlighted the inexperienced administration's dysfunctionality. When asked about Trump's tweets, Republican Senator Bob Corker, chairman of the Senate Foreign Relations Committee, was confused and asked who wrote those tweets and when they went out: "*The president? When did that occur?*"[40]

Yet, on the same the day which Trump tweeted his endorsement of the blockade, Tillerson and Secretary of Defense Jim Mattis began pressuring the president to take a more moderate and neutral approach to the Qatar crisis aimed at resolving the dispute to protect Washington's interests in the Middle East. Within three hours of Trump harshly accusing high-ranking Qatari officials of sponsoring terrorism in his tweets, the Pentagon officially stated that America's military was grateful for Doha's support and "*enduring commitment to regional security.*"[41] The Pentagon's spokesperson refused to comment on the president's tweets from that afternoon.[42]

TRUMP'S QUICK SHIFT ON QATAR

Soon after his controversial tweets in favour of the blockade, Trump completely changed his stance on the Qatar crisis. He not only quickly stopped accusing the emirate of sponsoring terrorism and extremism, but also expressed gratitude to Qatar's Emir Tamim for supporting America's struggle against terrorism and agreed to a USD 12 billion fighter jet deal with Doha—all that only a number of days after his tweets about Qatar.[43] In July 2017, Tillerson engaged in shuttle diplomacy in the GCC, travelling to Kuwait, Qatar, and Saudi Arabia with the

[39] Gaouette, N. and Starr, B. (2017). Trump Appears to Take Credit for Gulf Nations' Move Against Qatar. *CNN*, 6 June 2017.

[40] Geltzer, J. (2017). What Trump's Qatar Tweets Revealed. *The Atlantic*, 7 June 2017.

[41] Stewart, P. (2017). U.S. Military Praises Qatar, Despite Trump Tweet. *Reuters*, 6 June 2017.

[42] Al Jazeera. (2018). Qatar's Blockade in 2017, Day by Day Developments. *Al Jazeera*, 18 February 2018. www.aljazeera.com/news/2017/10/qatar-crisis-developments-october-21-171022153053754.html.

[43] Ajmera, A. and Stone, M. (2017). Qatar Signs $12 Billion Deal to Buy F-15 Jets from U.S. *Reuters*, 14 June 2017.

objective of resolving the diplomatic crisis.[44] By July 11, Washington and Doha signed a counterterrorism agreement, and in November the US and Qatar held their first counterterrorism dialogue in Washington.[45] America's then-Secretary of State praised Qatar's response to the quartet's actions as "very reasonable."[46] That month, Trump told *CBN News* that Washington is "*going to have a good relationship with Qatar and not going to have a problem with the military base [at al-Udeid].*"[47]

Ultimately, pressure from high-ranking officials within the Trump administration led to the American president reversing his stance against Doha. Clearly, the political establishment in Washington and many entrenched interest groups with stakes in keeping the US–Qatar alliance strong did not adopt the president's position against Doha expressed in his June 6, 2017 tweets. Fortunate for Qatar was Tillerson's support for Qatar, rooted in his service as ExxonMobil's CEO. As Ulrichsen opined, Tillerson "*knows probably more than anyone else in the US the true value of the Qatari partnership to the US.*"[48]

America and Qatar's military-to-military relationship has institutionalized since the strategic alliance began to take off in the 1990s, and especially so after the George W. Bush administration relocated US CENTCOM's forward headquarters from Saudi Arabia to Qatar in the early 2000s. Mattis was fully aware of how the US military presence in Qatar makes the emirate a vital ally as the al-Udeid base has for years enabled the US military to conduct military operations in conflicts across Afghanistan, Iraq, and Syria.[49]

[44] Qiblawi, T. (2017). Gulf Crisis: Tillerson Leaves Qatar After Saudi Meetings. *CNN*, 13 July 2017.

[45] Finn, T. (2017). U.S., Qatar Sign Agreement on Combating Terrorism Financing. *Reuters*, 10 July 2017; United States Department of State. (2017). First U.S.-Qatar Counterterrorism Dialogue. United States Department of State, 8 November 2017. www.state.gov/r/pa/prs/ps/2017/11/275409.htm.

[46] Finn, T. (2017). Visiting Doha, Tillerson Calls Qatari Position 'Reasonable'. *Reuters*, 11 July 2017.

[47] Al Jazeera. (2017). Trump: We Will Maintain Good Relations with Qatar. *Al Jazeera*, 15 July 2015. www.aljazeera.com/news/2017/07/trump-good-relations-qatar-170714230137824.html.

[48] Mudahka, F. (2018). Trump's Renewed Reconciliation Calls 'Could Help Solve Gulf Crisis'. *Gulf News*, 1 February 2018.

[49] Des Roches, D. (2017). A Base Is More Than Buildings: The Implications of the Qatar Crisis. *War on the Rocks*, 8 June 2017. https://warontherocks.com/2017/06/a-base-is-more-than-buildings-the-military-implications-of-the-qatar-crisis/.

Scores of neo-conservative voices in Washington, who have grievances with Qatar dating back to al-Jazeera's critical reporting on the US occupation of Iraq following Saddam Hussein's ouster in 2003, as well as former Secretary of Defense Robert Gates, have advocated that Washington threatens to relocate the US military base at al-Udeid to another location in the Gulf if Doha fails to sever ties with Islamist "terrorists" in the MENA region.[50] Yet a host of logistical and political factors have made it unlikely that the US would ever do so.

Put simply, for all Arab Gulf leaders there are political risks associated with these countries' indigenous populations seeing their rulers as "lackeys" of Western powers, chiefly the United States. Growing perceptions of Arab Gulf regimes being America's puppets is a factor that would give most GCC states second thoughts about agreeing to host US CENTCOM's forward headquarters. At a time in which perpetually low oil prices and regional unrest have, to varying degrees, challenged Arab Gulf leaders' legitimacy at home, Qatar stands out among GCC governments as the least threatened by any internal ideational threats. Qatar's small geography, tiny indigenous population of only 300,000, and financial resources, which the state has invested heavily in its own people via generous social programmes, have enabled the Al Thani family to avoid any credible threats to its legitimacy from any segments of its native citizenry.[51] Thus, for Qatar, the political risks of continuing to host the US military's largest installation in the Middle East are substantially lower than they would be for other GCC states which have been more challenged to preserve internal stability throughout the post-2011 period. In other words, the comparative strength of the social contract between Qatar's rulers and subjects has served to make the emirate a relatively safe place for US CENTCOM's forward headquarters.

Qatar's investments in the US economy, especially since the financial crash of 2008, have also curried Doha much favour among American officials. The Qatar Investment Authority, Qatar's sovereign wealth fund (SWF), helped the US economy recovery after the 2008 crisis through large investments in major American cities such as New York, Chicago, and Phoenix. The fact that major American academic institutions, such

---

[50] Karam, J. (2017). Sanctions, Leaving Military Base 'Possible Options Against Qatar'. *Arab News*, 27 May 2017.

[51] Adams, T. (2018). From Qatar's Blockade, a Bold, Unexpected New Vision Is Emerging. *The Guardian*, 6 May 2018.

as Cornell, Carnegie Mellon, Georgetown, Texas A&M, and Virginia Commonwealth universities, have branches in the emirate has further cemented the bonds between America and Qatar. Additionally, Doha, as a major purchaser of arms, is important to America's defence sector, having spent USD 9 billion on American weaponry between 2001 and July 2017, including US weapons systems such as Apache attack helicopters, Javelin missiles, and missile defence systems.[52]

Trump's firing of Tillerson on March 13, 2018 raised questions about how or if the US would change its stance on the Qatar crisis. With Pompeo replacing Tillerson, many analysts expected Washington to embrace a new stance on the Gulf dispute far more favourable to the quartet. Pompeo's record as being extremely hawkish on Iran and staunchly opposed to the Muslim Brotherhood informed such analyses, which predicted that the new Secretary of State would not share Tillerson's view that maintaining neutrality in the Gulf crisis and pushing for GCC unity would best serve Washington's interests. Given that the quartet did not share Tillerson's perceptions of the Qatar crisis, there was much speculation that Trump's decision to fire him was triggered by pressure from the Gulf. Shortly after the press reported on Tillerson's ouster, the Dubai-based Emirati political scientist Abdulkhaleq Abdulla labelled Trump's first Secretary of State "*the worst foreign minister in the history of America*" and suggested on Twitter that Saudi/Emirati dissatisfaction with Tillerson led to his firing.[53] Abdulla wrote, "*History will remember that a Gulf state had a role in expelling the foreign minister of a superpower and that's just the tip of the iceberg.*"[54]

Nonetheless, with Pompeo serving as Washington's chief diplomat, the US has stood by Qatar and refused to buy the quartet's narrative about Doha being a sponsor of violent extremism. Pompeo, while travelling from Europe to the Middle East within 48 hours of being sworn in as Secretary of State in April 2018, called for an end to the GCC crisis. He stated that "*enough is enough*" in a message intended for Riyadh.[55]

[52] Enos, E. and Stohl, R. (2017). Examining US Arms Sales to Qatar. *Stimson Center*, 20 July 2017. www.stimson.org/content/examining-us-arms-sales-qatar.

[53] Arab News. (2018). Gulf Arabs Relish Tillerson Firing; Iran Weighs Nuclear Deal. *Arab News*, 14 March 2018. www.arabnews.com/node/1266091/middle-east.

[54] Ibid.

[55] Harris, G. (2018). Pompeo's Message to Saudis? Enough Is Enough: Stop Qatar Blockade. *New York Times*, 28 April 2018.

Since becoming Secretary of State, Pompeo has clearly joined other high-ranking officials in Washington in viewing GCC unity as an important US national interest. The White House's efforts to unite America's Sunni Arab allies against Iran's expansion and consolidation of influence throughout the Middle East have suffered from the Qatar crisis, which the Trump administration recognizes has given Tehran yet another wedge in the Arab world to exploit for its own geopolitical and economic empowerment. As Simon Henderson argued, *"Pompeo's decision to take the Tillerson perspective on the Gulf crisis was probably a consequence of the simple judgment that there is a more important issue to focus on — namely, Iran."*[56]

Illustrative of how the US–Qatar alliance has only strengthened since Pompeo replaced Tillerson is the fact that in July 2018 Qatari and American officials announced the launching of a project to expand the US military presence at al-Udeid amid discussions about making it"permanent." Qatari state-owned media reported that

the construction of barracks and service buildings to support joint security efforts, as well as improving the quality of life of the troops stationed at the airbase… underscores Qatar's commitment to deepening its strategic military relations with the United States.[57]

CONCLUSION

Nearly two years into the Qatar crisis, the Trump administration faces a major dilemma albeit one that is largely of its own making through the White House's encouragement of hawkish conduct on Saudi Arabia and the UAE's part. With MbS and MbZ in power and Emir Tamim at the helm in Doha, odds are good that the Gulf Divide will become a permanent reality in the Arab world's geopolitical order with serious implications for alliances, strategic partnerships, and trade relationships in the increasingly polarized Gulf and beyond. How could

[56]Henderson, S. (2018). Pompeo Says 'Enough' to Gulf Royals' Rift with Qatar. *The Hill*, 30 April 2018. https://thehill.com/opinion/international/385435-pompeo-says-enough-to-gulf-royals-rift-with-qatar.

[57](2018). Qatar, US Plan 'Expansion' of Al-Udeid Airbase. *The New Arab*, 25 July 2018. www.alaraby.co.uk/english/news/2018/7/24/qatar-us-plan-expansion-of-al-udeid-airbase.

Trump get MbS and MbZ to make certain concessions to Qatar to resolve the *Khaleeji* dispute is the one-million-dollar question. His failure to, thus far, bring the leaders of the involved countries to a summit in the US suggests that certain GCC leaders' refusal to come tells us that Washington's mediation may fail to end the crisis.

Undoubtedly, aside from Iran, all states in the Gulf region—plus the US and other Western countries—are set to be long-term losers from the Qatar crisis even if such short-term gains are evident, highlighted by the boost to Oman's economy thanks to Qatar relocating its logistics hubs from Dubai to Sohar and increasing Qatari investment in the Sultanate on top of growing bilateral trade stemming from Muscat's "neutrality" in the crisis.[58] Trump's speech at the Riyadh summit in May 2017 emphasized the need for the Arab/Islamic world to unite against violent fundamentalists, which the president blamed Iran more than any other state for emboldening and sponsoring. If the White House remains set on pushing back against Iran's regional ascendancy, a functional GCC will be essential from an American perspective. At a time in which Tehran asserts influence in the Arab/Islamic world by supporting militias in Iraq, Syria, Lebanon, and elsewhere, difficult questions about how the US will interact with the Islamic Republic in a post-nuclear deal environment remain open. If Washington's allies in the Arabian Peninsula can move past this highly emotive dispute, which has been unprecedented for the GCC since its founding in 1981, the White House will be in a far stronger position to counter Iran.

If the US—or any other state in the world such as Kuwait, France, Oman, or Russia—will ever prove capable of providing Riyadh and Abu Dhabi with ways to ease their current stances against Qatar while maintaining a sense of dignity remains to be seen. If not, it would be safe to bet that future historians will interpret the institutionalization of the GCC's Qatar rift as a legacy of the Trump administration's first year in the Oval Office.

---

[58] Baabood, A. (2017). Oman and the Gulf Diplomatic Crisis. *Oxford Gulf & Arabian Peninsula Studies Commentary*, Autumn 2017. www.oxgaps.org/files/commentary_-_baabood.pdf.

CHAPTER 9

The Political Economy of the Gulf Divide

Steven Wright

INTRODUCTION

The coordinated campaign of Saudi Arabia, the United Arab Emirates, Bahrain, and Egypt, which culminated in the 5th June 2017 severance of diplomatic relations and enactment of an embargo on Qatar, can be understood from the outset as constituting a fundamental rupture of the regional order. The character and severity of the crisis is a watershed moment in regional relations as it has fractured commonly held outlooks on regional order to an extent where their incompatibility goes beyond manageable state-to-state friction over autonomy, to being one where national security and monarchical stability is seen to be threatened. While the six states which comprise the Gulf Cooperation Council have intermittently suffered from rivalry and actions that challenged both autonomy and security of fellow member states, a common understanding and outlook on regional order had largely prevailed that allowed for reconciliation and pragmatic cooperation.

While the consensus for cooperation and progressive cooperation between the GCC countries has stood since the organization was founded in 1981, the 'Ramadan Blockade' of 2017 is an action which reflects a fundamental difference in outlook between Qatar and the

S. Wright (✉)
Hamad Bin Khalifa University, Doha, Qatar
e-mail: stwright@hbku.edu.qa

© The Author(s) 2019
A. Krieg (ed.), *Divided Gulf*, Contemporary Gulf Studies,
https://doi.org/10.1007/978-981-13-6314-6_9

145

blockading states on regional order, in addition to the ideals of gradualist regional integration through the GCC as an organization. As highlighted above, while various historical grievances have undoubtedly existed between the six GCC states; it was the 2011 region-wide uprisings which were to be decisive in reshaping the geopolitical landscape of the wider region, and the legacy of which is still being felt in the contemporary age through the way it challenged the GCC consensus on regional order. These different outlooks by the Gulf States on regional order were to crystallize into incompatible positions, with Qatar taking the view that the region-wide uprisings, against long-standing rulers, heralded an opportunity for a new progressive era for the region. Essentially, Qatar's outlook has been one of gradualist and progressive-pragmatism, as it sees a greater emphasis on popular self-determination, the rule of law, and an opening of civil society, to be at the forefront of what the region needs for development and security to be achieved. Comparatively, the Saudi-led group is seeking maintenance of the traditional monarchical status-quo, as social or political liberalism, and an opening of civil society, is viewed as a threat to their national security and dynastic rule. Indeed, the manner in which the 2011 uprisings took place, in addition to a resurgent Iran, has heightened a sense of insecurity that has sharpened this interpretation of the risks of progressive-pragmatism and gradualist liberalism.

Such incompatible views on regional order are instructive given they are interpreted as detrimental to the 'others' national security as well as overall regional order. In light of these positions, and the actions taken against Qatar, the strategic goal of the 2017 Ramadan crisis can be understood as fixated on seeking regime change to force Qatar into a subservient vassal-state relationship that is contrary to international legal norms on the need to safeguard state sovereignty. While such motivations and the incompatible outlooks on regional order have clear longer-term ramifications, they are also useful in contextualizing the drivers behind the political economy impact of the actions taken, in addition to Qatar's response, and therefore aid in the below evaluation. In essence, it reflects incompatible conceptions of security needed for survival, and thus underlines the challenge of conflict resolution and reconciliation. Indeed, the character of mutual security guarantees, which would be needed to enable an easing of the crisis, seems to many seasoned observers as something which can both prolong the crisis in a manner which sees it become a new regional norm, which would shape security calculations and international relations.

From the outset, it is important to recognize that the March 2014 withdrawal of ambassadors by Saudi Arabia, the UAE, and Bahrain, which ended following Qatar signing the 2014 Riyadh Agreement, was a key event which impacted on Qatari decision-making about its neighbours during the reign of Qatar's Emir, Sheikh Tamim bin Hamad Al-Thani. The abrupt withdrawal of the ambassadors came within the first twelve months of Sheikh Tamim becoming Emir. Yet, the manner in which it occurred, in addition to how it was used to get Qatar to commit to the provisions of the Riyadh Agreement, which typified the outlook of the Saudi-led bloc on regional order, underlined a duplicity on behalf of the UAE, Saudi Arabia, and Bahrain, in their dealings with Qatar given the abrupt nature of the 2014 crisis. What is important here is that, for Qatari policymakers, it undoubtedly confirmed that such actions might reoccur in the future. While the 2014 withdrawal of the ambassadors did not extend to a maritime, air or land embargo, it is clear that it prompted contingency planning by the Qatari government for such a possibility, regardless of how remote. In terms of understanding how Qatar was able to respond to the June 2017 crisis and manage its economic impact, it is therefore necessary to contextualize it as a coordinated response which had been contemplated since the end of the 2014 crisis, which itself was a product if the incompatible views on regional order which had crystallized since 2011. Such contingency planning would have varied in its sophistication across different arms of the government, but it is sufficing to recognize that it existed.

As will be shown in this chapter, the impact of the 2017 Ramadan Blockade proved to have a controllable impact based on such planning and proved unable to destabilize the economy, thus impacting the political system, which was the strategic intention. During the crisis, it was progressively turned into an opportunity for economic diversification and self-sufficiency in crucial areas. In order to demonstrate this further, this chapter will engage with the three core issues of macroeconomic and financial resiliency, the impacts on trade, and finally the context of Qatar as an energy exporter. The central argument, however, remains that the embargo on Qatar failed to achieve its strategic objective based on the resiliency Qatar has shown for the reasons discussed above, in addition to it progressively building on the circumstances in a manner which spurred greater self-sufficiency and development.

Economic Resilience

A central aspect of the 2017 Gulf Crisis was an effort to undermine Qatar's economy as a means of applying pressure on the political system and leadership of the country. This was done through three main pillars: disrupting Qatar's trade, seeking to undermine confidence in the economy, and through attempting to destabilize Qatar's currency. While a discussion on Qatar' trade logistics will be discussed in a subsequent section, attention here will be given to the other two pillars identified.

A vital characteristic of the Ramadan Blockade has been the way cyber warfare has employed disinformation as Krieg writes in Chapter 6. This was directed towards impacting Qatar's international standing, fostering social divisions between society and the political elite, in addition to raising concern among investors and financial analysts towards impacting on Qatar's economic standing and suitability as a venue for foreign direct investment. Ultimately, Qatar proved resilient against these challenges and at a social level, the opposite impact was observed through social cohesion and support for the Qatari leadership intensifying among Qatari nationals and resident expatriates in the face of the existential threat. In the initial period of the blockade, disinformation created a climate of uncertainty internationally as the coordinate campaign was instigated. This manifested itself through Qatar's sovereign credit rating being downgraded by S&P Global Ratings on 7 June 2017 from AA- to AA, based on the concerns that were created by the enactment of the blockade and the disinformation that had been used to heighten a sense of alarm.[1] This was followed by a downgrading of one level by the agency Fitch, to AA- with a negative outlook. Such ratings are instructive as it underlines how global markets perceive Qatar's long-term and short-term foreign and local currency sovereign rating.

When viewed holistically, the crisis economically impacted all principal countries party to the dispute as the perception of regional risk was heightened. One of the more informative measures on the economic health of any country is its ability to raise capital, and also its ability to attract foreign direct investment. Indeed, the bond market can be understood as a national barometer on the robustness of a national economy. Regarding raising capital through sovereign bond issuances, Qatar issued a triple-tranche of bonds amounting to US$12 billion in April 2018,

---

[1] Anonymous. (2017). S&P Lowers Qatar's Credit Rating. *BBC News*, 7 June 2017.

and it proved to be oversubscribed with orders being estimated to have exceeded US$52–53 billion.[2] It is instructive that following Qatar's announcement for major bond issuance, Saudi Arabia unveiled a call for its own triple-tranche of sovereign bonds totalling US$11 billion, which was widely interpreted as a means of absorbing liquidity which would impact the success of Qatar's own bond sale. It is noteworthy that Saudi Arabia's own bond issuance attracted a comparable level of orders to Qatar's own sovereign bond sale, which given the comparable sizes of the economies, is an indicator of positive sentiment on Qatar's economy less than 12 months after the crisis had unfolded.

It was Vladimir Lenin who is said to have remarked that, '*the best way to destroy the Capitalist System was to debauch the currency*'[3]—Lenin was astute to understand the importance of a nation's currency and its link to political order. A destabilized currency has the potential to wreak economic instability that can have profound impacts on the social and political fabric of a country. Within the context of Qatar, monetary policy is shaped through the currency peg that Qatar has with the US dollar. A forced revaluation posed the threat of a spike in inflation, a decline in per capita purchasing power, in addition to impacting on broader international confidence in Qatar's economy. Luiz Pinto noted that the scale of the impact was significant as during the initial six months of the blockade, '*Qatari banks faced $35.4 billion in capital outflows and its central bank witnessed a $21 billion drop in official foreign exchange reserves*'.[4] According to S&P, Qatar was forced to inject around $43 billion into the local banking system during the first six months of the blockade.[5] The intention here was to impact Qatar's currency, yet it is essential to appreciate why this was unsuccessful:

> The [Qatari] government holds net financial assets of at least $331.1 billion or 203 percent of GDP, 87 percent of which is estimated to be held

[2] Al-Sayegh, H. (2017). Qatar Riyal Stabilizing in the Offshore Market After Central Bank Pledge on Dollar Supply. *Reuters*, 3 December 2017.

[3] Keynes, J.M. (1971). *The Collected Writings of John Maynard Keynes. Vol. 2, The Economic Consequences of the Peace*. London: Macmillan.

[4] Pinto, L. (2018). *Sustaining the GCC Currency Pegs: The Need for Collaboration*. Doha: Brookings Doha Centre.

[5] Sharif, A. (2018). Qatar Injected $43 Billion to Help Banks After Boycott, S&P Says. *Bloomberg*, 20 February 2018.

overseas or in hard currencies. This sovereign economic dominance was vital to withstanding what would have otherwise been a significant financial hit. Notwithstanding the blockade, economic factors commonly associated with a currency crisis or a devaluation are simply not found in Qatar. The country runs structurally large fiscal and current account surpluses and is able and willing to sustain the dollar peg with its external revenues and financial buffers.[6]

Despite these fundamentals, efforts were being made to influence the Qatari Riyal peg to the US dollar. Through the blockading countries and their citizens repatriating capital, it created downward pressure on the Riyal. Although Qatar's Central Bank guaranteed the official exchange rate to the US dollar for domestically exchanged currency, the rates in which Qatar's currency was being traded internationally went beyond the official rate which raised concerns that a forced devaluation would occur. This continued for a period of six months and culminated in the 5 December 2017 decision by MSCI, whose MSCI Global Investable Market Indexes (GIMI), is an industry leading indicator on market capitalization.[7] Following MSCI conclusion that Qatar's peg to the US dollar was sustainable, the speculation on the Qatari Riyal subsided and allowed Qatar to use its large fiscal and current account surpluses to further strengthen its banking sector and reserves to fortify its currency position.

The conclusion that can be reached here is that despite the concerted effort to destabilize Qatar's economy, with particular emphasis on its currency, its ability to attract international liquidity, in addition to the bond values of the country, it is the fundamentals that Qatar had which enabled it to withstand what can be understood as economic warfare. In essence, with global crude oil prices having been on a high-price cycle from around 2000 to 2014, Qatar was able to secure a vast financial surplus during this era which fed into its sovereign wealth fund being in a strong position. While the capital outflows and reduction in official foreign exchange reserves were considerable; it is essential to recognize that the country had both introduced counter-credit precautionary

---

[6] Pinto, L. (2018). *Sustaining the GCC Currency Pegs: The Need for Collaboration*. Doha: Brookings Doha Centre.

[7] Anonymous. (2017). UPDATE 1-MSCI to Continue Using Onshore FX Rates for Qatari Riyal for Now. *Reuters*, 6 December 2017.

policies following the financial downturn since 2003. This was promoted by Qatar Central Bank having encouraged all domestic banks to comply with the Basel Committee's guidance on Sound Practices for the Management and Supervision of Operational Risk.[8] This catered for greater liquidity which softened the full effects of the capital outflows and drops in official foreign exchange reserves. It was the size of the sovereign wealth investment fund, at over US$330 billion, which was a primary reason sufficient confidence was able to be restored to the international market. Ultimately, despite the upheaval, the crisis has proved to be an acceleration for national economic and monetary stability.

TRADE, FOOD SECURITY, AND SELF-SUFFICIENCY

The embargo closed off access for Qatari registered shipping, in addition to shipping carrying cargos to and from Qatar, and thus disrupted Qatar's logistics. It was fortunate for Qatar that in December 2016, Hamad Port became operational, and it was officially launched on the third month anniversary of the embargo on 5 September 2017. The construction of the Port began in 2010, but its importance to Qatar would have been underlined following the 2014 crisis which culminated in the Riyadh Declaration. Essentially, the strategic significance of the port is that it heralded the end of reliance on ports in the UAE for the shipment of goods to Qatar. The reason being that the long-standing and smaller Doha Port, was unable to handle the large container ships, which meant that Qatar was reliant on ports in the UAE, primarily Jebel Ali and Fujairah Port, for the larger ships to unload their cargos to smaller container ships which would then sail onwards to Qatar. This ability to move beyond the longstanding reliance on the UAE is an essential reason why the impact of the campaign on Qatar and suspension of relations was quickly overcome.

Hamad Port constitutes a US$7.4 billion investment over a space of 28.5 km², with a projected capacity of 7.5 million containers per year. At the point of completion, Hamad Port will be around the 20th largest port globally in term of container capacity. With it having become functional from December 2016, its role has proved to be timely and critical for the manner in which Qatar was able to handle the logistical challenge

---

[8] Qatar Central Bank (2011). *Instructions to Banks*, vol. 2. Doha: QCB.

of the closure of the Saudi border. To illustrate this, it is noticeable that before the embargo on 5 June, Hamad Port was receiving an average of 650 containers per day with a monthly average of around 20,000.[9] The impact of the embargo can be determined by the container traffic in the first four weeks of the embargo as container traffic dropped by around 38% to 250 containers per day, and a monthly average of 7000, which constitutes a drop of 35%. After mid-July 2017, the daily average had risen to 900–1000 containers per day which is a 46% increase in traffic since before the embargo, and a monthly average of 25,000 containers.[10] Interestingly, the impact was limited to the first month, but logistics had adjusted after this as supplies were re-routed. After the blockade, 70% of Qatar's imports were entering the country through the Port.[11]

According to Qatar's General Authority for Customs, most of its staff who were stationed at the Abu Samra customs facility on the Saudi Border were redistributed to both Hamad Port, Hamad International Airport, and Al-Rowais Port at the northern part of the Qatari peninsula. While Hamad Port is the primary facility for large cargo container ships, the Al-Rowais Port played a critical role in enabling Qatar to manage the impact of the closure of the Saudi border and its customs facility at Abu Samra. Al-Rowais Port was expanded within the first week of the blockade, most notably in terms of the development of a facility to receive camels and other livestock, in addition to refrigeration units to cater for perishable foods. The critical difference between Al-Rowais Port and Hamad Port is that the former can only cater for smaller cargo vessels such as wooden Dhows. Large and medium-sized Dhows were routed to the port to bring perishable goods, general supplies, in addition to both the livestock and belongings owned by Qatari nationals in the blockading countries. In total, Al-Rowais handled around 20% of Qatar's total imports.[12] Much of the traffic coming to this port came from Turkey, Iran, Kuwait, Oman, Azerbaijan, Sudan, and also Somalia. Given its location at the northern tip of Qatar's peninsula, goods could reach the port from Iran and Oman in under 12 hours. Qatar's General Authority for Customs cooperated with Qatar's Ministry of Economy and Trade to

[9] Qatar General Authority of Customs. (2017). *Magazine Customs*, vol. 66. Doha: GAC.
[10] Ibid.
[11] Ibid.
[12] Qatar General Authority of Customs. (2017). *Magazine Customs*, vol. 67. Doha: GAC.

find ways of expediting the clearance process of perishable goods, after implementing a new system within the first week of the blockade, the clearance time was reduced to 16–24 hours.[13]

The provision of high demand perishable goods was an activity which was coordinated by Qatar's Hassad Food, which is a wholly owned subsidiary of the Qatar Investment Authority (QIA) that focuses on food and agricultural investments. For the first month of the blockade, Hassad Food took the lead in sourcing high-demand perishable products for the Qatari market which included poultry, dairy, eggs, vegetables, fruits, and juices in addition to others.[14] For the first four weeks of the embargo on Qatar, Hassad Food coordinated the provision of these good through both air and sea freight. New logistical pathways were established through the Iranian port of Bushehr which received goods from Azerbaijan and Turkey. The first shipments of additional food items were delivered to Qatar by 6th June, and within under a week of the embargo, Hassad Food had secured 50% of the national food needs of Qatar. The nature of the response underlines both the pre-embargo contingency planning, the way the company was able to act, and also the financial reserves available to Qatar through QIA. After four weeks of Hassad Food began gradually handing over the food supply to the private sector as the impact was mitigated against.

These actions proved critical in maintaining stockpiles of perishable good in supermarkets to maintain public confidence. Such goods are important as they constitute key products which cannot be stockpiled and thus are visible indicators to the public on the impact of a disruption in logistics. Based on participant observation, what was noticeable to this author was that adequate stocks in significant supermarkets existed as both perishable and non-perishable goods were being proactively replenished, which underlined a recognition of the need to ensure public confidence through a visible abundance of consumer goods. The only immediate impact was mainly concerning poultry, eggs, and milk, yet within around 48 hours supply chains had responded to any discernible shortages of these products. Regarding non-perishable goods, shortages were not observable as a strategic stockpiling strategy had been

[13] Ibid.

[14] Anonymous. (2017). Hassad Hands Over Food Supply Task to Private Sector. *Gulf Times*, 14 November 2017.

prudently employed by the state in advance of the embargo to mitigate against any such eventualities. This was an important factor which bolstered societal confidence.

A goal for self-sufficiency was adopted as part of Qatar's National Development Strategy 2018–2022, which was released in March 2018. Even before its formal announcement as a national strategy, the drive for food security had seen emphasis given towards how self-sufficiency could be achieved in key areas. While the sourcing and provision of food items was the initial priority given the closure of the Saudi border, the embargo proved to be a catalyst in Qatar moving towards domestic self-sufficiency in key areas of food production. In the first six months of the blockade, Hassad Food undertook investments to develop 140,000 square metres of land for agricultural cultivation, which allowed Qatar to achieve a 20% self-sufficiency within 6 months for fresh vegetables, and with a declared target of 70% of domestic chicken needs being domestically produced within a period of two to three years following the embargo.[15] Adding to this, Hassad Food announced in July 2018, that it intended to invest US$500 million in Sudan's agricultural and food sector.

Regarding milk and dairy, before the embargo, Qatar was only able to produce around 10% of its needs and imported around 400 tonnes of milk and yoghurt daily from Saudi Arabia. As part of the drive towards self-sufficiency, a rapid expansion took place with the Qatari diary and meat company, Baladna, received its first batch of 4000 cows from the United States and Europe by August 2017.[16] As part of the drive towards greater self-sufficiency for food security, Baladna announced it planned to provide a sufficient quantity of milk and dairy for the country to be both entirely self-sufficient, but also emerge as a net-exporter, within a two-year time frame from the onset of the crisis.[17]

[15] Pathak, S. (2017). Qatar's Hassad Food Increases Vegetable Production by 35%. *Qatar Tribune*, 24 December 2017.

[16] Anonymous. (2018). Qatar Will Have Enough Milk by Ramadan: Baladna. *Al-Jazeera*, 10 March 2018.

[17] Ibid.

IMPACT ON ENERGY TRADE

While the embargo on Qatar by its neighbouring states has proved to have had a limited economic impact given the factors discussed above, what can be concluded is that its broader economic impact is one of opportunity cost. It is clear that the mainstay of Qatar's economy remains the export of its LNG, yet changes were occurring in the LNG sector which would necessarily have changed the calculations which feed into Qatar's LNG export strategy, and ironically had the potential to be a driver for greater economic integration between Qatar and its GCC neighbours given their own projected demand for natural gas.

In terms of rising demand for natural gas, it is noteworthy that Saudi Arabia, the UAE and Bahrain, are projected to progressively have an increasing demand for natural gas to meet their domestic needs. Indeed, such shortfalls in natural gas are part of a wider regional problem facing countries Gulf region: it is only Qatar and Iran that have ample supplies of this resource, while all other states need to rely on imports in the face of dwindling domestic supplies. For Oman and the UAE, they import gas from Qatar through the Dolphin pipeline. Yet for Oman, its own energy security needs to prompt it to act pragmatically by agreeing with Iran to enter into a gas supply agreement through new pipeline-based supply. While Oman has traditionally been a pragmatic and neutral actor, the same cannot be said for the United Arab Emirates, Saudi Arabia, and Bahrain, as the prospect of importing Iranian gas for their domestic needs remains politically unrealistic. It is in this context that a reasonable expectation as part of the drive for greater political and economic integration between the Gulf Cooperation Council member states would have seen Qatar fill that void providing a fair pricing regime could be achieved. Moreover, given that natural gas could be provided through a pipeline-based supply, it held the prospect of being more cost-effective than having to rely on imports from suppliers such as the United States which, as of 2016, saw the UAE and Kuwait become importers of US natural gas.

It is noteworthy however that despite the regional demand having grown, Qatar had not entered into further supply agreements with its neighbouring states prior to the cessation of relations with the GCC-3 in 2017. While Qatar had started supplying LNG through the first cross GCC pipeline in 2004 with Dolphin Energy Limited, it did not reach full operational capacity. The main reason for this has been established as one of opportunity cost for Qatar. Ultimately with the development of an LNG carrier fleet, Qatar was able to position itself as a global supplier which was driven by market fundamentals and profit maximization.[18] The rates to which Qatar supplied gas were done at a discounted rate. While the agreement for the supply of gas through the Dolphin pipeline is distinct from the commercially driven global LNG supply where Qatar focused on maximizing revenue, it should be recognized that the earlier agreement Qatar had with the UAE was very much an agreement of its time. Indeed, it is conceivable that the favourable contract Qatar agreed with the UAE not only served as a recognition of UAE's support for a transnational pipeline but also the political issues the Dolphin agreement heightened give Saudi Arabia's reticence on cross-regional projects which could traverse its demarcated territory. Equally with the UAE's increasingly divergent outlook from Qatar in the context of the regional upheaval of 2010 and 2011, the prospect of the UAE seeking to secure further gas from Qatar to meet its projected shortfalls faced practical political obstacles, and therefore the prospect of the UAE having a degree of energy dependence on Qatar would have served as a deterrent. This is despite the stated goals of the GCC collective seeking economic integration and thus underlines how broader political considerations and differing conceptions of regional order, proved to overwhelm the logic of greater cooperation and integration.

Although the further development of a regional gas market and higher gas supply agreements held the prospect of furthering integration which served all parties, the political obstacles which limited greater regional cooperation was a key factor which in Qatar deciding to maintain a globally orientated LNG strategy. On a broader contextual level, global changes in the market fundamentals of the LNG sector were observable which warrants placing Qatar's LNG strategy into perspective: in terms of global demand, the indicators underline a modest future demand with China and the Middle East being notable geopolitical exceptions where an increased demand is expected. Importantly, demand within Europe, in addition to the key markets of Japan and South Korea have peaked and show little indication of future growth in demand. Indeed, upwards of 60% of global demand comes from the combined markets of Japan, South Korea, and China, yet it is only China

[18] Krane, J. and Wright, S. (2014). *Qatar 'Rises Above' Its Region: Geopolitics and the Rejection of the GCC Gas Market*, vol. 35. London: LSE Kuwait Programme.

where demand is expected to grow, while the other countries demand has peaked and can be expected to decline slowly. The was illustrated in September 2018 with QatarGas signing a 22-year deal with PetroChina to supply around 3.4 million tonnes of LNG annually.[19] Nevertheless, while sluggish future demand is an important indicator; it is when this is considered in the context of an identifiable growth in supply that the complexity of the challenge facing Qatar comes into perspective.

Regarding the nature of the supply dynamics of the LNG sector, it is important to appreciate that the sector is in the midst of a transformational change. Less than a decade ago, the United States was projected to become the world's largest importer of LNG, yet in a reversal of fortunes that has been enabled from the exploitation of Shale, it has emerged as an actual exporter of LNG and is projected to be the world's largest exporter by 2022. As indicated earlier, as of 2016, it has begun exporting LNG to both Kuwait and the UAE, but it is also competing for market share in the key East Asian market which has been largely enabled through the landmark expansion of the Panama Canal. It is important to recognize here that with the expansion of the Canal, the transport time for LNG shipments from the United States to the lucrative markets in East Asia, has been cut to around 20 days. For US-based suppliers, it allows it to compete favourably against Qatar and other leading international suppliers and under its location, US suppliers are also in a favourable position to supply LNG to the European market. Adding to the increased projected competition from the United States, both Australia has rapidly expanded its production capacity of coalbed methane so a level which, as of 2018, allows a degree of parity with Qatar's export capacity. Russia too is striving, and in March 2017, President Putin stated ambition for Russia to be the largest producer of liquefied natural gas in the world.

The significance of the rapid increase in export capacity of operators in the USA, Russia, and Australia, translates to a new era of competition on a global scale in the face of a more challenging demand environment. At a geopolitical level, the rise of these major players in LNG means that existing and future consuming markets for LNG will increasingly be able to draw from the supply in North America, Central Asia, and Australasia,

[19]Anonymous. (2018). Qatargas Agrees on 22-Year LNG Supply Deal with China. *Reuters*, 10 September 2018.

which underlines the competition Qatar faces.[20] With short transit route times, a more global supply network can be drawn on by consuming countries that will be a beneficiary of lower process induced through competition. As countries seek to achieve energy security through a diversified energy supply base, these emerging competitors have the potential to make clear inroads in markets where Qatar is an established supplier. In essence, the LNG sector is heating-up to a new era of competition whose primary beneficiary will be consuming countries.

Adding to the complexity of the global LNG market is that while it is increasingly being dominated by the LNG giants of Qatar, USA, Russia, and Australia, there is little to indicate that these states will cooperate in a meaningful way given the context of an oversupplied market LNG market.[21] The rising quadripartite of Japan, South Korea, China, and India, constitute global LNG demand more than 60% of global market demand. The potential and logic for cooperation on LNG procurement have not been lost on these countries given their energy security and national economic interests and in that in 2018, Japan, China, and South Korea signed a tripartite agreement cooperate on LNG procurement. Such moves underline the nature of change and the way in which Qatar's economic mainstay will have to adapt with what is a trend towards more challenging conditions.

The breakdown in relations between Qatar and its gas-short neighbours, therefore, underscores a missed opportunity for all parties concerned. Cooperation and the supply of Qatari gas had the potential to ensure energy security, lower cost, and also to serve the interests of regional political and economic integration. For Qatar, the move towards supplying its regional neighbours would have allowed it to mitigate against the changing market environment which is becoming more competitive with the prospect of lower yields.

CONCLUSION: RESILIENCE AND OPPORTUNITY

What has come to be known as the Ramadan Blockade initiated by Saudi Arabia, the UAE, Bahrain, and Egypt, in addition to the severance or diplomatic downgrading of ties with Qatar by Comoros, Djibouti,

---

[20]Wright, S. (2017). Qatar's LNG: Impact of the Changing East-Asian Market. *Middle East Policy*, 24:1 (pp. 154–165).

[21]Wright, S. (2018). *Shifting Markets of Liquid Gas: Emerging Producers and Alternative Geo-Strategies*. Doha: Al Jazeera Centre for Studies.

Maldives, Mauritania, Jordan, Senegal, the Libya and Yemen; constitutes a fundamental rupture of the regional order. As has been highlighted above, the actions taken against Qatar underlines an incompatibility of world views. Such incompatibilities motivated Qatar's neighbours to take actions which are understood here to fixated on achieving regime change as a means of forcing Qatar into a subservient vassal-state relationship. While the actions instigated against Qatar are multifaceted and include cyberwarfare, disinformation, and efforts to foment social upheaval among others, it is clear that the economic and financial dimensions were a central pillar that was used to heighten pressure on Qatar as a means of this strategic objective being realized. While the immediate actions of the Ramadan Blockade had an impact, the overriding conclusion is that Qatar proved resilient given its forward contingency planning that had been initiated since 2014. Through new logistical infrastructure being completed, which allowed it to adopt new supply lines, it lessened the actual impact. Moreover, the financial reserves held by the state also allowed it to maintain the stability of the Qatari Riyals peg to the United States dollar, which as highlighted above, was one of the more acute threats Qatar faced given the implications of a revaluation.

While Qatar was resilient to the external pressures, one clear impact was the social solidarity that cross-cut all segments of society. Such social solidarity has proved an important means for both buttressing political support for the government, social optimism, and crucially feeding into a shared social understanding that Qatar's future success rests on self-sufficiency, diversification, and a gradual expansion of civil society. These have emerged as arguably a common zeitgeist within Qatar on what would be an effective means of both resistance and resiliency against the threats faced. Indeed, as greater understanding has permeated society in Qatar about the distinctions in political outlook between Qatar and its neighbours who have led such actions, it has become increasingly apparent of the need for a progressive strategy to be taken which transforms the embargo into an opportunity for social, political and economic growth in the country. On this basis, it can be characterized as a monumental turning point in Qatar's political and social fabric which can be used as a basis for future development. In terms of Qatar's political economy, the actions taken against Qatar has propelled a national drive for self-sufficiency in strategic areas, economic diversification, as well as social and political progress.

CHAPTER 10

The Future of the GCC Amid
the Gulf Divide

Abdullah Baabood

INTRODUCTION

The GCC is witnessing an unprecedent crisis in terms of its scale and magnitude. Since the inception of the GCC in 1981, by its current member states Bahrain, Kuwait, Oman, Qatar, Saudi Arabia and the United Arab Emirates, this regional organization has been having numerous disputes and disagreements. However, none has been as detrimental to regional integration and cooperation as the current one. Although the crisis is between some of its member states, one of its main impacts was on the regional organization itself and on its efforts for enhancing regional integration and cooperation. The blockade against Qatar does not only violate the letter and the spirit of the GCC but it also impinges on the fundamental principles of its core values, objectives and agreements. Thus, rendering the regional organization ineffective in the management and the resolution of the conflict but also effectively freezing most of its activities and undermining its regional and international status.

A. Baabood (✉)
Hamad Bin Khalifa University, Doha, Qatar

© The Author(s) 2019
A. Krieg (ed.), *Divided Gulf*, Contemporary Gulf Studies,
https://doi.org/10.1007/978-981-13-6314-6_10

161

The fact that Saudi Arabia, the UAE and Bahrain, the three GCC member states involved in the blockade, have totally ignored the organizational mechanisms for conflict resolution to deal with their grievances over Qatar's policies demonstrates that the trust in the organization appears to have vanished. Obviously the longer this crisis lingers the more entrenched the division becomes and the harder it will become for both a smooth reconciliation and for the GCC to regain its credibility. Largely due to this crisis, there are signs and beliefs that the GCC has lost trust if not momentum and its member states, although still trying to hold on to it, have started to consider other options not least the bilateral agreements between the Kingdom of Saudi Arabia and the United Arab Emirates as well as Kuwait through forming Coordinating Committees. These bilateral committees are constructed in such a way as to punish and reward members of the organization but not necessarily to enhance further regional integration.

GCC nationals especially the Gulf business community who are supposed to be the drivers of and the main beneficiaries from regional integration have also shown signs of fatigue and disappointment with the low level of achievements and the slow speed of cooperation especially on region-wide projects as well as disillusionment with the bad effects of conflicts and crisis on their common interests.

It is worth remembering that the GCC as an intergovernmental organization was conceived and designed at a time when Saudi regional hegemony and the smaller Gulf states had to be protected against Iranian expansionism and regional upheavals. Today, while external security concerns about Iran's covert operations in the region still feature widely in the security rhetoric of the Gulf States, the domestic security dimension relating to potential dissidence and violent non-state actors can no longer be served collectively by the GCC; the reason being that the organization has never been greater than the sum of its parts.[1] Despite some development in regional integration especially in the economic fields and common projects, there is no consensus on common foreign and security policy. Each member state appears to have a different perception of what constitutes security threat and take a different approach to liberalization, political opposition and the activities of non-state actors. This bewilders its security guarantor, the United States, that has

[1] Legrenzi, M. (2006). Did the GCC Make a Difference? Institutional Realities and (Un) Intended Consequences. *EUI Working Paper*, RSCAS 2006/01.

started in vain to get the GCC states to reconcile their differences and work together against common threats. Notwithstanding the GCC short comes, having a level of cooperation and coordination between its member states helps to face the multitude of threats and makes it easier for the United States and other security allies to function and cooperate with these Gulf states as a collective group.

Meanwhile, it is worth noting that other small states like Kuwait and Oman have become extremely apprehensive about actions taken against Qatar by one group of member states against another member state fearing that GCC membership might not shield them from the bullying of its bigger neighbours questioning the whole idea of GCC mutual defence and the idea of a "security community" after learning that military action was indeed considered against Qatar.

While the GCC may endure this unprecedented crisis, it will be hard to see how they can overcome the differences, bury their wounds and begin to trust each other and work as a collective and a cohesive group. For the GCC as regional organization to function, let alone prosper, there is an urgent need to build trust and gain respect for its rules and agreements, which may lead to demands that its objectives, structure and decision-making be restructured for it to have any meaningful purpose.

THE GULF COOPERATION COUNCIL

Given the myriad of economic, political and security challenges, the six-member states decided to form interregional integration projects that can help sustain these oil-rich but vulnerable states. The Gulf Cooperation Council was formally launched at a summit in Abu Dhabi on May 25.[2] Its founding Charter states that the GCC was formed to strengthen relations among its member states and to promote cooperation among their citizens.[3] Hence, the basic objectives as came in Article 4 of the GCC Charter is to deepen and strengthen existing relations and effect coordination, integration and interconnection between member states in all fields in order to achieve unity between them.[4]

---

[2] Hassan, O.A. (2015). The GCC's Formation: The Official Version. *Al Jazeera Studies Centre Dossiers*, 30 March 2015.

[3] GCC. (1981). *Charter of the Gulf Cooperation Council* (GCC). Riyadh, Saudi Arabia. Retrieved from https://www.files.ethz.ch/isn/125347/1426_GCC.pdf.

[4] Ibid.

In terms of governance and institution building, Article 9 of its Charter established the main GCC governing bodies, namely: the Supreme Council, which is the highest decision-making body, an "ad hoc" Commission for Settlement of Dispute, as well as the Ministerial Council and the Secretariat General. While Article 10 dealt with decision-making and voting in the Supreme Council where each of the six members of the Supreme Council are granted one vote. It also stipulates that resolutions of the Supreme Council are by unanimous approval in substantive matters, while those on procedural matters are by majority vote.

Since its foundation, the GCC has entered into several common agreements and joint projects. In the Economic sphere, for example, the GCC established a Unified Economic Agreement in 1981, Custom Union in 2003 and the GCC Common Market in 2008. The organization also planned to introduce a monetary union and single currency by 2010, but the process was delayed due to political hurdles. The Common Market, which created a single market with free flow of goods, capital and people, along with the Customs Union provided an appropriate platform for collective free trade negotiations and strategic dialogues with global partners. Besides that, the GCC initiated some common projects including power grid connectivity and a common rail network.

While the main reason for Gulf integration was the creation of a security community, it became clear quite early that economic and technical cooperation took precedence over security concerns. However, security cooperation was not totally neglected or forgotten. Cooperation in the security domain started with the foundation of the Peninsula Shield Force (PSF) in 1984, followed by the Joint Defence Agreement in December 2000, supervised by a Joint Defence Council and a Military Committee and later in 2013 a Unified Military Command.[5]

Through a series of security and defence agreements, the GCC was able to create a security community among its member states adding to building a robust regional security mechanism. Individually and collectively, the GCC states have succeeded in maintaining multi-faceted economic, defence and security cooperation with international partners including the U.S., European Union (EU), NATO, China, India, etc.

---

[5] See Guzanksy, Y. (2014). Defence Cooperation in the Arabian Gulf: The Peninsula Shield Force Put to the Test. *Middle Eastern Studies*, 50:4.

Such agreements have helped global economic cooperation and integration and aided in building further levels of security frameworks.[6]

Despite delays, hiccups and some occasional disagreements, not too uncommon among similar regional projects, regional cooperation in the Gulf was increasing among the GCC states and the organization became an active body in deepening integration and in representing the member states in international fora. Although the organization faced much criticism, the GCC has been somewhat effective in providing a semblance of security and stability to an otherwise unstable region. The GCC has acted as collectively with some measured effectiveness and success at both regional and international levels, e.g. at the UN, the Arab League, and the OIC among others.

While the Middle East region around the GCC began to unravel because of the Arab Spring, the GCC looked to be moving closer towards integration, culminating in Saudi Arabia's King Abdullah surprising many by calling at a GCC summit in Riyadh in December 2011 calling for deeper integration by transitioning the GCC from the level of cooperation to that of a union.[7] Notwithstanding this, the proposal of a Gulf Union never materialized into anything substantial as Gulf leaders had valid concerns that forming such a union may pave the way for further Saudi Arabia's domination of the organization.

These concerns have been validated by the recent crisis, which has emphasized the failure of the GCC as an organization in deepening further its integration process, improving its governance structure especially in dealing with disputes among member states or widening its membership. The crisis has also vindicated the long-held view that Saudi Arabia, being the largest and most powerful member of the GCC, is using the organization to dominate the smaller members.

Indeed, this current crisis has led to more fracture within the GCC and a serious Gulf Divide running in contradiction to the stated intent of the GCC to enhance regional cooperation and integration leading to a unity among its members based on their common objectives and their similar political and cultural identities, which are rooted in their Islamic

[6] Saidy, B. (2014). GCC's Defence Cooperation: Moving Towards Unity. Foreign Policy Research Institute. E-Notes, 15 October 2014.

[7] Khalaf, A. (2013). GCC Members Consider Future of Union. Al Monitor, 14 January 2013. http://www.al-monitor.com/pulse/politics/2013/01/saudi-arabia-gcc-announcement.html#ixzz55oCDc8k7.

belief. The current crisis has achieved nothing, apart from driving its member states apart and thus undermining the GCC and its common achievements of over 37 years of regional cooperation and integration.

THE GULF CRISIS

Much has been said and written about the current Gulf crisis and its aftermath.[8] Suffice to say that it began on 23 May 2017 with the hack of the Qatar News Agency and implantation of false statements attributed to Qatar's Emir that formed the basis for a subsequent media onslaught by Saudi and Emirati news outlets. Two weeks later, On 5 June 2017 three fellow GCC member states, Saudi Arabia, the UAE and Bahrain, along with Egypt, a fellow Arab League member, known collectively as Anti-Terror Quartet (ATQ), abruptly cut diplomatic ties with Qatar and imposed a comprehensive land, air and sea blockade as well as economic sanctions in a standoff that would have far-reaching consequences both regionally and internationally. In addition, the three GCC states prohibited their citizens from travelling to and residing in Qatar and gave Qatari citizens 14 days to depart from their territories.[9] Furthermore, all the blockading countries closed their airspace to Qatari aircrafts and demanded that foreign airlines seek permission for overflights to and from Qatar.

The ATQ countries accused Qatar of threatening regional security by sponsoring terrorist and Islamist organizations and aligning with Iran. Weeks after the blockade, they presented Qatar with a list of 13 sweeping demands to be fulfilled within 10 days in return for ending the blockade.[10] The ambiguous demands presented to Qatar on 22 June included but were not limited to; severing all ties and funding to terrorist and Islamist groups, curbing diplomatic relations with Iran, shutting

[8] See for example Ulrichsen, K.C. (2014). Qatar and the Arab Spring: Policy Drivers and Regional Implications. *Carnegie Occasional Paper*, 24 September 2014. https://carnegieendowment.org/2014/09/24/qatar-and-arab-spring-policy-drivers-and-regional-implications-pub-56723.

[9] BBC News. (2017). Iran Sends Food to Besieged Qatar. *BBC News*, 11 June 2017.

[10] Al Jazeera. (2017). Arab States Issue 13 Demands to End Qatar-Gulf Crisis. *Al Jazeera*, 12 July 2017. https://www.aljazeera.com/news/2017/06/arab-states-issue-list-demands-qatar-crisis-170623022133024.html; Wintour, P. (2017). Qatar Given 10 Days to Meet 13 Sweeping Demands by Saudi Arabia. *The Guardian*, 23 June 2017. https://bit.ly/2swYtXR.

down Doha's Al-Jazeera news network, closing a Turkish military base in Qatar, and the payment of reparations to Saudi Arabia. These demands were scaled back on 5 July to six broad principles that included commitments to combat terrorism and extremism and to end acts of provocation and incitement.[11]

As stated earlier in this book, Qatar has long practised an independent and ambitious foreign policy with different priorities to its neighbours which sometimes leads to their irritation or anger and there are at least two key issues which have enraged them in recent years.

First, it is Qatar's support for Islamist groups and especially the Muslim Brotherhood as outlined earlier by Davidson and Krieg in this book. While Qatar acknowledges that it has provided assistance to the Muslim Brotherhood, it vehemently denies aiding militant groups linked to al-Qaeda or the Islamic State (SIS).[12] Second, as Boussois highlights in this book, is Qatar's presumed relations with Iran, with which it shares the world's largest gas field.

Qatar, in return, denied accusations of terror finance and collusion with Iran. Doha has thus far refused to accept the quartet's demands, which in its views amount to surrendering its sovereignty and undermining the legitimacy of its ruling family. Although Qatar refused to capitulate and become a vassal state, it called on the blockading countries to come to the negotiating table to discuss all areas of concern.[13] At the time of writing, the ATQ countries have refused to accept this call and the crisis continues, with its harmful implications for the GCC, the wider region and the international community.

While the demands on Qatar are somewhat odd and difficult to placate, these tensions highlight deep differences and illuminate contrasting Qatari and Saudi-Emirati visions for the future of the Middle East that were greatly exacerbated by the parties varying perceptions.[14] As Krieg states in Chapter 6, Qatar's policy during the Arab Spring and its stand on the need for political change in the region were perhaps some of the main reasons for this current crisis. That is why this escalation in the Gulf

[11] BBC News. (2017). Saudi-Led Bloc Modifies Demands to End Qatar Crisis. *BBC News*, 19 July 2017.

[12] BBC News. (2017). Qatar Crisis: What You Need to Know. *BBC News*, 19 July 2017.

[13] Reuters. (2017). Qatar Rejects Arab States' Accusations; UK's Johnson Flies to Saudi. *Reuters*, 6 July 2017.

[14] Miller, R. (2018). The Gulf Crisis: How It All Started. *Al Jazeera*, 1 June 2018.

can be seen as one of a series of measures taken by the counterrevolutionary forces spearheaded particularly by Saudi Arabia and the UAE.[15]

The crisis with its attendant harsh measures and the public demands impinge on Qatar's sovereignty and contradict diplomatic protocols and neighbourly relations as well as international humanitarian law.[16] The continuation of the crisis also has an impact on global energy supplies as Wright writes in the previous chapter, disrupts existing international trade patterns as well as weakens the GCC as a regional organization, which for decades had guaranteed stability in an unstable region, playing a significant role in security and counterterrorism cooperation.

THE EFFECT OF THE CRISIS ON THE GCC INTEGRATION PROCESS

The sudden and unforeseen nature of this diplomatic spat is evidence of how policies and loyalties in this tumultuous region can shift overnight. After all, the nature of decision-making in the GCC states is based on personal views and preferences with very little input from formal institutions, international organizations or the public. In such circumstances, little attention is paid to the wider effects of such personalized decision-making.

Qatar is a member of the GCC and the blockade seriously undermines the letter and the spirit of the regional organization, its agreements and achievements. The blockade, in particular, runs against the spirit of the much-vaunted achievement of the GCC Common Market signed in 2007, which created a common free trade area and facilitated the free flow of people, goods and capital between its member states.[17] The blockade has impaired the GCC Common Market as, for example, the abrupt closure of Qatar's only land boundary effectively stopped the flow of goods and cut the country of its immediate neighbours. Qatar is undergoing vast development especially in preparing for the World Cup

---

[15] Krieg, A. (2017). The Gulf Rift—A War Over Two Irreconcilable Narratives. *Defense in Depth*, 27 June 2017. https://defenceindepth.co/2017/06/26/the-gulf-rift-a-war-over-two-irreconcilable-narratives/.

[16] Falk, R.A. (2018). A Normative Evaluation of the Gulf Crisis. *HSF Policy Brief*, 1:1, February 2018. http://humsf.org/wp-content/uploads/2018/02/HSF_PolicyBrief_2.pdf.

[17] Federation of Chambers of the Gulf Cooperation Council (GCC). (2018). *Gulf Common Market*. Riyadh: Saudi Arabia. http://fgccc.org/en/?page_id=3670.

2022 and it heavily relies on imported goods largely from Saudi Arabia and the UAE.[18] The blockade also restricted the freedom of movement enjoyed by GCC citizens, preventing families of different member states with marriage and tribal ties from visiting one another.[19] Furthermore, the lives of nationals from the ATQ countries living in Qatar have been disrupted due to having to leave the country, affecting their employment and the education of their children.[20]

The current crisis has also revealed the limitation and exposed the vulnerability of the GCC as it was completely sidelined and its absence from virtually every stage of the dispute rendered it to be almost irrelevant. In this sense, the decision to impose a blockade, which affects and disturbs common agreements, was not only taken outside the GCC and its problem-solving mechanisms, but the Gulf Cooperation Council has been completely ignored during this conflict. The GCC was excluded as the mechanism to discuss the dispute, communicate the initial grievances against Qatar and was not chosen as a facilitator of dialogue or mediator between the disputing members. It was even unable to prevent potential military escalation, which was a possibility—as stated by Kuwaiti Emir Sabah al-Ahmad al-Jaber Al Sabah during a September 2017 press conference at the White House with US President Donald Trump.[21]

Moreover, two GCC member states, Kuwait and Oman, were also not consulted or taken part in the blockade. Instead, they choose not to take sides and Kuwait, supported by Oman continued their efforts to foster mediation and reconciliation without much success so far.

GCC population and especially the business community as well as non-nationals residing in the GCC countries, even if they are not from the parties involved in the conflict, are facing difficulty in terms of travel and conducting business while investment climate is severely affected.

---

[18] OHCHR. (2017). On the Impact of the Gulf Crisis on Human Rights. *Report of the Technical Mission to the State of Qatar*, December 2017.

[19] Aljazeera.com. (2018). Qatar: UN Report Proof Saudi-Led Blockade Illegal. *Al Jazeera*, 8 January 2018.

[20] Raghavan, S. (2017). Qatari Capital Brims with Fear, Uncertainty and Resilience as Arab Crisis Intensifies. *The Washington Post*, 10 June 2017.

[21] Arab News. (2017). Full Anti-Terror Quartet Statement on the Emir of Kuwait's Comments in Washington. *Arab News*, 8 September 2017; Remarks by President Trump and Emir Sabah al-Ahmed al-Jaber Al-Sabah of Kuwait in Joint Press Conference. The White House, 7 September 2017. https://bit.ly/2Fexkkg.

The crisis has had an adverse effect on the social, economic and political relations of the GCC states and the wider region.

At the international level, the GCC is involved in a number of strategic dialogues and trade and economic negotiations with international partners including the United States, the EU, China, India and Turkey. With a disunited GCC these international negotiations and dialogues have become hard to pursue causing puzzlement and disenchantment among its global interlocutors.

This blockade has not only severely impaired the GCC's own cooperation, integration and common projects, but it has also reflected negatively on its credibility in international cooperation with other regional and international countries and organizations. It highlights the volatility and vulnerability of the GCC as a regional organization and raises serious questions and concerns about its future role as a collective group.

The quartet's precarious endeavour to bring Qatar to heel has been met with stout and surprising resilience by the small Gulf nation, leading some to question whether the Saudi-led bloc's plan may have had the opposite effect.[22] Internally, the blockade has fuelled nationalist sentiment in Qatar and rallied its citizens behind their leader Emir Tamim al-Thani, as Al-Muftah writes in Chapter 14. The deep wound caused by the blockade to the Qatari people and its government would make them ever more suspicious about the intentions of its neighbours. For example, it is hard to see how Qataris could ever again trust an organization that manifestly failed to prevent three of its members from turning against them twice in three years.[23] At the same time, officials and public in Kuwait and Oman have watched with wariness and apprehension that they, too, could be vulnerable to Saudi or Emirati pressure to follow a particular line in regional policy-making, especially if and when they undergo their eventual transition to new leadership. Kuwait, in fact, had requested the British government to establish a preeminent military presence in the country as a way to sure up its security.[24] While Oman that enjoys historical military cooperation with UK, is considering

[22] Hassan, H. (2018). Qatar Won the Saudi blockade. *Foreign Policy*, 4 June 2018.

[23] https://www.aljazeera.com/indepth/features/2017/06/timeline-qatar-gcc-disputes-170605110356982.html.

[24] https://www.forces.net/news/exclusive-britain-considering-permanent-military-presence-kuwait.

establishing a permanent army training base in Oman, according to the British defence secretary Michael Fallon.[25]

In some sense, the current crisis with Qatar is seen as only the tip of an iceberg of a joint Saudi-Emirati policy to dominate and reshape the region, causing serious damage to trust and confidence of further GCC integration.

BILATERAL AGREEMENTS—A SUBSTITUTE?

As the GCC stagnated and was unable to function because of the crisis, there was much hope that the GCC annual summit in Kuwait City on 5 December 2017 would be an opportunity for reconciliation between the disputing parties, which would allow the organization to function smoothly. However, that summit had in fact turned into more of a disappointment for those supporting reconciliation. The level of representation was low with only the Emir of Qatar attending and the Emir of Kuwait present as the host.[26] The summit itself fell apart within hours as it was concluded after less than a session of the planned two-day meeting, that a resolution of the spat was not on the table casting doubts if there were ever to be any future GCC summits.[27] In fact, the day before the summit, the foreign ministers meeting provided an indication of the acrimonious positions taken by the blockading countries, when they started to resort to recrimination and finger-pointing.[28] Moreover, in the morning of the GCC Summit, the details of a bilateral partnership agreement between Saudi Arabia and the United Arab Emirates were announced[29] outlining a far-reaching agreement allegedly concerning

[25] https://www.arabianbusiness.com/uk-seeks-permanent-army-training-base-in-oman-626900.html.

[26] Krieg, A. (2017). The Saudi-Emirati Axis: United Against Gulf Unity. *Middle East Eye*, 7 December 2017.

[27] Al-Jaber, K. and Cafiero, G. (2017). The GCC's Worst Summit. *Al Jazeera Online*, 9 December 2017. https://bit.ly/2GRU3mr.

[28] Kristian Coates Ulrichsen. (2018). Missed Opportunities and Failed Integration in the GCC. In Zeina Azzam and Imad Harb (eds.). *The GCC Crisis at One Year, Stalemate Becomes Reality*. Arab Center Washington DC.

[29] Langton, J. (2017). Sheikh Khalifa Forms Joint Military Alliance Between UAE and Saudi Arabia. *The National*, 5 December 2017. https://bit.ly/2AFjhi3.

"all military, political, economic, trade and cultural fields".[30] Although this agreement remained vague on how this new strategic partnership would go about devising and implementing policy, the message it sent to the rest of the group of six, was that at least in Abu Dhabi and Riyadh the utility of the GCC as a regional organization was no longer appreciated. Since the organization has effectively been frozen in time. A further declaration by Kuwait and Saudi Arabia to set up a bilateral cooperation council on 18 July 2018 just reinforced the perception that multilateralism in the Gulf was not in demand.[31]

These bilateral agreements are not necessarily meant to create a two-speed GCC, but they seem to be constructed to intentionally isolate Qatar further and perhaps other member states that do not follow the Saudi–Emirati line. Rather than enhancing further GCC integration, these bilateral moves could deter future region-wide development efforts and sound the potential death knell for the GCC.

Is an Arab NATO an Alternative?

The Trump administration has since been quietly working on creating a new security alliance comprised of the six GCC member states plus Egypt and Jordan, unofficially known as the "Arab NATO" and dubbed the "Middle East Strategic Alliance"(MESA). The alliance's objectives—formally announced during a ministerial meeting between Secretary of State Mike Pompeo and the GCC+2 on 28 September 2018 on the margins of the UN General Assembly in New York—suggest that this US-led alliance is supposed to function as a loose bulwark against perceived Iranian expansionism.[32] Mike Pompeo emphasized the need for Middle East stability, defeating terrorist organizations like ISIS, bringing an end to the on-going conflicts in Syria and Yemen, helping to stabilize Iraq and *"stopping Iran's malign activity in the region"*.[33]

---

[30]Wintour, P. (2018). UAE Announces New Saudi Alliance That Could Reshape Gulf Relations. *The Guardian*, 5 December 2017.

[31]AlSharq Al-Awsat. (2018). Saudi Arabia, Kuwait Sign Deal to Establish Joint Coordination Council. *AlSharq Al-Awsat*, 18 July 2018.

[32]US DoS. (2018). GCC+2 Ministerial Meeting Readout. *US State Department*, 28 September 2018. https://www.state.gov/r/pa/prs/ps/2018/09/286302.htm.

[33]The New Arab. (2018). US Pressing Ahead with 'Arab NATO' to Confront Iran. *The New Arab*, 29 September 2018.

The idea of establishing a broad Arab alliance dates to the beginning of the Arab uprisings in 2011 and was again considered in 2015. Yet, the Obama administration, had given priority to constructively engaging Iran in an effort to find a diplomatic solution to the ongoing "nuclear crisis". The five permanent members of the UN Security Council; namely China, France, Russia, the UK and the United States, plus Germany, had reached a nuclear deal with Iran on 14 July 2015 in Vienna known as the Joint Comprehensive Plan of Action (JCPOA), aiming to resolve the conflict with Iran over its clandestine nuclear programme.

However, the Trump administration, Cafiero writes in Chapter 8, had bought into the neo-conservative securitization of the JCPOA as a "bad deal". In May 2018 the US President announced his withdrawal from the Iran Deal and reimpose more stringent sanctions, thereby jeopardizing the landmark arms control agreement under which Iran dismantled much of its nuclear programme under the supervision of international inspectors who had repeatedly certified Iran's compliance.[34]

Indeed, President Trump has shown more interest in the region through his tough rhetoric on Iran, accusing it of being the *"head of international terrorism"* and demonizing it not only as a vital threat to US national security, but also to the GCC and its long-time ally Israel. As a consequence, Trump seemed to have invested heavily into the hawkish Saudi Crown Prince MbS who together with Abu Dhabi's Crown Prince has presented himself as a champion of confronting Iran. Together they used the Riyadh Summit in May 2017, where massive arms deals for the kingdom were announced, as a platform to ostracize the Islamic Republic.[35]

In this context, it is worth remembering that there had been previous attempts at constructing a string of security alliances across the Middle East, but all ended in failure. It must be recalled that Britain and the United States made several attempts in the 1940s and 1950s to build pan-Arab alliances such as the Baghdad Pact or the Central Treaty

---

[34]Williams, J. (2018). Read: Trump's Iran Nuclear Deal Speech Full Text. *Vox*, 8 May 2018.

[35]Mehta, A. (2017). Revealed: Trump's $110 Billion Weapons List for the Saudis. *Defence News*, 8 June 2017. https://www.defensenews.com/breaking-news/2017/06/08/revealed-trump-s-110-billion-weapons-list-for-the-saudis/.

Organization (CENTO), all had short lives, often ending in acrimony.[36] Following the 1991 Gulf War and the defeat of Iraq, a similar attempt at creating a military alliance between Arab members of the US-led coalition force was made. It comprised members of the GCC plus Egypt and Syria, known as the Damascus Declaration, and equally failed to bear any fruit.[37]

It is worth noting that, despite the GCC being based on a collective defence agreement, the organization failed to respond adequately to the 1990 Iraqi invasion of Kuwait.[38] The creation of the Peninsular Shield Force as a collective defence mechanism has always lagged behind the ambitions of being a joint expeditionary force that could quickly respond to emerging threats across the Gulf. Problems with force integration, command and control as well as adequate capacity and capability relegated the Peninsular Shield Force to a mere force on paper.

Furthermore, in early 2015, the Arab League countries decided to set up a 42,000 men strong joint Arab force—an endeavour that never materialized due to differences of opinions over the definition of threats and scope of operation especially between Saudi Arabia and Egypt. Cairo and Riyadh, two of the largest Arab militaries, were unable to resolve differences in opinion about how the force should be deployed and against whom. This led Saudi Arabia, later in the same year, to announce a wider alliance through the creation of the Islamic Military Counter-Terrorism Coalition (IMCTC).[39]

Although the GCC+2 Ministerial meeting on 28 October 2018 in New York shows according to a US State Department statement that "*all participants agreed on the need to confront threats from Iran directed at the region and the United States*",[40] the perception of Iran and its

---

[36]Gorvett, J. (2018). 'Arab NATO' Faces Challenges, Question Marks. *Asia Times*, 14 August 2018. http://www.atimes.com/article/arab-nato-faces-challenges-question-marks/.

[37]Whitehall Papers. (1993). The GCC: Alliance Politics. *Whitehall Papers*, 20:1 (pp. 35–50), https://doi.org/10.1080/02681309309414506.

[38]Ahady, A.U.H. (1994). Security in the Persian Gulf After Desert Storm. *International Journal*, 49:2; (1993). The GCC: Alliance Politics. *Whitehall Papers*, 20:1 (pp. 35–50).

[39]Gorvett, J. (2018). 'Arab NATO' Faces Challenges, Question Marks. *Asia Times*, 14 August 2018. http://www.atimes.com/article/arab-nato-faces-challenges-question-marks/.

[40]US DoS. (2018). GCC+2 Ministerial Meeting Readout. *US State Department*, 28 September 2018. https://www.state.gov/r/pa/prs/ps/2018/09/286302.htm.

activities in the region varies intensely from one Gulf state to the next. The securitization of Iran, mostly driven by Riyadh and Abu Dhabi, has been a major obstacle to regional security integration. The reason being that Kuwait, Oman and Qatar do not necessarily share the same threat perception as their GCC partners. After all, one stated reason for the current Gulf Crisis was Doha's more nuanced and pragmatic relationship with Tehran, which diverged from Saudi Arabia and the UAE.

The statement of Qatar's Foreign Minister Sheikh Mohammed bin Abdulrahman Al Thani at a news conference following the 28 October 2018 meeting that *"the alliance should be built on existing institutions"* case in point. The Qatari minister raised the pertinent question of how regional integration around an external threat could be achieved when the GCC countries themselves remain internally divided.[41]

However, despite its early prevacation and hiatus on the crisis, the US administration very soon recognized that stability of the region requires GCC coherence, cooperation and unity and tried to exercise some pressure on the blockading countries to end the dispute with little success so far.[42] The United States tried to show its displeasure with the prolonging of the conflict by indefinitely postponing the scheduled US-GCC Summit and scaling back on some of its joint military exercises.[43]

There seems to have been a realization in the Trump administration that any US policy against Iran requires the buy-in of its local Arab allies with the GCC being at the forefront of any such strategy. Any effort to move forward on the idea of an Arab NATO requires Trump to help America's partners in the Gulf to overcome the self-inflicted divide. The GCC+2 meeting in New York was a means of GCC states to express their support for US leadership on jointly tackling regional security threats without having to make any binding commitments. Yet, it was not until the fallout of the Khashoggi affair in October 2018 that Washington had the means to exercise pressure particular on Saudi Arabia and its Crown Prince MbS to make concessions in the Gulf Divide. With mounting evidence that the US-based, Saudi journalist Jamal Khashoggi was killed in a premediated operation plausibly

[41] AP. (2018). US Pushes Forward With Plans for Anti-Iran Arab Alliance. *The New York Times*, 28 September 2018.

[42] Harb, I.K. (2018). Trump, a Mediator in the GCC Crisis? *AlAraby*, 13 March 2018.

[43] De Petris, D. (2017). America's Role in the Qatar Crisis. *The Huffington Post*, 28 July 2018.

authorized by MbS himself, the Crown Prince had no choice but to demonstrate that he was eager to make progress in resolving the blockade of Qatar.[44]

Conclusion

The GCC was set up as a tool for regional integration among the Arab Gulf States thirty-seven years ago in reaction to the multitude of security threats following the Iranian Revolution and the start of the Iran-Iraq War. Despite some measurable achievements in economic, social as well as security cooperation, the GCC remains more of a shallow intergovernmental body that never achieved deep integration in key policy domains. Little progress has been made in terms of its structure, its institutional design and decision-making mechanisms. The current crisis dividing the Gulf is now clearly revealing its vulnerability and testing its durability and its resilience. The utility of the rule-based regional organization is questioned by its inability to resolve a crisis that challenges its core values, objectives and agreements. Qatar's growing frustration with the organization is shared by the other two small states, Kuwait and Oman, who are facing looming leadership successions, which might leave them exposed to the same hawkish policies of their bigger Gulf brothers.[45]

The GCC, despite its many achievements, has failed so far in resolving the crisis mainly due to its weak intergovernmental institutional setup. The lack of any supranational decision-making authority or dispute resolution mechanism leaves the future of the organization largely determined by the whims of some of its more powerful leaders.[46]

This raises many questions about the future of GCC amid an ongoing Gulf Divide. The GCC has prevailed as an institution through a variety of regional crises and conflicts, including the Iraqi invasion of Kuwait in 1990, and the diplomatic dispute between Qatar and its neighbours in 2014.[47] Although no member state has so far expressed its wish to

[44] https://www.aljazeera.com/news/2018/10/pushing-saudi-arabia-gcc-crisis-yemen-war-bloomberg-181030052111400.html.

[45] Ulrichsen, K.C. (2017). Is the GCC Worth Belonging To? *Chatham House Expert Opinion*, 20 June 2017. https://www.chathamhouse.org/expert/comment/gcc-worth-belonging.

[46] Ibid.

[47] Ibid.

leave the organization, the persistence and the endurance of the crisis will lead Qatar and to a certain extent Kuwait and Oman, to begin to question the benefit of belonging to a dormant organization incapable of overcoming an unprecedented divide. The current status may over time become the norm given the declaration of Adel Al Jubeir, Saudi Arabia's Foreign Minister, that:

> "Relations will be frozen until they (the Qataris) change and I hope they will change, and if they don't change we're a patient people. We'll wait for 10-15, 20, 50 years. How long did it take you [the US] with Castro and Cuba? We can do the same with Qatar!"[48]

This led Qatar's Foreign Minister Sheikh Mohammed bin Abdulrahman Al Thani to respond saying that *"A year from now, no one will know what the future of the countries will be... Qatar can also wait forever"*.[49]

Alternatives to the GCC like the idea of bilateral cooperation agreements or even that of an Arab NATO will undermine attempts to resolve the current crisis as it will distract from the actual underlying differences and grievances. Qatar's Foreign Minister declared that unless the issue of the blockade is addressed first, the envisioned regional alliance will not be effective. Referring to the Arab NATO meeting in New York he said that *"This gathering is important. But we need to address the challenges among these countries"*, to prove the *"credibility"* of the alliance.[50]

The persistence of the crisis has not only managed to harm GCC regional integration efforts, limited as they may be, but will also offer ample opportunities for opponents such as Iran to benefit from the disintegration of the organization.[51] The short-sightedness of the blockading countries in managing this current crisis has in fact resulted in undermining one of the most promising regional integration efforts in the Arab region.

In sum, the region is better with the GCC than without it and it is likely to survive and endure this crisis rather than be formally terminated

---

[48] Toumi, H. (2018). Quartet to Wait 50 Years for Qatar 'Right Move'. *Gulf News*, 22 September 2018.

[49] Al Jazeera. (2018). Qatar's Top Diplomat Says Gulf Crisis at a 'Stalemate'. *Al Jazeera*, 28 September 2018.

[50] Ibid.

[51] Ulrichsen, 'Is the GCC Worth Belonging To?'

or dissolved. However, experience elsewhere in the Arab World suggests that it may simply become ever more marginal or irrelevant to the point where it effectively disappears from the policy-making landscape altogether. The region after this crisis will never be the same and the GCC project will have to evolve in a meaningful manner to be relevant to its member states, the public and the international community at large.[52]

---

[52] Stratfor. (2017). The Gulf Cooperation Council Will Never Be the Same. *Stratfor*, 6 December 2017. https://worldview.stratfor.com/article/gulf-cooperation-council-will-never-be-same.

CHAPTER 11

The Libyan Revolution Undone—The Conversation Will Not Be Televised

Anas El Gomati

INTRODUCTION

It is tempting to see the progression from peace to conflict as linear with a simple beginning, middle and end. This is often not the case, the beginning and the end of a conflict is a matter of perspective, one that is often fiercely contested. The 2017 Gulf Crisis is the result of a fiercely contested set of underlying dynamics, with little consensus regarding what Qatar had done to trigger the crisis, and importantly which day, year or decade the crisis begins?

For some, as Cafiero suggests in this book, it was the Trump administrations alleged 'green light' to UAE crown prince Mohamed Bin Zayed days before the QNA hack that triggered the crisis. For others, a Qatari ransom fee paid in Iraq, in the months preceding the crisis that offered impetus to the UAE to act, as Boussois highlights in his chapter. The arrival of the Bin Khalifa clan into power in 1995, without expressed

A. E. Gomati (✉)
Sadeq Institute, Tripoli, Libya
e-mail: anas.elgomati@sadeqinstitute.org

© The Author(s) 2019
A. Krieg (ed.), *Divided Gulf*, Contemporary Gulf Studies,
https://doi.org/10.1007/978-981-13-6314-6_11

Saudi permission decades earlier has also been sounded out as the underlying trigger for the crisis.[1]

Closer scrutiny of the UAE led coalition's set of 13 demands and allegations labelling Qatar a terrorist sponsoring State offers insight into the life span and age of the crisis. A surface analysis of the demands, notably to shut down the Al Jazeera Network and to sever ties with groups ranging from the Muslim Brotherhood to states like Iran, led observers to remark they had seen this before.

At first sight the blockade and crisis of 2017 was not the beginning, but the middle of an earlier crisis that began three years earlier. In 2014, Riyadh, Abu Dhabi and Manama sparked a diplomatic crisis in the Gulf, recalling their ambassadors, and then issuing similar demands to shut down Al Jazeera and sever ties with the Muslim Brotherhood and Hamas.

These explanations however only serve as a timeline of disputes and a history of their escalation, but not the reasons that underline the demands being made by the UAE-led quartet, which led to the crisis. They do not offer an understanding of why the UAE and Saudi Arabia view Al Jazeera and the Muslim Brotherhood as such a threat, and how a news channel or a political movement could create such anger, that the quartet was willing to go as far as taking military action against Qatar only days into the crisis according to senior US officials.[2]

To understand these demands, is to understand the reasons behind the crisis. As such, for outside observers it is the recent history and political events of 2011 in North Africa that offer a clearer picture of the reasons underlying the crisis. The political upheavals and uprisings in North Africa—beginning with the Jasmine revolution in Tunisia—and the interaction between Gulf states in this geographically distant theatre, demonstrate how and why the Gulf divide came about. It is in northern Africa at the beginning of the Arab Spring that the UAE and Saudi Arabia for the first time reveal their fear of Al Jazeera and the Muslim Brotherhood.

As such to understand the Gulf crisis and its beginnings, we must understand the story of a fruit and vegetable vendor in the North African town of Sidi Bouzid in 2010. Moreover, it is how this story was told

---

[1] Ramesh, R. (2017). The Long-Running Family Rivalries Behind the Qatar Crisis. *The Guardian*, 21 July 2017.

[2] Emmons, A. (2018). Saudi Arabia Planned to Invade Qatar Last Summer. *The Intercept*, 1 August 2018. https://theintercept.com/2018/08/01/rex-tillerson-qatar-saudi-uae/.

to the world that reveals the seeds of political discomfort and difference that transitioned to political crisis and near direct military conflict in the Gulf.

From Riot to Revolution

Far from the local aristocracy of Carthage, and the coastal European resorts of Tunis, in the heart of Tunisia's deep southern Kasserine pass, lays the town of Sidi Bouzid. Whilst northern Tunisia, has traditionally been home to a host of colonial rulers and foreign aristocracy who ruled the country from the north, gasping in awe of its stunning cliffs and views of the Mediterranean coastline, Tunisia's forgotten south has for centuries been a breeding ground for political neglect, marginalized by foreign rulers and local elites alike. This was all to change, in the winter of 2010, when Mohamed Bouazizi, a jobless Tunisian university graduate, turned street vendor, changed the history of Sidi Bouzid and the Arab world forever.

On 17 December 2010 Bouazizi, with around 200 US dollars' worth of fruits and vegetables, bought on credit the night before, arrived to downtown Sidi Bouzid to begin work at 10 a.m. Harassed by a police officer to a pay a bribe to operate without a licence, which he refused, Bouazizi had his scales and produce seized by the police, and when he protested, he was allegedly assaulted. Bouazizi frustrated and helpless sought justice attempting to lodge a complaint at the governor's office. When the authorities refused to meet him, Bouazizi, frustrated and humiliated, covered himself in gasoline and self-immolated in front of the governor's office in the crowded streets of Sidi Bouzid.[3] Within days, Bouazizi's story sparked national anti-government protests and clashes that led Tunisia into crisis and former President Ben Ali to flee to Saudi Arabia within weeks of the protests.

In the first days of the protests, the story was covered by international media as popular riots,[4] with the French foreign minister Michele Alliot Marie even offering to send French *'savoir faire'* in the form

---

[3] Fisher, M. (2011). In Tunisia, Act of One Fruit Vendor Sparks Wave of Revolution Through Arab World. *The Washington Post*, 26 March 2011.

[4] Saleh, H. (2010). High Unemployment Sparks Tunisian Riot. *Financial Times*, 21 December 2010.

of the Gendarmerie to the Tunisian autocrat to crush the revolt and restore calm.[5]

It wasn't until the Qatari-based pan-Arab news channel Al Jazeera began to cover the events a different story began to emerge, told from the perspective of its citizens. The story of a man humiliated by a regime burning hopelessly in the streets of Sidi Bouzid[6]; the story of young dissidents refusing to return home[7]; and finally a new set of questions, about whether this was the story of Tunisia, or of much of the Arab World?[8] Viewers across the Arab world tuned into Al Jazeera to hear debates that had never been televised, and questions never publicly asked. If Tunisians could have a revolution, could Egyptians[9] or Libyans for that matter? What Al Jazeera's coverage did was thrusting both a popular sense of urgency and instilling a need to act to end autocratic rule in the Arab world.

Qatar's Al Jazeera was not just covering the revolutions of the Arab World, it was covering the revolution through the stories of its citizens and became a platform for revolutionary discourse to take place, in ways that had never been imagined before.

The new language used to describe the politics of the Arab world captivated viewers and was revolutionary in itself. These weren't new ideas, but the conversations around social justice, accountability and political pluralism had challenged the myth of authoritarian stability. More important however, was that Arab viewers were inspired by these conversations to act and follow the Tunisian model. Tunisian revolutionaries were offering inspiration to Egyptians, and likewise to Libyans, as the conversations spread like wildfire. It was Al Jazeera's positive and emotional coverage of these revolutionary youth and their ideas, as well as

[5]Willsher, K. (2011). French Minister Defends Offer of Security Forces to Tunisia. *The Guardian*, 18 January 2011.

[6]Ryan, Y. (2011). The Tragic Life of a Street Vendor. *Al Jazeera*, 20 January 2011. https://www.aljazeera.com/indepth/features/2011/01/201111684242518839.html.

[7]Ryan, Y. (2011). How Tunisia's Revolution Began. *Al Jazeera*, 26 January 2011. https://www.aljazeera.com/indepth/features/2011/01/2011126121815985483.html.

[8]Andoni, L. (2010). The Rebirth of Arab Activism. *Al Jazeera*, 31 December 2010. https://www.aljazeera.com/indepth/opinion/2010/12/20101231161958792947.html.

[9]Bayoomi, Al. (2011). Can Egyptians Revolt? *Al Jazeera*, 26 January 2011. https://www.aljazeera.com/indepth/2011/01/2011126105953366758.html.

the interactive nature of its platform, that was both unique to the Arab world and captivated viewers across the world.

The thought of a new pluralistic and democratizing phenomenon spreading across the Arab world, featuring heroic civilians bravely tearing down autocratic foes was barely imaginable before the story of Mohamed Bouazizi. Whilst Al Jazeera's viewers and many citizens across the Arab were inspired by these conversations, it sparked fear for others in the region as Krieg, Ulrichsen and Davidson highlight earlier in this book.

For Qatar's neighbours in the UAE and Saudi Arabia in particular, these conversations could inspire their citizens to act in kind, if they believed it could work. It would only take a single individual to take inspiration, to protest and start the conversation to spark crisis for the regimes in Riyadh and Abu Dhabi. If these revolutionary Saudi or Emirati conversations were televised, around the world, the Saudi and Emirati regimes could only be cast as the villains to a global audience cheering on the revolutions and the conversation.

It is here that the Gulf crisis begins. In fear of a debate that had never been televised, and that once started, could not be stopped. Al Jazeera's platform had become as revolutionary as the revolutions it was covering, and its power to inspire people and create change was feared by those resisting the Arab Spring and its consequences.[10] The seeds of the Gulf divide were sewn by the revolutionary coverage of the Arab revolutions by Qatar and the way the narratives of revolutionaries were broadcast to form a revolutionary Arab public sphere.[11]

Libya, the first armed conflict in the Arab Spring, is where this chapter argues the crisis between Qatar and the UAE transitioned from difference and discomfort to a military confrontation. Libya offers a perfect case study to see the full potential of Qatar's foreign policy reach and the soft power of Al Jazeera in particular. The chapter argues that it was Qatar's ability to leverage strategic relationships with opposition groups, many of which Islamists, and rebrand them for elections using Al Jazeera's extensive reach, that seemingly offered Doha a competitive advantage in the race for political control in post-revolutionary Libya.

[10] See Cherribi, S. (2017). *Fridays of Rage: Al Jazeera, the Arab Spring, and Political Islam*. Oxford: Oxford University Press (Chapter II).

[11] See Krieg, A. (2017). *Socio-political Order and Security in the Arab World*. London: Palgrave (Chapters IV and V).

The chapter will contrast Qatar's soft and later hard power engagement in Libya with the Emirati response to the fall of the Gadhafi regime. The aggressive Emirati political engagement and ambitious military strategy in Libya surpassed the expected survival instinct triggered by the Arab Spring. Abu Dhabi's contrasting geopolitical and foreign policy ambitions eventually led to a military confrontation by proxy between the two countries in Libya and provided much of the fuel behind the Gulf divide—all that after both Qatar and the UAE had participated in the same NATO-led operation against the Libyan dictator.

From Coalition to Competition

The Libyan revolution that began with protests in Eastern Libya in February 2011, and rapidly descended into a military campaign that pitted local Libyan revolutionary groups supported by a broad NATO-led coalition against the Libyan regime, looked like a unique moment that brought the Arab and Western world together. After the US-led invasion of Iraq in 2003, without the authority of the UN Security council, Libya seemed to open a new chapter of multilateralism in 2011. The UN Security Council led with resolution 1973 in March 2011, and NATO and Arab nations including Qatar and the UAE began to ready themselves to engage militarily in Libya.[12] The intervention in Libya was an opportunity to protect a peaceful popular movement calling for social justice and socio-political change, after Gadhafi sent troops to the gates of Benghazi, the birthplace of the revolution, calling for the city to be cleansed of 'rats and cockroaches'.[13]

The UN under the banner of the 'responsibility to protect' (R2P) doctrine offered a compelling set of conditions under which minimal use force could be used with broad international legitimacy and a clear UN mandate. The Obama administration, already bogged down in Iraq and facing chaos in Afghanistan, were neither elected for nor confident to lead a third war in the Muslim world in less than a decade. Obama, in relinquishing the lead political and military role, created a leadership vacuum for the Libyan military operation. Whilst NATO fulfilled much

---

[12]BBC. (2011). Libya: UN Backs Action Against Colonel Gaddafi. *BBC*, 18 March 2011.

[13]Kirkpatrick, D. and Fahim, K. (2011). Qaddafi's Grip on the Capital Tightens as Revolt Grows. *The New York Times*, 22 February 2011.

of the military planning and execution, the UK, France, Qatar and the UAE played a crucial role within the military leadership and coalition. Qatar and the UAE organized shipments of weapons and led training and equipping missions into Libya in support of the most powerful armed groups in the country.[14] The most important of these groups were trained in Libya's Western Nafusa mountain region. As NATO provided air support against Gadhafi's nearby troops, the Emirati and Qatari Special Forces used the air cover to launch a joint military assault and capture the capital from the Gadhafi regime. Initially the surrogate operation looked promising, as Libyan rebel groups began to descend from the mountains towards Tripoli in August 2011. What emerged was a race between UAE and Qatar-backed rebel groups to reach the capital. The idea was that whoever arrived in Tripoli first would eventually control the country and the effort to dictate the outcome of the revolution.

The Race to Tripoli

The first signs of conflict between Qatar and the UAE in Libya began on 19 August, the 20th day of Ramadan. The date holds much significance in Islamic history. It is also known as '*Fatah Mecca*'—the day that the holy city of Mecca, was liberated by the prophet Mohamed in 630AD, and the day chosen by Libyan revolutionaries and NATO to launch an assault to liberate Tripoli.[15] In the sweltering heat of the summer, revolutionary armed groups trained by the Qatari and Emirati Special Forces advanced on the city in search of Colonel Gadhafi. The armed groups, with aerial support from NATO began to coalesce around the infamous *Bab Al Azizia* compound, home to Gadhafi, where he had controlled the country for over 42 years.

As the walls of the compound began to fall, and rebels entered, one news channel arrived to document the historic moment differently to any other: Al Jazeera. Whilst other news channels and journalists began to enter, chaotically shooting footage of the conflict that ensued, Al Jazeera's team were preparing to document a moment of immense political significance—the moment Gadhafi lost control of his military

---

[14]Nakhoul, S. (2011). Special Report: The Secret Plan to Take Tripoli. *Reuters*, 6 September 2011.

[15]Denyer, S. (2011). Tripoli's Sudden Fall Revealed Rotten Heart of Gaddafi's Regime. *The Washington Post*, 31 August 2011.

compound, and the country. The cameras were pointed at the armoured vehicle of Abdel Hakim Belhaj, a revolutionary military leader, and head of a powerful Tripoli brigade. As Belhaj made his triumphant entrance in front of the camera into Gadhafi's compound, he introduced himself to Libyan viewers and the world as one of the most powerful men in Libya.[16] Al Jazeera had offered a platform to Belhaj at a historic moment in the country, positioning him as one of the main leaders of today, and perhaps the future. For Belhaj this marked a pivotal moment in his political journey. Later that week he was elected as the head of the Tripoli Military Council[17]; the de facto military authority in charge of all rebel groups in Libya's capital. The reach and scope of Qatar's foreign policy was spectacularly demonstrated. Not only were Qatar's military allies in Tripoli first, and now militarily in control of the capital, but they were being prepared for a crucial transformation, with the help of Al Jazeera. Qatar were strategically positioning Belhaj into more than just a fighter, or a hero of the Libyan revolution, but as a potential future leader of the country.

For the UAE, Belhaj's entrance to Bab Al Azizia and subsequent perceived military control of Tripoli was taken as not only a crucial loss in the race for military control and political influence in Libya but represented a much deeper fear. For the Emiratis, it wasn't just that they were losing in Libya, it was the question of whom they were losing to that had sparked so much fear. For the Emiratis, Belhaj was no ordinary revolutionary; and in many ways personified Emirati paranoia.

A COMPETITIVE TRANSFORMATION

The transformation of Belhaj into a potential leader of post-Gadhafi Libya seems almost impossible to imagine before the Arab Spring. Belhaj was formerly the leader of the Libyan Islamic Fighting Group, a paramilitary group that according to the US government had links to Al Qaeda. Belhaj, had spent years being tortured in Gadhafi's prison, after being illegally extradited oversees by the British and American intelligence

---

[16]Youtube. (2011). Belhaj Entering Bab Al Aziziya Compound. Posted by NWKuwait, 25 August 2011. https://www.youtube.com/watch?v=a8aWOD37I94.

[17]Nordland, R. (2011). In Libya, Former Enemy Is Recast in Role of Ally. *The New York Times*, 2 September 2011.

services to the Gadhafi regime in 2004.[18] The regime had led a de-radicalization and dialogue programme with Belhaj, members of the LIFG, and the Muslim Brotherhood whilst they were in prison in 2007.

In 2010, the regime freed Belhaj and others, promoting their release as the abandonment of their religious ideology and violence. In reality, the regime demanded that the LIFG, Belhaj and anyone seeking release from prison, renounce and abandon any and all forms of violent and non-violent political opposition, activism or dissidence. Whether they held used religious or secular narratives to do so, was beside the point. Yet, in little over than eighteen months from Belhaj's release from prison, the unthinkable had happened. Belhaj was standing triumphantly, Kalashnikov in hand, in Gadhafi's compound, whilst the former leader was on the run. Moreover, he was rebranding himself in front of a global audience from a former 'terrorist' to a potential leader of a democratic Libya as he prepared to contest elections less than a year later.[19]

For the Emiratis, this transformation showed not only what Al Jazeera was capable of, but how deeply diverse the range of political challengers could be in the Arab World. Everyone was committed to elections, including alleged former Salafi-Jihadists, and were speaking the language of democracy. Moreover, they believed they stood a chance at winning elections. For the Emirates, this marked a turning point, and they would invest heavily to win the next battle for control of Libya.

Power in Libya—Between Influence and Control

The race for political control of Libya took shape in 2012, after the first elections in Libya's modern history had taken place in July 2012. Libyans were optimistic and enthusiastic with around 80% turning out for the elections. For Libyan politicians, and their international backers, the formal race to succeed Gadhafi had begun.

The UAE prepared well for the race for power, after their initial loss to Qatar during the race to control to Tripoli. The UAE, like others, had cultivated links to various politicians and armed groups during the

---

[18] Human Rights Watch. (2011). US/UK: Documents Reveal Libya Rendition Details. *Human Rights Watch*, 8 September 2011. https://www.hrw.org/news/2011/09/08/us/uk-documents-reveal-libya-rendition-details.

[19] Labib, N. (2011). Libyan Islamist Commander Swaps Combat Rig for Suit. *Reuters*, 11 November 2011.

revolution but had strengthened these ties in the run-up to the elections for the General National Congress (GNC).

Whilst in neighbouring Egypt and Tunisia, Islamist parties emerged as the most powerful forces in the political process, the election results were entirely different in Libya. The elections in Libya, were not designed for control, but for inclusivity and consensus. The GNC offered 200 parliamentary seats, 120 of them for independent candidates, and only 80 available for political parties. The parliament was designed to be an inclusive political landing ground for all of Libya's political trends and interests to be represented instead of a place for one or two parties to dominate and exclude others. However, the resulting political pluralism, compromise and consensus required for legislating and decision-making frustrated politicians and their international backers alike.[20]

For the UAE, who had hoped to buck the trend of Islamist parties coming to power in the post-revolution elections, the initial results in Libya seemed to be in their favour. The Muslim Brotherhood's Justice and Construction Party (J&C) lost the political party votes, only winning 15% of their allocated 80 party seats. The UAE backed secular party—the National Forces Alliance (NFA) led by Mahmoud Jibril—won around 40% of the political party votes. However, the 120 independent seats, of which 25 had affiliation to the NFA was not enough for the NFA and Jibril to control the parliament. Indeed, Jibril later lost in a parliamentary vote to become prime minister, demonstrating how difficult it was to translate popularity and electoral victories into political power.[21]

The Emiratis had invested a significant amount of their hopes around the NFA. They built a close political relationship with Jibril, and another NFA official—Abdul Majid Mlegta. Mlegta, a senior figure in the party, brother of Othman Mlegta, the leader of a powerful Tripoli-based brigade—the *Qa'qaa* brigade–that the UAE funded.[22]

Despite their best efforts, the political and military situation only offered the Emiratis partial influence in the parliament with the NFA, and partial control of Tripoli with the *Qa'qaa* brigade. Like the parliament, the capital was dominated by armed groups, many of whom had

---

[20] Interview, former member of the GNC, Istanbul, September 2018.

[21] Author's Interview with Mahmoud Jibril, Rome, December 2017.

[22] See Ulrichsen, K.C. (2016). *The United Arab Emirates: Power, Politics and Policy-Making*. London: Taylor & Francis (p. 198).

received weapons from Qatar during and after the revolution. Between 2012 and 2014, at the end of the mandate of the GNC, the status quo showed no signs of change, and the race for political power and military control of Tripoli and Libya, remained contested. This was to change in the months following the military coup in Egypt in June 2013 replacing the elected Muslim Brotherhood-led government with a secular military President. A failed attempt at a coup, opened opportunities for the UAE in Libya, as a love story began between the UAE, and a retired Libyan general.

The Love Story Behind Libya's Civil War

General Khalifa Hafter, a former Libyan army general, who had defected from the Gadhafi regime in the late 1980s, to return to join the Libyan revolution in 2011 only to find himself marginalized by 2012, first attempted to change Libyan history on St. Valentine's Day 2014. On 14 February 2014—Hafter, announced he would be ousting the elected parliament and government on behalf of the Libyan people, and that a 'Libyan National Army' under his command would take control of the country.

Hafter's first attempt at a military coup was an utter failure. He tried to stage a popular military coup following the example set by the Egyptian military some months earlier. But he did so without any popular support or prominence amongst the revolutionaries—most importantly, he lacked the coercive military power that Sisi was able to rely on in Egypt. Hafter held a coup, but no one turned up, and he literally disappeared, as the Libyan government issued an arrest warrant.[23] Hafter's first attempt was so badly organized, that he was forced to become the first person in history to announce a military coup via YouTube.[24] However, he had set in motion a love story on Valentine's Day with the Emirati leadership, who saw in Hafter the potential political and military partner they had been waiting for. With Hafter they found a man who ideologically catered to the UAE's anti-Islamist narrative, and with the

[23]Abdallah, K. (2014). The Coup That Never Was. *Al Ahram*, 20 February 2014. http://weekly.ahram.org.eg/News/5470.aspx.

[24]YouTube. (2014). .حفتر خليفة ف براير 14 يوم ال ليبي ال جيش تحرك. Posted by Libya Hura, 14 February 2014. http://www.youtube.com/watch?v=R5uXd3oGDTw.

political and military ambitions to restore an order that would put the revolutionary genie back into its bottle.

Hafter re-emerged 91 days later, on 15 May 2014, with Emirati and Egyptian military and political support and direction. He launched a new political and military campaign, under the banner of an alleged 'Counterterrorism Operation'—dubbed *Operation Dignity*.[25] On Hafter's second attempt, he triggered a civil war that engulfed the country, and almost changed the country within 5 days.

On day one Hafter announced his coup live on television and invited Libyans to join Operation Dignity alongside a self-styled Libyan National Army. A day after, he took action, he launched airstrikes with Emirati and Egyptian support in Benghazi, against both tribal and revolutionary armed groups and a single Salafi-Jihadist group, Ansar Al Sharia. On the third day, groups from Zintan, supported by the UAE, attacked the elected, and now electorally expired, parliament's headquarters, in an attempt to oust it from power.[26] Two days later, on day five, Hafter had cultivated together with his Emirati and Egyptian sponsors, what he had previously given little thought to when he first uploaded his coup to YouTube on Valentine's Day: a powerful new narrative. In an interview offered to Saudi-owned Al Sharq Al Awsat newspaper on 20 May, Hafter declared 'There is only one enemy, and that is the Muslim Brotherhood, the malignant disease which is seeking to spread throughout the bones of the Arab world', a disease he intended to purge from Libya.[27] Hafter had declared war on tribal militias, an entire elected parliament with over 120 independent candidates, a self-declared Salafi-Jihadist group, revolutionary militias who had fought against Al Qaeda affiliates, and a political party. All were labelled as being part of one enemy which he would 'purge' from Libya—the Muslim Brotherhood. The entire operation, and all of the targets were legitimized by a narrative of 'countering terrorism'.

Whilst, Hafter did not take the country on the 5th day, he did spark a civil war between disparate numbers of groups that still rages five years

---

[25] Kabbous, S. (2014). A Q&A with Khalifa Hifter, the Mastermind Behind Libya's New Revolt. *The Washington Post*, 20 May 2014.

[26] Laessing, U. (2014). Gunmen Loyal to Ex-general Storm Libyan Parliament, Demand Suspension. *Reuters*, 18 May 2014.

[27] Mahmoud, K. (2014). Khalifa Haftar Pledges to "Purge" Libya of Muslim Brotherhood. *Al Sharq Al Awsat*, 20 May 2014.

later. Libya's sovereign institutions are split. For a time, there were two parliaments, and three governments. Despite significant efforts by the United Nations to negotiate an end to the conflict since 2014 in Morocco and Algeria, and the announcement of a peace accord and unity government in 2016, Hafter has refused to enter political dialogue or enter a ceasefire. He has been able to do so through a combination of significant Emirati and Egyptian military backing and political support. However, the key to his success lays in the creation of a powerful narrative, which would help him justify his actions and would be re-employed by the UAE and Saudi Arabia amid the Gulf Crisis of 2017, as Krieg illustrates.

OPERATION DIGNITY: REHEARSING THE GULF CRISIS

Central to Operation Dignity's military campaign has been a strategic narrative promoted by the Emiratis and Egyptians and echoed in Libya by their partner Khalifa Hafter. Behind these statements lays a political strategy to label all domestic opponents to Hater and his patrons in Cairo and Abu Dhabi as extremists and terrorists. And by extension Qatar as the main promotor of the revolutionary dynamic in 2011, was labelled a terrorism sponsor.[28]

In support of the UAE, Hafter has built a narrative that it was Qatar, and to a lesser extent Turkey, that were behind the rise and support of terrorist groups in Libya. Indeed, in the early days of Operation Dignity, Hafter even issued a demand that Qatari citizens had 48 hours to leave the country, for supporting terrorism in Libya.[29]

The efficacy of the narrative is in the perceived legitimacy given to the UAE, Egypt and Hafter for 'fighting terrorism' regardless of the political nature, institutional characteristics or behaviour of the target labelled as terrorist. Once a group or individual is labelled a terrorist, the use of military force by Hafter and his patrons are given justification and seen to be legitimate without any real scrutiny or accountability.

---

[28] Al Arabiya. (2017). Haftar Accuses Qatar of Supporting Terrorism in Libya. *Al Arabiya*, 29 May 2017. http://english.alarabiya.net/en/News/north-africa/2017/05/29/Haftar-accuses-Qatar-of-supporting-terrorism-in-Libya.html.

[29] Reuters. (2014). Renegade General Urges Turks, Qataris to Leave East Libya. *Reuters*, 22 June 2014.

The lethality of the narrative, is in its ability to block any attempt, by an external actor to engage any actor labelled a terrorist. Any attempt to reframe the narrative, and label it a 'conflict between two sides' or 'civil war' as opposed to a war on terror is criticized as 'terrorist sympathizing'. Any attempts to mediate, negotiate, or halt violence in favour of a peaceful settlement is rebuked by the UAE, Egypt and Hafter using the popular maxim that *'we don't negotiate with terrorists'*.

The almost global consensus in classifying self-identifying Salafi-Jihadists such as ISIS and Al Qaeda as a terrorist group, and refusing to mediate with such groups, is not necessarily controversial, in view of the limited policy options available for engagement. The fact that Salafi-Jihadists tend to refuse engagement and dialogue, in favour of promoting violence, often necessitates states to prioritize means of violence to confront them in an act of last resort.

However, the UAE, Egypt and Hafter employ the terrorist label to stigmatize and delegitimize groups in Libya who did not only oppose Salafi-Jihadism but actively sought dialogue and engaged in competitive political discourse. Nonetheless, these groups, in particular the Muslim Brotherhood and affiliates, members of the GNC, and armed groups that participated in anti-ISIS operations, were described as terrorists, and subsequently became military targets in the Operation Dignity during the civil war.[30]

In an attempt to resolve the military stand-off in the civil war, the UN invited representatives from all of the major political actors and armed groups to participate in peace negotiations, shortly after the conflict began. Whilst all groups accepted the invitation and participated in the UN-sponsored dialogue in Morocco and Algeria between 2014 and 2016, Hafter refused to participate, labelling the UN effort a *'dialogue with extremists'*.[31] In fact, Hafter went as far as bombing Tripoli's last functioning civilian airport on 24 November 2014,[32] as his rival political

---

[30]Author's Interview with Libyan member of UN led dialogue in Algeria, April 2014.

[31]France24. (2017). Exclusive: Only Military Solutions Will Be Used Against Terrorists, Says Libya's Haftar. *France24*, 17 July 2017.

[32]NBC News. (2014). Airstrike Hits Last Functioning Airport in Tripoli, Libya. *NBC News*, 25 November 2014. https://www.nbcnews.com/news/world/airstrike-hits-last-functioning-airport-tripoli-libya-n255631.

participants were boarding their flights to attend the UN dialogue, delaying the talks by two days.[33]

For the two years of attempted peace talks, Hafter justified obstructing the political dialogue and refusing attempts at ceasefires in favour of pursuing the conflict by constantly declaring he would 'never negotiate with terrorists'.[34] Hafter was threatened with sanctions by the European Union in 2015 if he did not allow the UN dialogue to resume. Hafter's spokesman replied the sanctions were '*meaningless...if the West calls us criminals, it makes no difference, because we are fighting terrorism*'.[35]

Since, Hafter has been able to successfully hijack the UN political process alongside Emirati support. The UN eventually decided to announce a unity government before the Libyan parliament approved it. The head of the Libyan parliament Agila Saleh and a bloc loyal to Hafter in parliament refused to vote or accept the Libyan Political Agreement over an article that would remove Hafter from his position.[36] This agreement that took almost two years to draft had already lost significant legitimacy when it was revealed through email leaks that the UAE had been meddling in the peace process. Email leaks made to the Guardian newspaper indicated the UN's chief negotiator Bernadino Leon had been secretly taking instruction from MbZ whilst negotiating a lucrative contract for his next job for the UAE government throughout the dialogue process.[37]

Libya today remains politically divided amid a state of civil war that looks like it will continue for years to come. Whilst Hafter and his sponsors in the UAE and Egypt have invested heavily in building their narrative as 'counter terrorists', meddling in the political process, little attention was directed by Hafter's coalition towards the real Salafi-Jihadist threat of IS in the country that many of his opponents fought

---

[33] Author's Interview with Suliman Faqih, head of Misratan delegation leaving Tripoli in November 2014, in Misrata 2015.

[34] Mohamed Al Hejazi, LNA Spokesman on Libya's Al Ahrar Television, November 2014.

[35] Paton, C. (2015). Libya: Armed Forces Brush Off Threat of EU Sanctions Against General Khalifa Haftar. *International Business Times*, 22 July 2015.

[36] Author's Interview with House of Representatives member who led boycott of the UN Libyan Political Agreement, March 2016.

[37] Ramesh, R. (2015). UN Libya Envoy Accepts £1,000-a-Day Job from Backer of One Side in Civil War. *The Guardian*, 4 November 2015.

in Sirte and Derna. This begs the question of what constitutes the real threat to the UAE, Egypt and Hafter in Libya?

WHAT TERRIFIES THE UAE IN LIBYA?

As Krieg argues earlier in this book, from the Emirati point of view, pluralist institutions, political parties and dissidents who oppose, fund or challenge authoritarian rule broadly fall into the category of 'terrorism'. Institutions that enshrine civilian authority, political parties that act as shadow governments outside of power are at the core of what the UAE and Egypt determine to be terrorism in Libya. These institutions, bodies and groups are the products of free speech, and act as a check on power against the kind of authoritarianism that the UAE seeks to promote.[38]

When Hafter's forces launched an attack against the Libyan parliament headquarters in 2014, and almost burnt it the ground, his spokesman described the parliament as *'supporting extremist Islamist entities... under the cloak of politics'*.[39] The UAE and Hafter went that far as to designate democracy as both a process and pluralist institution as terrorism. For two years, the UAE had tried in vain to conquer Libya's pluralist 200-seat parliament and source of political power in the country. When the UAE had failed, they decided to destroy the parliament and sent in the UAE-funded Zintan brigades, now loyal to Hafter to oust them from power.[40]

Political parties, NGOs and elected municipal councils have also been framed as terrorists. Hafter's forces have since 2016 began removing local elected mayors in Libya, and replacing them with military councils, loyal to him.[41] Civil society organizations and journalists across Libya, particularly in Benghazi, now under the control of Hafter's forces, have been labelled as 'secret members of the brotherhood', and terrorist sympathizers, particularly those working on human rights, elections or human rights.[42]

---

[38] Krieg, A. (2017). The Saudi-Emirati Axis: United Against Gulf Unity. *Middle East Eye*, 7 December 2017.

[39] Mohamed Al Hejazi to Libya Al Ahrar Television, 17 May 2014.

[40] Mohamed, E. (2014). Rogue Libyan General Launches Anti-Islamist Raid on Parliament. *The National*, 18 May 2014.

[41] Author's Interview with former head of municipal elections in Libya, July 2018.

[42] Author's Interview with exiled human rights activist in Istanbul, September 2018.

What the UAE and its partners find terrifying in post Arab Spring Libya, is the presence of institutions, groups and individuals that threaten the authoritarian model and monopoly of power. Political parties, parliaments, civil society by their very nature force societies to engage in a conversation about power between the Governor and the Governed, which the UAE in particular find terrifying as it opens the door to political debate over the very legitimacy of the political status quo. Particularly in response to socio-economic and political grievances, this type of civil society activism could become a source of legitimacy for an alternative power undermining the existing political status quo in a country—something that Abu Dhabi fears might one day bring regime change to the Gulf.

CONCLUSION

The clash over narratives between Doha and Abu Dhabi that Krieg highlights in his chapter could first be observed in northern Africa amid the immediate post-revolutionary years of the Arab Spring. Whilst Qatar used its soft, and in the case of Libya, its hard power to promote socio-political pluralism and open dialogue undermining the political status quo of decades of secular authoritarianism, the UAE emerged as a status quo power, vigorously trying to push back the tide of revolutionary upheaval.

In Libya, Qatar and the UAE initially engaged together under the umbrella of NATO-led military operation to remove Gadhafi from power—both countries doing so using local surrogates on the ground. With the regime in Tripoli collapsing, there began a race to controlling the revolutionary aftermath not only in an effort to increase the two Gulf states' political and economic power in northern Africa, but also as a means to control the socio-political narrative that was to dominate the Arab world in the years to come.

In a first instance, Qatar with its soft power reach seemed to have taken the lead in Libya. Al Jazeera's influence was able to present revolutionary Islamists as legitimate contenders for political office. Suddenly, seemingly anyone could potentially rise to political power and direct the fortunes of an Arab state—an idea that shook the UAE, 'Little Sparta', to its core.

Qatar and the Emirates differed on one crucial strategic objective in a post-revolutionary Libya. Initially, Doha had offered support to its surrogates in Libya first by training and equipping them during the revolt, before using Al Jazeera to help rebrand and equip them to compete for post-revolutionary power in Libya. The UAE by contrast were willing to go much further. Their aim was not to support, but to install a new political and military order in Libya. The 'counterterrorism narrative' in conjunction with extensive use of military force to confront and eradicate any political, institutional and military opposition in their way demonstrated the distance the Emiratis were willing to go in Libya.

The 'terrorism label' and the linked narrative framing everyone as a terrorist who would dare to challenge or question the political status quo, was successfully introduced to Libya's public discourse. Moreover, by the time the crisis unravelled in June 2017, the UAE had created a self-sustaining narrative that any form of opposition in Libya, armed and unarmed, could be blamed on Qatar. Demonizing Qatar and its Islamist surrogates as terrorists, sources of instability and chaos in Libya, Hafter was not only able to undermine the reputation of his opponents but has also become a crucial partner to the UAE's offensive information warfare, as Krieg defines it in Chapter 6.

The Libyan experience showed the UAE quite plainly the power of narratives whilst simultaneously enforcing their paranoias in a post-revolutionary Arab world. Since 2011, Abu Dhabi has been feeling a real and palpable threat by nascent or maturing forms of political opposition, dissidence and difference of opinion in the Arab World.

Socio-political pluralism in the form of political parties, civil society and social movements would be able to hold governments to account, and critically challenge the Emirati narrative of authoritarian stability. Allowing individuals and groups to engage in critical discourse in an emerging public sphere, somewhat unrestrained by the reach of authoritarian governance, would directly challenge UAE regime security. Al Jazeera had offered its unconstrained and inclusive platform to the Arab people during the Arab Spring, acting as a force multiplier to already existing currents challenging the status quo. For the UAE, the unconstrained conversations about accountability, pluralism and social justice, were at the heart of the Arab revolutions that had brought some of the old powerhouses of the region to its knees. Thereby, Qatar had helped sowing the seeds for social and political upheaval that could no longer be controlled by *ancien regimes.*

CHAPTER 12

The Evolution of Turkey—Qatar Relations Amid a Growing Gulf Divide

Ali Bakir

INTRODUCTION

In the mid-seventeenth century, Qatar became part of the Ottoman Empire. Although the Ottomans ruled the region for nearly four centuries from 1538 to 1916,[1] the local dynamics in the Arabian Peninsula and the intervention of foreign powers dominated the landscape at the time, quite like the situation we see in the region today. In 1871, the Ottomans dispatched the ruler of Kuwait, Sheikh Abdullah bin Sabah, to Qatar to persuade the Al Thani family to accept Ottoman rule. A powerful ally of the High Porte, the ruler of Kuwait feared the territorial ambitions of Saud bin Faisal Al Saud, who had toppled his brother Abdullah bin Faisal Al Saud as ruler in Saudi Arabia (Emirate of Nejd).[2]

---

[1] Levitt, P. (2015). *Artifacts and Allegiances*. Berkeley: University of California Press (p. 116).

[2] Rahman, H. (2005). *The Emergence of Qatar: The Turbulent Years 1627–1916*. London: Thames and Hudson (p. 94).

A. Bakir (✉)
Independent Political Risk Analyst, Ankara, Turkey

© The Author(s) 2019
A. Krieg (ed.), *Divided Gulf*, Contemporary Gulf Studies,
https://doi.org/10.1007/978-981-13-6314-6_12

At the time, Al Sabah reached out to Sheikh Qassim bin Mohammed Al Thani, the de facto ruler of Qatar who governed on behalf of his father. Sheikh Qassim accepted Ottoman sovereignty hoping this would help fend off Bahraini schemes against Qatar and acquire the needed support to retake control of Khor al-Adaid region—located with the border of modern-day Saudi Arabia—from the British-backed Abu-Dhabi.[3] Qatar then continued to be part of the Ottoman Empire until 1916, when it became a British protectorate.[4]

In 1971, the State of Qatar gained its independence. From this point onwards, modern Qatari–Turkish relations underwent three distinct phases. The first saw the establishment of diplomatic relations in 1972, followed by the opening of a Turkish Embassy in Doha in 1980; yet a Qatari embassy in Ankara would not open until 1992. In the second phase, in 1980s, the two countries began to enter into legal treaties by signing several bilateral agreements in 1985. In the third phase, Doha and Ankara began to consolidate their relations after two main events paved the way for this: The rise of Sheikh Hamad bin Khalifa Al Thani to power in Qatar in 1995, and the rise of the Justice and Development Party (AKP) to power in Turkey in 2002.

Charting a New Path

By the time Sheikh Hamad bin Khalifa became the Emir of Qatar in 1995, he had realized in face of Saudi Arabia's helpless defence of its own country against Saddam's aggression in 1990, that relying on Riyadh for regional security might not be the right policy. He believed that it needed a different approach. The Emir, thus, resolved to chart out a new path for his country to guarantee its security and prosperity.[5]

Qatar, henceforth, invested massively in its national brand. As a small nation that lacked the means to protect itself from its two big neighbours, Saudi Arabia and Iran, Doha needed to put itself squarely on the world map and make itself visible. The creation of Al Jazeera in 1996

---

[3] Ibid.

[4] Leonard, T.M. (2006). *Encyclopedia of the Developing World.* New York: Routledge (p. 1339).

[5] سالم، بول، و دي زينو، ويب. (2012). السياسة الخارجية القطرية: الديناميات المتغيرة لدور إستثنائي. مركز كارنيجي للشرق الأوسط، 31 ديسمبر 2012.
http://carnegie-mec.org/2012/12/31/ar-pub-51004.

helped achieve this goal in record time as the media network quickly became the main source of Qatar's soft power. Doha coupled this move with a pragmatist and shrewd foreign policy, steering itself close to Arab popular attitudes, leveraging Iran to counter-balance Saudi Arabia, and using Israel to secure security partnerships with the United States. In 2002, the US military deployment in the Udeid air base was formalized,[6] and the base subsequently became the headquarters of the US Central Command in the Middle East in 2009.[7]

In 2002, AKP took power in Turkey, precipitating radical transformations in the country's foreign policy that redefined Turkey's role and status regionally and globally. The new foreign policy sought to expand the Eurasian nation's range of available options and transform itself from a peripheral state in the words of Samuel Huntington to a geopolitically pivotal state.[8] The goal was to fulfil the ambitious project of the new leadership to turn the Turkish Republic, on the centenary of its founding in 2023, into an influential power both regionally and globally, by becoming one of the top ten most powerful economies in the world.[9]

The Middle East region has immediately occupied an important position in the new Turkish agenda. Except for a short period of time during the mid-1950s,[10] Turkey had avoided any deep involvement in Middle Eastern affairs; but with the rise of AKP to power, this changed as the new government began to implement radical shifts in both Turkey's domestic and foreign policies.

[6] Gordon, M.R. (2003). Aftereffects: Bases; U.S. Will Move Air Operations to Qatar Base. *The New York Times*, 28 April 2003.

[7] CENTCOM. (2009). CENTCOM Exercises New Forward Headquarters in Qatar. *U.S. Central Command*, 14 October 2009. http://www.centcom. mil/MEDIA/PRESS-RELEASES/Press-Release-View/Article/903774/ centcom-exercises-new-forward-headquarters-in-qatar/.

باكير، علي حسين. (2010). صعود تركيا الإقليمي: تصورات عن دور أنقرة المفترض عام 2030. *مجلة آفاق المستقبل*، مركز الإمارات للدراسات[8] والبحوث الإستراتيجية،عدد 4، مارس- أبريل 2010، ص80.

[9] Davutoglu, A. (2011). Vision 2023: Turkey's Foreign Policy Objectives. *Speech at the Turkey Investor Conference*, Turkey's Ministry of Foreign Affairs, 22 November 2011. http://www.mfa.gov.tr/speech-entitled-_vision-2023_-turkey_s-foreign-policy-objectives__-delivered-by-h_e_-ahmet-davutoglu_-minister-of-foreign-af.en.mfa.

[10] Larrabee, F.S. (2011). Turkey and the Gulf Cooperation Council. *Turkish Studies*, 12:4, December 2011 (p. 690).

The AKP government build their foreign and security policy around engagement with the Middle East. At the heart of this policy shift lay the rapprochement with the Arab monarchies of the GCC. The geo-economic motive was the main imperative for Ankara's engagement with that regional bloc, as trade and investment were key components of Turkey's grand strategy. The GCC nations' massive financial capabilities and huge oil reserves made them instrumental in Turkey's regional agenda.

Meaningful economic cooperation between the two sides was first raised at a meeting of the GCC in June 2004, which paved the way for signing an economic cooperation agreement in May 2005 in Bahrain. In parallel, trade between Turkey and the GCC rose from $2.1 billion in 2002 to $16.6 billion in 2008.[11] As rapid and concrete progress was achieved on the geo-economic front, a memorandum of understanding was signed in Jeddah in 2008 establishing the Turkey-GCC High-Level Strategic Dialogue Mechanism. Ankara was recognized as the GCC's First Strategic Partner outside the Gulf region,[12] paving the way for Turkey's entry into the geopolitical and security spheres of the Gulf region.[13]

For the GCC, the geo-security component was paramount in the kind of relationship the bloc was seeking with Ankara.[14] This was because of the traditional security challenges to GCC nations arising from Iran's domination of Iraq shortly after the US-led invasion in 2003; the expansion of Tehran's regional influence though a network of armed extremist militias led by Lebanese Hezbollah; the Islamic Republic's development of its conventional missile capabilities and nuclear programme; as well as the threat posed by the rise of extremism and terrorism in the region.

باكير، علي حسين. (2010). صعود تركيا الإقليمي: تصورات عن دور أنقرة المفترض عام 2030، مرجع سابق، ص81.[11]

[12] MoFA. (2018). Körfez Arap Ülkeleri İşbirliği Konseyi (KİK), T.C. Dışişleri Bakanlığı. http://www.mfa.gov.tr/korfez-arap-ulkeleri-isbirligi-konseyi.tr.mfa.

[13] Kalin, I. (2017). Turkey, the Gulf and Regional Ownership. *Daily Sabah*, 17 February 2017.

[14] Martin, L.G. (2009). Turkey and Gulf Cooperation Council Security. *Turkish Studies*, 10:1, March 2009 (pp. 75–93).

The key objective of the GCC was to achieve geo-strategic balance with Iran through Turkey.[15] The bloc was increasingly unable to safe-guard the collective security of its member states alone, while reliance on the United States as the sole security guarantor had become a political burden due to popular opposition, undermining the legitimacy of some Gulf regimes such as the Saudi monarchy[16] besides helping rally some support for radical elements in these countries.

Ultimately, the Sunni-majority GCC countries saw Sunni-majority Turkey as a capable power led by a government with a moderate Islamic background and an independent foreign policy.[17] In addition, the Arab public had generally positive perceptions of Turkey. Taken together, Turkish geo-economic motives and the Gulf geo-security imperatives, would later become the entry point for the development of Turkish–Qatari relations.

RISING STARS

Between 2007 and 2010, Turkey and Qatar were both rising stars in the region. Both countries also had several similar features, including a proactive, bold, and independent foreign policy; emphasis on diplomatic mediation to resolve regional conflicts; a high level of pragmatism regarding political events; and religious moderation. These features gave Ankara and Doha a huge reservoir of soft power, allowing them to present themselves as modern Muslim states. In Turkey's case specifically, its political model/experience quickly became a source of inspiration[18] for the peoples of the region. Turkey's economic and political transformation as well as its new independent foreign policy had created an interest in the country across the Middle East and was seen positively by different

---

15) باكير، علي حسين. (2008). نحو علاقات تركية-خليجية إستراتيجية. مجلة آراء حول الخليج، مركز الخليج للأبحاث GRC، أكتوبر، عدد 49 (، 2008.

[16] Otterman, S. (2005). Saudi Arabia: Withdrawl of U.S. Forces. *Council of Foreign Relations (CFR)*, 7 February 2005. https://www.cfr.org/backgrounder/saudi-arabia-withdrawl-us-forces.

[17] Martin, *Turkey and Gulf Cooperation Council Security* (pp. 82–83).

[18] Ülgen, S. (2011). From Inspiration to Aspiration: Turkey in the New Middle East. Carnegie Endowment. *The Carnegie Papers*, December 2011.

segments of the Arab people. More importantly, Turkey was also seen as a successful example of the compatibility of Islam with democracy and thus Turkey's experience[19] was considered by many as a model for the Arab world.[20]

Before the outbreak of Arab uprisings, the Turkish government led by the AKP had succeeded in fostering excellent relations with several Middle Eastern governments and civil society groups, pursuant to the 'zero-problem' policy[21] and the 'strategic depth' doctrine[22] developed by Ahmet Davutoglu, top advisor between 2003 and 2009 to the then-prime minister Recep Tayyip Erdogan. For decades before that, the region had been living in a political impasse, which made it easier for Turkey to set the agenda and pursue its proactive policy, relying on its soft power—a soft power, which stemmed primarily from its experience of moderate Muslim democracy, its independent foreign policy, and economic success.

Together, these elements charmed the Arab grassroots, and it seemed that Turkey was developing an independent and alternative path relative to the one pursued by the two main regional alliances existing at the time: The *Mumana'a* camp (Axis of Defiance), comprised of Iran, Hezbollah, and the Syrian regime, with Qatar and the Palestinian resistance factions such as Hamas leaning towards it; and the Axis of Moderation, comprised of Saudi Arabia, the UAE, Egypt, Jordan, and the Palestinian National Authority.

At the end of 2010, a wave of Arab uprisings erupted in Tunisia, quickly spreading to other Arab nations including Egypt, Libya, Yemen, Syria, and Iraq. Officials in Turkey had to make a crucial decision on whether to side with the regimes or with the citizens revolting against them. In some cases, Ankara tried to leverage its relations with some

---

[19] Kujawa, K. (2011). Turkey and Democratization in the Arab World: Between an Inspiration and a Model. *PISM, Policy Paper*, no. 12, August 2011.

[20] Akgun, M. et al. (2011). The Perception of Turkey in the Middle East 2010. *TESEV*, February 2011; Akgun, M. and Gundogar, S. (2012). The Perception of Turkey in the Middle East 2011. *TESEV*, February 2012.

[21] Davutoglu, A. (2010). Turkey's Zero-Problems Foreign Policy. *Foreign Policy*, 20 May 2010.

[22] Yesiltas, M. and Balci, A. (2013). A Dictionary of Turkish Foreign Policy in the AK Party Era: A Conceptual Map. Center for Strategic Research (SAM). *Sam Papers*, no. 7, May 2013 (p. 8).

regimes, for example in Syria and Libya, to persuade them to change track.[23] However, when this effort failed, Turkey decided to quickly side with the demands for democratic change.

This Turkish policy converged to a large extent with the regional vision of Qatar who has sought to stay close to the pulse of the Arab peoples in its foreign policy and through Al Jazeera. For this reason, Qatar also decided to forgo its good ties[24] to Iran, Syria, and Libya and sided instead with the revolutionary forces.

This major alignment of Turkey and Qatar's positions on hot regional issues, especially in Tunisia, Egypt, Libya, and Syria, produced a set of shared interests between the two sides, which boosted their bilateral collaboration. Both Ankara and Doha were convinced that their home fronts were sufficiently strong and immune, believing that these revolutions posed no threat to them, unlike other countries of the region. Both judged that adopting a proactive foreign policy and riding the wave of change sweeping across the region would produce a new era where Turkey and Qatar could play a pioneering role by filling the vacuum of normative regional leadership.

The Egyptian revolution in 2011 gave a strong impetus to the regional agendas of the two countries. At the time it seemed that a new axis was being formed, between Doha, Ankara, and Arab revolutionary forces. But when the Arab revolutions brought Islamists to power in Tunisia and Egypt alarm bells sounded in the region's capitals.[25]

As a result, Turkey and Qatar found themselves on a collision course with regional players such as Iran, the UAE, and Saudi Arabia. While Iran strongly opposed Turkey and Qatar's policy in Syria, offering support to the Assad regime against the Syrian revolution, the UAE and Saudi Arabia led counter-revolutionary efforts in a number of Arab states affected by the Arab Spring—most notably in Egypt, a major and pivotal

أونيش، ضياء. (2012). تركيا والربيع العربي: بين الإعتبارات الأخلاقية والمصالح الذاتية. رؤية تركية، عدد 3، خريف 2012.23

[24] Bakir, A. (2017). Demystifying Qatar-Iran Connection in GCC Crisis. *Anadolu Agency (AA)*, 20 June 2017. https://www.aa.com.tr/en/analysis-news/demystifying-qatar-iran-connection-in-gcc-crisis/845650.

[25] Boduszynski, M.P. (2017). The Anti-Islamist campaign and Arab democracy. *Open Democracy*, 27 October 2017. https://www.opendemocracy.net/north-africa-west-asia/mieczys-aw-p-boduszy-ski/anti-islamist-campaign-and-arab-democracy.

power in the Arab world where change could precipitate major shifts in the region.

In 2013, the authority of King Abdullah bin Abdul-Aziz Al Saud began to wane, and it is believed that Khalid al-Tuwaijri, Chief of the Royal Court, and private secretary of the custodian of the two holy mosques became in charge of much of the kingdom's affairs.[26] As he was known for his hostility to political Islam and the Muslim Brotherhood in particular, al-Tuwaijri brought Saudi Arabia closer to the visions of the United Arab Emirates.[27] While Turkey and Qatar were engaged in supporting the revolutions and countering Iranian influence in the region, the UAE and Saudi Arabia were staging a reactionary effort to unleash a wave of counter-revolutions.[28] On 25 June 2013, the Qatar's Emir HbK abdicated voluntarily in favour of his son, the young Emir Sheikh Tamim Al Thani.[29] This shrewd move was in line with the exceptional developments unfolding in the Arab world, and it shored up Qatar's credibility and soft power. Nearly two weeks later, on 3 June, a military coup backed by the UAE and Saudi Arabia toppled Egypt's first democratically elected president in the country's history. Egypt's Minister of Defense Abdul-Fattah al-Sisi took power afterwards. The success of the coup in Egypt gave the counter-revolutionary axis led by the UAE and Saudi Arabia a major regional boost.

However, the implementation of Abu Dhabi's anti-Muslim Brotherhood narrative,[30] outlined by Krieg and Davidson earlier in this book, caused four major shifts in the region[31]: it triggered intra-Sunni

[26] The New Arab. (2015). Rise and Fall of Saudi Arabia's al-Tuwaijri Family. *The New Arab*, 28 January 2015.

[27] Bakir, A. (2015). Kral Selman'ın dış politikası: Değişimin boyutu ve fırsatlar. *Aljazeera Turk*, 15 Şub 2015. http://www.aljazeera.com.tr/gorus/kral-selmanin-dis-politikasi-degisimin-boyutu-ve-firsatlar.

[28] Kamrava, M. (2012). The Arab Spring and the Saudi-Led Counterrevolution. *Orbis*, 56:1, 2012 (pp. 96–104); Dorsey, J. (2014). Reshaping the Middle East: UAE Leads the Counter-Revolution. *Huffpost*, 14 December 2014. https://www.huffingtonpost.com/james-dorsey/reshaping-the-middle-east_b_5981492.html.

[29] Doherty, R. (2013). Qatar's Emir Hands Power to Son in Unusual Gulf Abdication. *Reuters*, 25 June 2013.

[30] Lynch, M. (2016). *The New Arab Wars: Uprisings and Anarchy in the Middle East.* US: Public Affairs, 2016 (pp. 153–154).

[31] باكير، علي حسين. (2015). هل ستدفع التحديات الجيو-أمنية الإقليمية السعودية والإخوان للتقارب؟. عربي 21، 17 يناير 2015.

conflicts on several fronts including one with Doha and Ankara; it harmed the unity and power of the GCC; it enabled the rise of Iranian influence to unprecedented levels; and it facilitated the rise of Islamic State group *(DAESH)* in the shadow of a regional divide.[32]

Subsequently, relations between Turkey and Saudi Arabia cooled, and Riyadh suspended the joint bilateral and multilateral platforms it had shared with Ankara. Taking advantage of the vacuum left by the Obama Administration's pivot away from the region, this reactionary axis proceeded to put pressure on Qatar, which led to the Gulf Divide that caused the Gulf crises of 2014 and 2017.

The Birth of an Alliance

Traditionally, Doha often relied on hedging[33] to counter-balance Saudi Arabia and deflect its attempts to meddle in its internal affairs. In this context, it maintained good relations with Iran as an insurance policy. However, this time the situation was different, and Doha was not able to counter-balance Riyadh through Tehran because of the profound differences it has had with Iranian policies. In addition, the new Emir did not want to be drawn into a confrontation with his Gulf neighbours and sought to consolidate his authority first. From this standpoint, Doha signed[34] two internal GCC agreements, one in November 2013 and a complementary one in November 2014, to try to address its neighbours' grievances.

These shifts pushed Doha closer to Ankara, as their positions, interests, and the regional challenges became largely identical. This took place in conjunction with a shift in Turkey's political system that installed Erdogan as the first president of Turkey to be directly elected by the people, amid ambitions to shift Turkey's foreign policy away from idealism and soft

---

[32] https://goo.gl/7ndbHV.

[33] Guzansky, Y. (2015). The Foreign-Policy Tools of Small Powers: Strategic Hedging in the Persian Gulf. *Middle East Policy*, XXII:1, Spring 2015 (pp. 114–115).

[34] Trabouls, K. (2017). Qatar Downplays CNN Leaks of Riyadh-Agreement Stating that the Current Crisis Bears 'No Relation'. *The New Arab*, 11 July 2017.

power to realism and hard power. The convergence between Turkey and Qatar was culminated in December 2014 with the signing of an agreement establishing the Qatar–Turkey Supreme Strategic Committee. In parallel, a defence cooperation agreement,[35] the first of its kind between the two countries, was signed, paving the way for the evolution of the partnership between Ankara and Doha into a fully fledged alliance.

On 22 January 2015, King Abdullah of Saudi Arabia passed away, triggering another reshuffling of the deck in the region. Riyadh was strongly seeking to roll back Iran's influence, which had reached new heights in Yemen, Syria, and Iraq, after the Obama administration allegedly turned a blind eye to Tehran's expansionism to safeguard the nuclear negotiations. The Kingdom needed all the regional support it could get for this effort, particularly from Turkey and Qatar.

The Turkish President and the Qatari Emir both saw this event as a precious opportunity to extend bridges to Saudi Arabia. The calculus was that an agreement with Riyadh would help heal the rift in the Gulf bloc and strengthen Turkish–Gulf relations, in a way that would ultimately weaken the counter-revolutionary axis and neutralize the Egyptian crisis. At this stage, the anti-Muslim-Brotherhood policy was no longer a Saudi priority[36] as Riyadh converged with the Turkish–Qatari regional agenda in an unprecedented manner. For King Salman, a pan-Arab alliance with Turkey against Iran was supposed to take precedence over feuds over the role of political Islam in the Arab world.

In 2015, relations between Ankara and Doha gained unprecedented momentum, with the Emir of Qatar visiting Turkey four times that year. This year of bilateral engagement culminated in the first summit of the Qatar–Turkey Supreme Strategic Committee in Doha in December. At the end of the summit, 15 wide-ranging agreements covering security, banking, energy, transport, education, the environment, media, and information, were signed.[37] An informal agreement was reached

[35] Hurriyet. (2014). Qatar, Turkey Take Bold Step for Strategic Cooperation. *Hurriyet Daily News*, 19 December 2014.

[36] Atkinson, M. (2015). Saudi Arabia Has 'No Problem' with Muslim Brotherhood: Foreign Minister. *Middle East Eye*, 13 February 2015.

[37] بيان مشترك بين دولة قطر والجمهورية التركية. (2015). وزارة الخارجية القطرية، 2 ديسمبر 2015. https://goo.gl/U1djyF

to mutually waive visas for the two countries' citizens,[38] the first of its kind for a Gulf nation. During that year, Ankara and Doha stepped up their roles in the military operations of the international coalition fighting *DAESH*, as well as increasing their support for the Syrian opposition. The two countries also gave support to the operation launched by the Saudi-led Arab coalition in Yemen, and Doha even sent troops to help defend the Saudi border with its southern neighbour.

An Alliance Put to the Test

On the evening of 15 July 2016, Turkey underwent a violent coup attempt by elements in the armed forces targeting the government. The coup was short lived and was fully foiled within the early hours of the next morning, thanks to the joint efforts of Turkish civilians and security forces.

Following the failed coup attempt, a reconfiguration of regional and international attitudes vis-à-vis Turkey ensued. Doha quickly condemned the attempted coup, and the emir was the first leader to contact the Turkish President that night to offer his country's support.[39] At the end of that month, Qatar's Foreign Minister Sheikh Mohammed bin Abdulrahman Al Thani became the first foreign official to visit Turkey after the coup attempt.[40]

By contrast, other Gulf countries during the early hours of the failed coup adopted a political and media discourse sympathetic to the putschists. UAE-based Sky News Arabia claimed that Erdogan had fled to Germany,[41] while Al-Ghad TV funded by the UAE, and later

---

[38] TCCB. (2015). Türkiye ile Katar Arasında Vizeler Kaldırıldı. (2015). *T.C. Cumhurbaşkanlığı*, 2 Aralık 2015. https://www.tccb.gov.tr/haberler/410/36170/turki-ye-ile-katar-arasinda-vizeler-kaldirildi.html.

[39] https://goo.gl/ أردوغان: أمير قطر أول من اتصل بي ليلة محاولة الانقلاب. (2016). *وكالة الأناضول للأنباء*، 31 يوليو 2016. yzFmva.

[40] MoFA. (2016). The Visit of the Foreign Minister of Qatar to Turkey. (2016). *Turkey's Ministry of Foreign Affairs*, 30 July 2016. http://www.mfa.gov.tr/the-visit-of-the-foreign-minister-of-qatar-to-turkey.en.mfa.

[41] https://goo.gl/ هل أسقط انقلاب تركيا الفاشل قناع المهنية عن "سكاي نيوز"؟. (2016). *الخليج أون لاين*، 20 يوليو 2016. hDrA2P.

Saudi-owned Al-Arabiya TV, hosted Fethullah Gulen,[42] the man who was accused by the Turkish authorities of masterminding the coup attempt.

Ironically, over the course of the rest of 2016, Saudi Arabia and UAE on one side, Turkey on the other side, paid efforts to mend relations between each other. The Turkish government launched a flurry of diplomatic activities to prove to the United States and European powers that it was not isolated in the region. For their part, the Gulf countries wanted to deflect accusations that they had backed the coup in Turkey financially and through their media arms. Meanwhile, in the shadow of worsening relations between Turkey and other Gulf monarchies, the rapprochement between Qatar and Turkey continued. By December 2016, the emir had met Turkey's president five times in a year with new bilateral agreements being signed.[43]

The diplomatic crisis that unfolded in May 2017 and peaked in the blockade in June 2017, posed a serious test to the Turkish–Qatari alliance. Many at the time might suggest that Ankara had been unwise in rushing to stand with Qatar without considering the consequences.[44] However, Turkey's actions on the ground were moderate and incremental, although the rapid pace of events forced the gradual response to be decisive and swift. From a Turkish perspective,[45] the crisis was not just a bilateral problem between Qatar and its neighbours; rather, its context and roots could not be isolated or confined to the Gulf geography. The new US President provided an additional element: On 20 May 2017, President Trump arrived in Saudi Arabia for his first foreign visit as president, attending a grandiose summit with a number of Arab and Muslim

---

[42] 2016 أغسطس 3 ،الغد قناة.(2016).غولن الله فتح مع خاص لقاء https://www.youtube.com/watch?v = HXvFqAa2uzY; 2016 أغسطس 20 ،برس ترك.(2016) واسعة احتجاج موجة إثر غولن مع مقابلة تحذف "العربية" https://www.turkpress.co/node/25142.

[43] MoFA. (2016).The Second Session of the Supreme Strategic Committee Between Turkey and Qatar. (2016). *Turkey's Ministry of Foreign Affairs*, 18 December 2016. http://www.mfa.gov.tr/the-second-session-of-the-supreme-strategic-committee-between-turkey-and-qatar.en.mfa.

[44] Özdemir, C. (2017). Turkey's High-Stakes Game Supporting Qatar. *Deutsche Welle*, 5 July 2017. https://www.dw.com/en/turkeys-high-stakes-game-supporting-qatar/a-39541631.

[45] 2017.يوليو 28 ،بوست نون.الخليج في الإقليمي النظام أزمة.(2017) أحمد ،أوغلو داوود http://www.noonpost.org/content/19090.

leaders. The gathering, which was not attended by the Turkish President, is believed to have provided the green light for the subsequent Gulf crisis.[46]

At the beginning of June, a few days after the hacking of QNA and the campaign against Qatar, Erdogan tasked a high-level delegation, which included members of his innermost circle, İbrahim Kalın—special adviser to the President and the Presidential Spokesperson of Turkish President, and Berat Albayrak—Turkey's energy minister and son-in-law of President Erdogan—to make a secret visit to Saudi Arabia. The delegation's mission was to examine the true extent of the crisis and its root causes, and how Turkey could help resolve it quickly. The Turkish delegation returned without satisfying answers but understood that a major escalation was unfolding.[47]

When the three Gulf countries decided to sever diplomatic ties and embargo Qatar, Turkish officials called for a rapid and peaceful resolution of the crisis through dialogue. In parallel, Ankara launched a multi-faceted diplomatic effort to contain and resolve the crisis, including marathon phone calls and shuttle diplomacy. The Turkish President closely engaged Muslim and world leaders to urge them not to be drawn into the allegations made by the blockading countries. On June 14, Turkey's Foreign Minister Mevlüt Çavuşoğlu was dispatched to Qatar, Kuwait, and Saudi Arabia, followed by a tour on July 23, that took Erdogan to the three countries as part of his effort to find a negotiated settlement.

The Turkish effort stemmed from rational calculations reflecting a more moderate and realistic policy for the region drawing on the experience of the Arab Spring. Turkish officials didn't rush to take sides, and most importantly didn't promise things that they could not fulfil. Moreover, they kept diplomatic channels open with both sides of the

[46] MEE Staff. (2017). Steve Bannon Says Trump's Saudi Visit Started Qatar Crisis. *Middle East Eye*, 24 October, 2017. http://www.middleeasteye.net/news/steve-bannon-says-trumps-visit-saudi-sparked-qatar-blockade-1719031821; Lander, M. (2017). Trump Takes Credit for Saudi Move Against Qatar, a U.S. Military Partner. *The New York Times*, 6 June 2017.

[47] باكير، علي حسين. (2017). ما لا تعرفه عن جهد تركيا لحل الأزمة الخليجية. *صحيفة القبس*، 11 يونيو 2017. https://alqabas.com/406089/.

divide and increased the diplomatic efforts with the aim to contain and ultimately solve the crisis. However, Ankara's position in the region and its military involvement in Syria and Iraq meant it could not afford to lose any more regional allies and that is why it showed readiness to wield hard power, if necessary, to maintain regional stability. Ankara feared that the crisis would escalate in a way that would shake up the map of alliances in the region and push it towards chaos, as the propaganda campaign against Qatar was suggesting it could happen. According to leaked e-mails from the account of UAE Ambassador to Washington Yusuf al-Otaiba, Doha was not the only target, so there was a realization that as soon as Qatar would be subjugated, Turkey would be the next.[48] Some even went that far to argue that Turkey was the real target.[49]

UPGRADING THE ALLIANCE

By the standards of conventional power, the Saudi-led quartet overwhelmingly outmatched Qatar. For this reason, the quartet apparently bet on this material superiority and the sheer shock effect from the blockade leaving no room for Doha to manoeuver or hold its ground. The hope was that Qatar would therefore be forced to surrender and accept the quartet's terms before any external party could intervene. The quartet consequently obstructed all attempts of mediation launched early on by both Turkey and Kuwait.[50] Once Ankara realized that the anti-Qatar bloc wanted escalation rather than containment, and to bring about regime change in Doha, Erdogan went public with his opposition to the measures adopted by the Saudi-led bloc, voicing strong criticism and demanding an end to the blockade—at a time when—former US Secretary of State Rex Tillerson was only calling for it to be eased.[51]

---

[48] Varol, Z. (2017). Hacked Emails of UAE Ambassador to US Reveal Alleged Role in Turkey Coup Attempt. *Daily Sabah*, 3 June 2017.

[49] Akit. (2017). Asıl hedef Katar değil Türkiye. *Yeni Akit*, 5 June 2017. http://www.yeniakit.com.tr/haber/asil-hedef-katar-degil-turkiye-341885.html.

[50] Bakir, A. (2017). GCC Crisis: Why Is Kuwaiti Mediation Not Working? *Aljazeera Opinion*, 11 August 2017. https://www.aljazeera.com/indepth/opinion/2017/08/gcc-crisis-kuwaiti-mediation-working-170807093244546.html.

[51] Butler, D. (2017). Turkey's Erdogan Calls for Lifting of Qatar Blockade, Approves Troop Deployment. *Reuters*, 9 June 2017.

Taking this into account, Turkey, as Qatar's main regional ally, took two strategic decisions. First, it decided to establish an airlift to break the economic embargo of Qatar. Second, it decided to expedite the deployment of Turkish troops to the small Gulf emirate. The Turkish President gave out instructions to meet all Qatari needs, and in the early hours of the blockade, Turkish goods were flown to Doha by Turkish Airlines cargo planes. The cargo planes were joined by Qatari military planes and Qatari Airways aircrafts. As the daily flights between the two countries reaching a record number, the Turkish government dedicated a separate terminal for Qatar Airways at Istanbul's Sabiha Gökçen International Airport. Within 48 hours, Turkish goods had re-stocked the Qatari market, helping avert Qatar's sudden and complete isolation.[52]

On 7 June, a day after Trump tweeted in support of the blockading countries,[53] the Turkish Parliament accelerated procedures required to approve a draft law allowing for the deployment of Turkish troops on Qatari soil. The Turkish President signed the legislation the following day, and on June 22, Ankara sent a new detachment of forces comprised of 5 armoured vehicles and 23 soldiers, joining around 88 Turkish soldiers already deployed at the Tarik bin Ziad base. Batches of Turkish troops continued to arrive in Qatar, most recently on 26 December 2017, with the two sides looking to increase the number to 3000 Turkish soldiers at a base that can accommodate up to 5000 troops.[54]

Ankara's deployment of hard power during the Gulf crisis was a sign of the major shift that took place in the Turkish leadership's response to quick and violent developments in the Middle East. Up until 2016, Ankara's regional policy relied primarily on its soft power accumulated between 2002 and 2011, that is before realizing it would be impossible to push its regional agenda forward by using soft power alone. The shift began with Recep Tayyip Erdogan taking over in 2014 as the first president directly elected by the people. This helped him to advance the

[52] باكير، علي حسين. (2018). الدور التركي والإيراني في مسارات الأزمة لإسناد قطر. في صمود قطر: نموذج في مقاومة الحصار وقوة الدول الصغيرة. تحرير: هزالدين عبد المولى. مركز الجزيرة للدراسات. بيروت: الدار العربية للعلوم ناشرون، ص80-67.

[53]The American Interest. (2017). Trump: I Decided to Take Action Against Qatar. *The American Interest*, 9 June 2017. https://www.the-american-interest.com/2017/06/09/trump-i-decided-to-take-action-against-qatar/.

[54] باكير، علي حسين. (2018). الدور التركي والإيراني في مسارات الأزمة لإسناد قطر. في صمود قطر: نموذج في مقاومة الحصار وقوة الدول الصغيرة. تحرير: هزالدين عبد المولى. مركز الجزيرة للدراسات. بيروت: الدار العربية للعلوم ناشرون، ص80-67.

execution of the new vision based on the need to activate Turkish hard power.

At the end of 2014, Turkey and Qatar had signed a defence agreement, followed by supplementary defence agreements in 2015 and 2016.[55] These same agreements allowed Ankara to deploy troops to Doha and activate its hard power immediately in the heart of the Arabian Gulf region for the first time since the collapse of the Ottoman Empire.

Turkey's forward military deployment outside its borders was aimed at achieving several objectives, most of which revolved around building up the military and security capacities of its regional partners, strengthening regional alliances, and sending political messages as show of force.[56] All these reinforced Turkey's ability to influence regional and international efforts to reconfigure the Middle East on the geopolitical and geo-security levels, which have intensified greatly following the wave of Arab revolutions and counter-revolutions.

Consequently, the Turkish President did not hesitate to approve the decision to deploy troops to Doha. Although these initial deployments were limited in number, the timing of the Turkish decision as well as its substance sent out a strong and clear message to those concerned, signalling that Ankara was willing to defend its Qatari ally, militarily if necessary.

The goal of this measure was not to antagonize the other Gulf countries, as much as to preclude any military escalation of the crisis and protect Qatar by establishing an equilibrium in the balance of power between the rival parties in preparation for a negotiated settlement of the crisis.

Turkish officials also distrusted the US position and were afraid that the splits within the US administration along with Trump's initial support for the quartet's move against Qatar would tempt the quartet to launch a military assault against Doha.[57] Moreover, there were concerns that a coup would be orchestrated against the Emir Sheikh Tamim bin Hamad Al Thani, especially as Qatar's hosting of the largest US military base in the Middle East failed to dissuade Saudi Arabia and the UAE

---

[55] Ibid.

[56] Kasapoglu, C. (2017). Turkey's Forward-Basing Posture. *EDAM*, Foreign Policy and Security Paper Series 2017/4, July 2017 (p. 3).

[57] الدور التركي والإيراني، مرجع سابق.

from bullying their small neighbour, threatening Doha, and imposing a blockade on it.[58] Erdogan therefore had to make a crucial decision in the first few hours of the blockade, at a time when no one had yet understood the full magnitude of the game.

Many observers ignore this aspect of the crisis, but it is critically relevant. The Turkish decision at the time greatly shaped the trajectory of the crisis. If Doha had yielded at the start of the blockade, the US role would have borne no importance after that as all sides would have had to accept that outcome as a *fait accompli*. Although the blockading countries had denied any intention to carry out military action, resort to force, or stage a coup to topple the Qatari Emir, there were many indications suggesting otherwise.[59] One of them came in a joint press conference between the Emir of Kuwait Sheikh Sabah Al Ahmad Al Sabah and Donald Trump on 7 September 2017, during which the emir suggested mediation efforts had succeeded in preventing military action against Qatar.[60]

CONCLUSION

The Gulf crisis left a deep rift across the region especially between the GCC member states. The crisis has thus invalidated the function of the GCC, having split it into two main camps, undermining the organization's humble achievements, and destroying all trust among Gulf nations.

But one of the most prominent outcomes of the Gulf crisis concerning Turkey's regional role and Turkish–Qatari relations, is the rapid and unprecedented integration and cooperation between the two countries, reaching new levels in terms of both scope and pace. Politically, the two sides have a clear desire to continue the alliance in its new form. Turkey was the first stop for Sheikh Tamim's overseas tour during the

[58] Ibid.

[59] Bakir, A. (2017). Why Saudi Arabia's Attempts to Topple the Emir of Qatar Will Fail. *The New Arab*, 7 September 2017.

[60] هل كان الخيار العسكري مطروحًا في الأزمة القطرية؟". (2017). سي ان ان بالعربية، 8 سبتمبر 2017 https://arabic.cnn.com/middle-east/2017/09/08/qatar-crisis-military-action-option.

blockade,[61] followed by a meeting of the Qatar–Turkey Supreme Strategic Committee in Doha in November 2017. The two sides are also seeking to turn the temporary boost in their bilateral trade into a sustainable economic relationship especially in food production, construction, pharmaceuticals, transport, plastic industry, and other sectors.[62]

Militarily, the alliance between the two sides appears stronger than ever in their history, with Doha hosting the first Turkish military base in the Arab world. The arms deals signed by Doha with Turkish defence companies at the Doha International Maritime Defence Exhibition and Conference[63] also present a glimpse into the future of the alliance and Ankara's commitment to contributing effectively to Doha's defensive posture.

Thus, the Gulf crisis accelerated the geo-strategic component of Ankara's Gulf policy, with Turkey becoming a key player in the security of the Arabian Gulf region for the first time since the collapse of the Ottoman Empire. Paradoxically, the crisis has proven that Ankara could play the role the GCC had intended it to play when Turkey was named as the first strategic partner in 2009. However, instead of only counter-balancing Iran, this role now also includes counter-balancing states within the GCC itself. The crisis has also profoundly affected the credibility of Washington's security guarantees to small states in the region, which now fear the consequences of relying exclusively on the United States to guarantee their national security following Qatar's experience.

On the other hand, the Gulf crisis has forced Turkey to partially reassess its position vis-à-vis Iran, as the latter took advantage of the crisis politically and economically. Indeed, to accelerate the flow of assistance to Qatar, Doha, and Ankara were forced to selectively and partially open up to Iran. It is not clear how long this could last, but it will depend on the balance in the region and the attitudes of the other powers. The

---

[61] أول جولة خارجية منذ الحصار.. أمير قطر يزور تركيا وألمانيا وفرنسا. (2017). الخليج أون لاين، 13 سبتمبر 2017 https://goo.gl/GgxfEs.

[62] Kaplan, E. (2017). Turkey, Qatar Sign Deals During Erdogan's Visit to Doha. *Anadolu Agency (AA)*, 15 November 2017. https://www.aa.com.tr/en/middle-east/turkey-qatar-sign-deals-during-erdogans-visit-to-doha/966252.

[63] Daily Sabah. (2018). Turkish Defense Firms Ink Nearly $800M of Deals at Doha Exhibition. (2018). *Daily Sabah*, 16 March 2018.

only thing sure a year after the crisis is that Qatar and the Turkish–Qatari alliance have emerged stronger than before.

In this sense, the crisis brought some unintended positive outcomes for Turkey. One of the most prominent of these is deeper bilateral relations between Ankara and some Arab counties looking to diversify their alliances and partnerships to deflect the threat from Riyadh and Abu Dhabi. In this regard, it has been proven that Turkey's decision to stand with Qatar in the crisis was the right call, not only because it has demonstrated that Ankara is ready to use both hard power and soft power to achieve regional balance and stability, but also because it has shown Turkey to be a reliable ally in times of crisis. This will most likely improve Ankara's position and future role, in a way that makes it difficult to exclude it from any political and security arrangements in the region.

Finally, the Gulf crisis has demonstrated that for Ankara values still matter and play an important part in its foreign policy. Because although Turkey seems to be paying more attention to material interests in its relations with other countries in the last few years, it potentially sacrificed a more lucrative relationship with the Abu Dhabi and Riyadh to stand with Qatar, for something Ankara considered to be the right thing to do.

CHAPTER 13

Iran and Qatar: A Forced Rapprochement

Sébastien Boussois

INTRODUCTION

By deciding in June 2017 to severe diplomatic relations and establish a maritime and an air blockade against Qatar, the self-proclaimed 'anti-terror quartet' put an end to the apparent unity of the Arabian Gulf. At the heart of the accusations against Qatar was the emirate's relationship with Iran with whom it shares the largest gas field in the world. It is a story of regional rivalry that dates back to the Islamic revolution in Iran in 1979. Both Abu Dhabi and Riyadh have securitized the 'Iran issue' extensively since, accusing neighbours such as Kuwait, Qatar and Oman of maintaining too close relations with declared foe on the other side of the Gulf.

Since the beginning of the crisis, the blockading countries are playing Iran's alleged game: the art of division. Kuwait, Oman, the emirate of Dubai and Qatar have traditionally positioned themselves more neutrally towards Iran, trying to find a beneficial balance between exploring economic opportunities with the Islamic Republic while not antagonizing the Saudi kingdom. Despite this, particularly Abu Dhabi and Riyadh have invested heavily into securitizing Iran's foreign and security policy.

Sébastien Boussois is the author of "Pays du Golfe, les dessous d'une crise mondiale" (Armand Colin, 2019).

S. Boussois (✉)
Université Libre in Bruxelles, Brussels, Belgium

© The Author(s) 2019
A. Krieg (ed.), *Divided Gulf*, Contemporary Gulf Studies,
https://doi.org/10.1007/978-981-13-6314-6_13

The pressure being exercised by Riyadh and Abu Dhabi towards its Gulf Cooperation Council (GCC) neighbours has confronted partners and friends to choose first between Qatar and the quartet, and secondly also between the quartet and Iran. However, this divisive agenda has so far not been fruitful. Both Qatar and Iran have arguably emerged from the crisis stronger than before.[1] Driven to preserve its relations with Tehran for economic and energy-political reasons, Doha remains resilient amid the imposed blockade by its bulky neighbours.[2]

To date, it is above all a strong economic relationship between the two countries, Qatar and Iran, that provides both with political stability. Together with Russia, both own half of the oil resources of the planet making them a powerful troika not just within OPEC but in the wider region. Prioritizing economic pragmatism, Doha has never jumped on the Saudi bandwagon of demonizing Iran, which does not mean that Qatar shares Iran's political or ideological vision.

First, this chapter will commence by looking at the relations between Iran and the Gulf countries to understand how the GCC was created as a bulwark against Iranian influence in the region, before discussing the historical relations between Iran and Qatar. This part will also provide an explanation of the deep ideological discrepancies between the two countries when it comes to regional security and stability.

Consequently, after shedding light on the securitization effort by Saudi Arabia and Abu Dhabi against Tehran, the chapter will go on to look at how the Gulf Crisis has paradoxically provided Iran with the tools to strengthen its position within the Arabian Gulf by positioning itself as a saviour of Qatar, a country 'under siege'.

The chapter will conclude by showing how the violent crisis in the Gulf since June 2017 is reshuffling the cards within the GCC, creating a de facto division and thereby reinforcing the weight of the alleged 'Iranian enemy'. While some go as far as to speak of the end of the GCC[3]; it has become increasingly obvious that by isolating Qatar, Riyadh has undermined the primary mechanism of countering Iranian influence in the Gulf.[4]

---

[1] Carey, G. and Champion, M. (2017). Saudis Have a Lot to Lose in Fight With Qatar, Even If They Win. *Bloomberg*, 9 June 2017.

[2] Macheras, A. (2018). Here for the Long Haul: How Qatar Is Overcoming the Aviation Blockade. *The New Arab*, 8 January 2018.

[3] Khouri, R.G. (2017). Will the GCC Fall Apart? *Al Jazeera*, 7 November 2017.

[4] Ulrichsen, K. (2017). Implications of the Qatar Crisis for Regional Security in the Gulf. *Sharq Forum*, 29 June 2017.

THE HISTORIC RELATIONS BETWEEN IRAN
AND THE GULF COUNTRIES

Iran's rise to power can be linked to three crucial developments in the region since 2003: first, regime change in Iraq in 2003; second, the rise of Hezbollah to power in Lebanon in 2006; and third, the Civil War in Syria since 2011. It managed to exploit the absence of Saudi leadership and the increased ideological division of the Arab world since the Arab Spring.[5] The narrative put forward by the Arab Gulf countries, most importantly Saudi Arabia, has been that Iran's interference in the fragile states of the Arab world is exacerbating regional instability and insecurity.

Although concepts such as the sphere of influence, empire and expansion are not new to the Persian vocabulary, it has been the Islamic Revolution of 1979 that has made Iran unpredictable and potentially dangerous in the eyes of the West and the Arab Gulf countries. At the time of the Shah there has been a degree of convergence between Saudi Arabia and Iran on how to look upon regional security and stability—Iran was conceived as a manageable and controllable entity. All this changed with the disruptive event of the Islamic Revolution marrying theocratic Shia Islamist elements with Socialism and creating an arguably internationalist vehicle to export a new socio-political model to the region that neither the Arab powers nor the West could control. The 1979 Embassy hostage crisis accompanied by an inherently anti-Western rhetoric, severed relations between Tehran and the West—and with it the relationship between Tehran and the mostly Western client states in the Gulf. Iran was increasingly viewed as a regional peril advancing an agenda that would run counter to Western interests. Particularly America's agenda to contain Iran through the funding of proxies in the region, most notably Saddam's Iraq, further exacerbated the Islamic Republic's inferiority complex and security paranoia. A vicious insecurity cycle emerged between the United States and its regional proxies on one side and Iran on the other, which threatened to explode over Iran's nuclear programme in the late 2000s. All along, the GCC allegedly stood as a bulwark against Iran's policies in the region.[6]

[5] Kellner, T. and Reza Djalili, M. (2018). L'antagonisme irano saoudien et le nouveau grand jeu au Moyen Orient. *Diplomatie*. No. 91, March/April 2018.

[6] Kinninmont, J. (2015). Iran and the GCC: Unnecessary Insecurity. *Chatham House Research Paper*, July 2015.

FROM THE ISLAMIC REVOLUTION TO THE CREATION OF THE GCC

Since the 1950s, Arab regimes have been worried that Iran could eventually turn into a nuclear power. The question had become more tangible since the early 1970s when Tehran signed the Nuclear Non-Proliferation Treaty. In 1979, after the Islamic Revolution, Iran lost its status as America's 'Middle Eastern policeman' as part of the US' Twin Pillar Policy. But it is mainly in the late 1980s, during Iran's war with Iraq, that the suspicions of the international community about Iran's alleged enrichment in secret facilities was reinforced as it was widely feared that Baghdad's use of chemical weapons and its race for developing weapons of mass destruction amid the war could have pushed Tehran to consider non-civilian uses for its nuclear power. Iran's resilience amid a material onslaught by the highly armed Iraqi forces and the fear that Tehran could go nuclear-triggered paranoias in Saudi Arabia that Iran might be out to expand across the Gulf. The kingdom's initiative to bundle military capabilities of the Arab Gulf monarchies under the GCC, founded in 1981, has to be understood within this rapidly changing geo-strategic context.[7]

Although the GCC intended to provide a framework for regional integration of trade and economic policies, the defence aspect remained one of the most important. In 1984, the 'Peninsula Shield Force'[8] was created to deter any potential adversaries from threatening the relatively young states. Constituted by the national armies of the various monarchies, the Peninsula Shield was to function as a rapid reaction force to be deployed against any military intervention from outside. Further, the GCC was to establish a joint mechanism to maintain internal security in the six Member States allowing for the integration of internal security forces and intelligence services. When put to the test in 1990 to protect Kuwait from an Iraqi invasion, the force failed to provide the desired deterrent. It proved to be a lot more effective in helping Bahraini

---

[7] See Barzin, N. (2005). *L'Iran nucléaire*. Paris: L'Harmattan; Delpech, T. (2006). *L'Iran la bombe et la démission des nations*. Paris: Autrement; Géré, F. (2006). *L'Iran et le nucléaire: les tourments perses*. Paris: Éditions Lignes de repères; Grandperrier, C. (2011). *Regards croisés sur un Iran nucléaire*. Paris: L'Harmattan.

[8] Reder, J. (2017). The Peninsula Shield Force: The Gulf Cooperation Council's Vestigal Organ. *International Policy Digest*, 8 May 2017.

security forces to restore order amid the Arab Spring protests in 2011 when Saudi and Emirati forces moved into the capital Manama to protect key installations. After all, regional military security was not provided by the GCC alone but by the United States who had moved extensively into the region after the 1991 Gulf War. The United States as a protector of the oil monarchies meant that Washington would provide a guarantee that Iran would not dare to cross the Gulf—a scenario that remains to be highly unlikely considering Iran's widely defensive security posture.[9]

BRINGING IN IRAN FROM THE COLD AFTER 2015

In face of growing regional instability post the Arab Spring, the Obama administration had realized that it might serve US interests more to make Iran a partner through trust-building measures instead of further alienating the Islamic Republic. The traditional allies of the United States, Israel, Saudi Arabia and the Gulf monarchies, had to be convinced that Iran could be partner—something that would prove difficult after decades of securitizing the regime in Tehran. Despite objections to a nuclear deal in neo-conservative circles in Washington, Israel and Saudi Arabia, the Obama administration helped by the EU, China and Russia were able to negotiate a deal with the Islamic Republic that would be mutually acceptable, not touching upon Iran's regional policies but focusing on its nuclear programme. The signing of the so-called JCPOA on 14 July 2015,[10] marks a watershed moment in the relationship between the West and Iran potentially opening the door for a more far-reaching rapprochement between Tehran and the Arab World. Through positive engagement on a level playing field the Islamic Republic had shown that it would be willing to make concessions and compromises. Meanwhile in the GCC the 'Iran Deal' was received with mixed feelings as particularly Riyadh feared that the United States could return to a twin pillar policy playing the kingdom against the Islamic Republic[11]—a fear that might have been widely reversed by Trump's unilateral withdrawal of the deal in May 2018.

---

[9]Krieg, A. and Rickli, J.M. (2018). *Surrogate Warfare—A Mode of War for the 21st Century.* Washington, DC: Georgetown University Press (See Chapter 7).

[10]Fitzpatrick, M. (2015) Iran: A Good Deal. *Survival*, 57:5 (pp. 47–52).

[11]Pengelly, M. (2018). Trump Will Pull Out of Iran Nuclear Deal, Leading Senator Predicts. *The Guardian*, 18 March 2018.

THE SECURITIZATION OF IRAN BY SAUDI ARABIA AND THE UAE

Since the Islamic Revolution in 1979, Saudi Arabia in particular has been obsessed with the rise of an alternative Islamic power potentially challenging the aspired monopoly of the kingdom as an Islamic power. As the custodian of the two holiest sites in Islam, Saudi Arabia had arguably developed since the 1930s into the ideological leader of the Islamic World; at least within the Sunni Arab World. The new theocracy in Tehran posed a direct challenge to this ideological hegemony claiming to provide an alternative form of Islamic jurisprudence and governance to the bipolar socio-political model of the Wahhabist kingdom. Thus, the Islamic Republic and its revolution was not just framed within the context of potential Persian expansionism but framed as an ideological threat to the kingdom and its order on the Arab shores of the Gulf.[12] The fact that Iran could now acquire influence not just through transactional military or financial means but through transformational means, potentially tying Shia Arabs to its grand strategic narrative, was seen as a fundamental threat by the Al Saud. And Saudi Arabia was not alone: conservative circles in the United States and Israel echoed these security concerns.[13] The antagonist narratives disseminated by Iran in the wake of what the Mullahs perceived to be an American-led campaign against the Islamic Republic, did not help. In particular the rise of the neo-cons to power just before 9/11, tasked to manage the response to the atrocious terror attacks, reinforced Iranian paranoias. The neo-conservative narratives placing Iran on the 'Axis of Evil' and framing the 'Global War on Terror' as a struggle of good against evil, resonated well with like-minded fear mongers in Riyadh, Tel Aviv and other Gulf states. But the process of securitizing Iran is older than this.

Already in the 1980s Saudi Arabia led a campaign to stigmatize and securitize the Islamic Republic. Securitization refers to a process of subjective framing of an issue as an existential security issue by a political authority.[14] Saudi Arabia invested heavily into portraying the Islamic

---

[12]Wehrey, F. et al. (2009). *Saudi-Iranian Relations Since the Fall of Saddam Rivalry, Cooperation, and Implications for U.S. Policy*. Santa Monica, CA: Rand Corporation (see Chapter 2).

[13]Moghaddam, A. (2007). Manufacturing War: Iran in the Neo-Conservative Imagination. *Third World Quarterly*, 28:3.

[14]Buzan, B., Wæver, O., and de Wilde, J. (1998). *Security: A New Framework for Analysis*. London: Lynne Rienner.

Republic as an urgent, existential threat to regional security and stability, thereby constructing a security perception about Iran that was adopted not only in most other GCC countries but also within conservative and neo-conservative circles in the United States.[15] The Saudi narrative of Iran as the 'evil empire' resonated well with the fear-based approaches taken by conservative thinkers in Washington and security officials in Israel. Viewing Iran as a threat rather than an opportunity has dominated the foreign and security policy approach by the Saudi kingdom to the Islamic Republic—a war over narratives that predates the joint Emirati-Saudi securitization campaign against Qatar.

Abu Dhabi's dispute with Iran over the control over several islands in the Gulf had made it adopt a more confrontational stance with Tehran than other emirates. With the shift of the balance of power in the UAE in favour of Abu Dhabi after the financial bailout of Dubai in 2008, the UAE's Iran policy had become more antagonist overall.[16] MbZ's administration increasingly bought into Saudi's securitization of the Islamic Republic as a threat to regional security.[17]

It's All About the Gas—Qatar and Iran Relations

The bilateral relations between Iran and Qatar rest primarily on economic and diplomatic agreements relating to the extraction of gas from the North Field. Iran and Qatar, together with Russia, represent a global force in the production of gas in the world—a force often dubbed the gas troika. The fact that both countries share the largest independent gas field has created a powerful bilateral relationship between both countries that rests on mutual commercial and economic interests that are of critical importance to both Tehran and Doha. The gas field, known as North Dome in Qatar and South Pars in Iran, was unearthed in 1971 by the Dutch Oil Company (Shell) and straddled the territorial waters of both countries. Qatari authorities have assessed the reserves of this

[15] Mabon, S. (2017). Muting the Trumpets of Sabotage: Saudi Arabia, the US and the Quest to Securitize Iran. *British Journal of Middle Eastern Studies*.

[16] Roberts, D. (2017). Qatar and the UAE: Exploring Divergent Approaches to the Arab Spring. *Middle East Journal*, 71:3 (p. 551).

[17] Buzan et al. *Security*.

deposit at close to 25 trillion cubic meters.[18] Nearly 40% of Qatar's gas field is located under Iran's maritime waters. In less than thirty years, Doha has become the largest exporter of liquefied natural gas (LNG) on the planet with nearly 30% of the world market share. The move from a mediocre producer of oil to becoming one of the largest producers of LNG in the world has transformed the emirate of Qatar into the richest country in the world setting in motion an unprecedented hyper-development in the emirate. For Qatar, then, the exploration and extraction of gas from the North Dome is the centre of gravity for the survival of the country.[19]

Iran is playing an important role in ensuring the security of extraction along its maritime border with Qatar. Further, Iran's antiquated hydrocarbon infrastructure along the South Pars has long been seen in Doha as a business opportunity for Qatari companies and their partners to invest. In 2017, after the beginning of the recent crisis, a new agreement worth 4, 8 billion USD was underway with the French oil and gas giant Total, a partner of Qatar Petroleum, for the operation of South Pars—an agreement whose future is uncertain amid US pressure to sanction trade with Iran.[20] It was considered to be one of the first major investments by a Western company into Iran since its rehabilitation in 2015 whereby Total could rely on Qatar to facilitate the deal.[21]

Although the bilateral relationship between the two countries rests on mutual economic interests, regional security and stability in the immediate vicinity of the North Field plays an important role in this hydrocarbon partnership. Although their visions for the future of the region divert drastically, Doha and Tehran have understood that pragmatism requires priority in dealing with one another. Thus, while those who have securitized Iran have eyed Qatar's relationship with Iran suspiciously, it is important to note that relations between the two countries

[18] Qatar Gas. (2018). The World's Premier LNG Company. Website http://www.qatar-gas.com/english/aboutus.

[19] Al Jazeera News. (2015). Qatar-Iran Ties: Sharing the World's Largest Gas Field. *Al Jazeera News*, 15 June 2017. https://www.aljazeera.com/indepth/interactive/2017/06/qatar-north-dome-iran-south-pars-glance-lng-gas-field-170614131849685.html.

[20] BBC News. (2018). Total Set to Pull Out of Iran Gas Deal Without Sanctions Waiver, *BBC News*, 16 May 2018. https://www.bbc.com/news/business-44147814.

[21] Reuters. (2017). Total Marks Iran Return with South Pars Gas Deal. *Reuters*, 3 July 2017.

are not friendly, but technocratic and pragmatic. Maritime security agreements between Qatar and Iran dating back to June 2011 entailing clauses about border protection, ensuring freedom of navigation and confronting organized crime,[22] have to be viewed within the context of ensuring a secure environment for exploring and extracting gas from an offshore field dozens of miles away from either shore. Cooperation on maritime security is critical to maintaining a secure access to the hydro-carbon infrastructure on top of the field.

In 2010, the former Iranian President Ahmadinejad and the Qatari Prime Minister Hamad Bin Jassim Al Thani defended the idea of coop-eration as a means of strengthening regional security.[23] This involved an increase in military and naval cooperation for the control of territorial waters. Strengthening naval cooperation was also an important part of the agreement mostly to protect the maritime borders between them. Ahmadinejad's words at the time were clear: '*Through consultation and harmony, Iran and Qatar can strengthen unity among the countries of the region and implement security and stability*'.[24] The Emir added at the same time: '*The cooperation between Iran and Qatar can guarantee security and stability in the region*'. In 2011, Qataris and Iranians dis-cussed military cooperation agreements, first and foremost to secure their own financial windfall.[25] One of the main goals of the agreement beyond increasing bilateral security was to set an example for regional cooperation on matters of regional interest. According to the agreement, Qatar and Iran decided to exchange specialized and technical commit-tees, share mutual cooperation in training and conduct joint campaigns against terrorism and insecurity in the region.

Moving away from the immediate vicinity of the Gulf, the bilateral cooperation between Iran and Doha appears to vanish. The Syrian Civil War might be the best example, where both sides take irreconcilable stances. While Iran has long provided the regime of Bashar al-Assad's

[22] Tehran Times. (2010). Iran, Qatar Sign Defense Cooperation Agreement. *Tehran Times*, 25 February 2010.

[23] AFP. (2010). Iran, Qatar Vow Cooperation for Security. *Agence France Presse*, 20 December 2010.

[24] Ibid.

[25] Burt, E.W. (2017). Qatar and Iran: Odd Bedfellows: United States Institute for Peace. *The Iran Primer*, 18 January 2018.

regime with financial, material and military support,[26] Qatar has since 2011 followed a policy of regime change in Syria supporting a range of opposition groups. In regard to Hamas, Tehran and Doha have taken divergent approaches since 2012 as well. The Islamist movement officially broke with Bashar al-Assad in 2012 by acknowledging the legitimacy of the opposition agenda and the organization's offices were moved from Damascus to Cairo. Despite Hamas' refusal to publicly support the Syrian dictator, Iran continues to support the Islamist organization as a potential surrogate on the ground against Israel. Qatar on the other hand, despite continuously funding reconstruction efforts in Gaza, has distanced itself from the Muslim Brotherhood affiliate amid the Gulf Crisis. Nonetheless, Qatar remains dedicated to the fate of the Gazan people living under Israeli siege, even cooperating with Israeli agencies and authorities to deliver humanitarian assistance to the strip.[27]

TEHRAN AT THE HEART OF THE GULF CRISIS

Within a climate of neo-conservative securitization of Iran after the election of Trump in Washington, the revived demonization of the Islamic Republic by both Saudi Arabia and the UAE fell on fertile ground. Amid this climate, Doha was faced with a dilemma of having to negotiate the release of Qatari hostages that had been held for over a year by the Shiite militia Kitaib Hezbollah affiliated with Iran in southern Iraq. The 26 Qatari falconers, among them members of the royal family, were kidnapped in December 2015 not far from the Saudi border by more than 100 armed militia men. Despite warnings of the Qatari government not to travel to the militia areas in southern Iraq, temptation was too big and the government now had to find avenues to open lines of communication with the non-state actor with apparent links to Iran. Naturally, negotiation about the release of the hunters would be led through a variety of different channels in Tehran, Baghdad and Syria.[28]

---

[26]Behravesh, M. (2017). But Really, Why Is Iran Still Backing Assad? A Psychological Analysis. *Middle East Eye*, 11 February 2017.

[27]API. (2018). Qatar Working Closely with Israel to Channel Aid to Gaza, Says Doha Official. *Times of Israel*, 9 February 2018.

[28]Worth, R.F. (2018). Kidnapped Royalty Become Pawns in Iran's Deadly Plot. *New York Times Magazine*, 14 March 2018.

While details about the ransom and the nature of the ongoing negotiations remain speculative at this point, reports about hundreds of millions of dollars began to surface in early 2017—money that was allegedly
hand-delivered to Baghdad by Qatari government officials.[29] In addition, allegations were made that Qatar had agreed with Iran to facilitate
the evacuation of Shia villages in Syria via Syrian opposition forces in
exchange for Tehran exercising pressure on Ketaib Hezbollah to release
the hostages.[30] For Saudi Arabia in particular these kinds of direct dealings with Iran involving large sums of ransom to Iranian surrogates in
Iraq, were a red line that was seemingly crossed by Doha. For the deputy
Crown Prince of the kingdom, Mohammad bin Salman, the hostage deal
might have been the stroke that broke the camel's back.[31] After all, the
security paranoia in Riyadh were newly inflamed by the suspicion that
a GCC neighbour could have directly negotiated over hundreds of millions of dollars with the archenemy itself.

TEHRAN'S SOLIDARITY SINCE THE BEGINNING
OF THE DOHA BLOCKADE

After the beginning of the blockade in June 2017, faced with rising tensions with its neighbours Doha saw an opportunity to upgrade its relationship with Tehran. Less than three months into the crisis, Qatar sent
a strong signal to the blockading countries by announcing on August 24
the return of its ambassador to Tehran. Qatar had downgraded its diplomatic relations with Iran under Saudi pressure following an unwillingness of Iranian authorities to stop protestors in Tehran setting fire to the
Saudi embassy in 2016. With the crisis in full swing and without being
provided with an avenue out, Qatar was in dire need of regional partners. Plus, the political directive of Riyadh to maintain severed relations

[29] Arango, T. (2017). Big Ransom and Syria Deals Win Release of Royal Qatari Hunters.
The New York Times, 21 April 2017.

[30] Chulov, M. (2017). Qatari Jet Sits on Tarmac in Baghdad as Royal Hostages Await
Release. *The Guardian*, 19 April 2017.

[31] Solomon, E. (2017). The $1bn Hostage Deal That Enraged Qatar's Gulf Rivals. *The
Financial Times*, 5 June 2017.

with Iran in solidarity with the kingdom was no longer valid. At first sight, Qatar was '*being pushed into the arms of Iran*'.[32]

Despite a sovereign wealth fund of $335 billion and strategic investments across the world, Doha had to quickly react to an unprecedented and unexpected situation in absence of a contingency plan. In particular in the field of food and water security, Qatar had to swiftly reorganize logistics to compensate for imports from the blockading countries. The emirate managed to put in place a crisis strategy based on proactive and effective economic measures aimed at curbing the effects of the blockade.

Tehran sensed an opportunity to come to Qatar's aid. Iran managed to score points politically and commercially against its Gulf Arab rivals. A few days after the start of the embargo Iran took a lead to counter the embargo imposed on Qatar by delivering 350 tons of food stuff via air and sea corridors. Iran's show of solidarity towards Qatar, a country felt abandoned by its neighbours during the holy month of Ramadan, went a long way. Iran together with Turkey was able to fill the void left by the loss of Saudi and Emirati imports. Although Qatar had to compensate for the increased logistical costs, the emirate has since been able to diversify its food imports decreasing costs via economies of scale.[33] Iranian producers were able to cash in and received access to a powerful consumer market that had long been closed to them due to Qatar's solidary import policies favouring GCC products over external products—often despite them being less desirable in both quality and pricing.

Towards Deeper Integration with Iran?

In the greater game of dominoes in the Middle East, the rivalry between Riyadh and Tehran seems to have been decided temporarily in favour of Iran. While Saudi Arabia has lacked a coherent strategy to deal with the aftermath of the Arab Spring, Iran was able to provide the strategic narrative of the Islamic Revolution to disenfranchised communities across the Arab world. Saudi Arabia, bogged down in a political, economic and identity crisis, was unable to assume regional leadership. Iranians have

[32] Dudley, D. (2017). How Qatar Is Being Pushed into the Arms of Iran by Saudi Arabia and Its Allies. *Forbes*, 27 November 2017.

[33] Livingstone, D. and Saha, S. (2017). Beyond the Qatar Crisis. *Diwan*, 14 August 2017.

meanwhile skilfully taken advantage of the absence of an American and Saudi regional strategy over the past fifteen years to strategically place their pawns in what Saudi Arabia might have once considered its sphere of influence. The small states of Qatar and the UAE appear to have been more successful in advancing their own and Arab interests, at times against the interests of Iran. Yet, Iran had been more strategic and more ambitious in increasing influence across the region—the notion of the 'Shia Crescent' seems to be not too farfetched if one considers how Iran has been able to consolidate its power in Beirut, Damascus, Baghdad and Sanaa. Unable to control these states, the Islamic Republic is nonetheless able to disrupt activities of declared adversaries in these areas. Iran could even present itself as a major power in the defeat of Daesh. While the West's airpower warfare against the self-declared Caliphate found it difficult to strategically weaken the group, Iran was able in cooperation with Russia in Syria to regain lost territories from the jihadists.[34]

The Qatar Crisis is just another prestige exercise: with little effort Tehran was able to expand influence and reach into the Gulf at the expense of Saudi Arabia. Iran's strategy of mosaic defence, creating buffer zones around its heartland, might not be able to consolidate Iranian power in these territories but disruptive influence might still serve its strategic end games. After all, Iran's achievements in the Gulf regarding the Qatar Crisis are more constructive than disruptive. Like its relations with Moscow and Baghdad, Iran's relationship with Qatar is strategic and pragmatic. It provides the Islamic Republic with relief of political and diplomatic pressure as the GCC; and the United States as its protector, are preoccupied with trying to solve what appears to be a pointless and unnecessary move to self-inflict harm on a rather homogenous group of countries.

A GCC in Crisis Faces an Iran That Is Stronger

The GCC is in a state of disintegration as Iran strengthens its regional influence and consolidates its pragmatic alliances. However, the reputation of Iran continues to degrade in the Arab world. At the same time, many of them wish a change of regime, which might not be a good idea as Tisdall claims in a recent Guardian article as '*Iran's enemies would be*

---

[34]Krieg, A. and Rickli, J.M. (2018). *Surrogate Warfare—A Mode of War for the 21st Century*. Washington, DC: Georgetown University Press (see Chapter 7).

wise not to wish for regime change. Tensions with Saudi Arabia are high, and any weakening of the Iranian government could lead to a danger- ous escalation'.[35] As Saudi Arabia enters into a state of uncertainty amid MbS' consolidation of power and an ever more failing rentier state, the region requires an Iran that is stronger. As the regional centre of gravity has shifted to the Gulf, a collapse of Iran simultaneously with a weaken- ing of Saudi Arabia would leave Qatar and the UAE as the only regional powerhouses—two small states whose feud undermines the unity of the GCC. The Gulf Divide paradoxically has not helped the Saudi cause, it has actually strengthened Iran relatively to its neighbours.

Today, the GCC as an organization remains in name only as Baabood highlights in Chapter 10, paralyzed by the unwillingness of the blockad- ing countries to honour their commitment to regional unity and com- mon measures to conflict resolution. The first summit during the crisis in December 2017 illustrated the damage that the Gulf Crisis has caused, and the Emir of Qatar was the only senior dignitary following the invita- tion of Kuwait's Emir. No major officials from Saudi Arabia, the UAE or Bahrain attended. Even worse, Saudi Arabia and the UAE used the occa- sion to proclaim a *'joint commission for political, military and economic cooperation'.*[36] The alignment of Abu Dhabi and Riyadh seems to prior- itize an unforgiving policy of 'take it or leave it' over Gulf unity. Their unwillingness to concede and to compromise on what appear to be quite radical views, has not only pushed Qatar outside the union of six but has increasingly put pressure on Kuwait and Oman as well to consider their unique relationship with the Islamic Republic.[37]

Oman has always taken more of an outlier approach to dealing with Iran due to long-lasting historic relations between the two coun- tries founded on commercial and ideological interests. Kuwait has also rather been pragmatist in their dealings with Iran due to societal ties of minorities to Persia. While both Oman and Kuwait have traditionally favoured a coherent approach to Iran within the context of the GCC, the 2017 Crisis has pressured both countries to reconsider. In absence of

[35] Tisdall, S. (2018). Iran's Enemies Would Be Wise Not to Wish for Regime Change. *The Guardian*, 1 January 2018.

[36] Krieg, A. (2017). The Saudi-Emirati Axis: United Against Gulf Unity. *Middle East Eye*, 7 December 2017.

[37] Wheeldon, T. (2017). Why Iran and Oman Are Strengthening Relations. *France 24*, 13 July 2017.

assurances that unity stands above individual interests, both Oman and Kuwait have taken a silent stance for Qatar as another small state being bullied by the great power ambitions of Saudi Arabia and the UAE. Kuwait quickly positioned itself to mediate between the feuding countries. It has been the traditional role of the Emir of Kuwait, Sheikh Sabah al-Ahmad Al-Sabah, within the Gulf as the GCC's older eminence, yet, both Riyadh and Abu Dhabi have clearly disavowed his efforts to bring the parties together. The Emir's ambitions to find common grounds for a rapprochement were disregarded by the two regional strongmen, MbZ and MbS.[38]

Conclusion

The lessons of the Gulf crisis are already multiple. In just a few months, Qatar has managed to save itself from one of the most serious political crises in its recent history as an independent state. Despite its small size, Doha managed not only to dismiss its accusers for lack of evidence of what they were advancing, but also to judge and gauge the strength of its alliances for counter the blockade. The priority in the coming months in the Gulf now split into two unequal blocks, will be to contain Saudi Arabia and maintain the dialogue with Iran where internal tensions seemed to rise in January 2018. From this turmoil to the East, it seems to emerge the voice of smaller countries who try to maintain balance and resist the influence of the greatest.

The role that Iran will play in the coming years in the world is at the heart of all the speculations and regional tensions in the Middle East. The crisis triggered by Riyadh and Abu Dhabi in June 2017 was aimed at Doha, but indirectly was meant to isolate Iran on the regional and international scene. This has not been the case and Iran continues to rise. Despite the embargo, Qatar has managed to adapt and has not strengthened its relations with Iran. Nonetheless, although Qatar was provided with an umbilical cord amid the embargo, the small emirate has not opted to further integrate policies with Iran beyond the dimensions of trade and hydrocarbon exploration. Qatar has no choice than to maintain good relations with Iran because the shared gas field remains the centre of gravity for the Qatari rentier state. If it had not been for the wealth

---

[38] Krieg, A. (2017). The Saudi-Emirati Axis: United Against Gulf Unity. *Middle East Eye*, 7 December 2017.

generated from LNG, Qatar would not have been able to weather the crisis as successfully as it did.

Doha's policy towards Iran remains therefore a pragmatic one not overshadowing the fundamental differences in values and ideology between the two countries. While Saudi Arabia might have been reasonably successful in securitizing Iran together with a powerful coalition of the Trump White House, Abu Dhabi and Israel, Iran has so far benefitted from the crisis exploiting the situation economically and politically to present itself as a reliable partner in times of crisis. The primary victim of the crisis is the GCC that has never been so divided and weak in its more than three decades history: originally intended to stand as a bulwark against Tehran after the Islamic Revolution, it is now little more than the shadow of its past ambitions.

In the face of a Saudi-UAE-led initiative to reconsolidate the Gulf around their narratives, Qatar, Kuwait and Oman might be more inclined to develop their own autonomous policy towards the Islamic Republic. The question is whether Iran can actually develop a new sustainable relationship with its Arab neighbours while the GCC goes into hibernation mode.

CHAPTER 14

Qatar's Response to the Crisis: Public Diplomacy as a Means of Crisis Management

Hamad Al-Muftah

INTRODUCTION

In the current setting of politics and political crisis in Qatar, numerous solutions largely dependent on the context of the crisis and the involved political parties have been presented. Communication has been identified as an effective tool for resolving and managing crisis, and strategic communication offers efficient tools for crisis management. Public diplomacy has traditionally been applied by international entities in an effort to realise the objectives of their foreign policy by interacting with foreign populaces.[1] Public diplomacy can be defined as the communication and dissemination of messages by governments aimed at foreign publics with the view of creating public discourse around a matter of concern either influencing or informing an overseas audience. Cull[2] illustrates that public diplomacy can also be referred to as *"the diplomacy of the*

[1] Grigorescu, A. and Fawaz, A. (2014). Public Diplomacy. *Valahian Journal of Economic Studies*, 5:1 (pp. 103–111).

[2] Cull, N. (2009). *Public Diplomacy: Lessons from the Past: Center on Public Diplomacy (CPD)*. Los Angeles, CA: Figueroua Press.

H. Al-Muftah (✉)
Georgetown University, Washington, DC, USA

people". Even though the definition of public diplomacy is dynamic, it is normally adopted through various instruments and tools, ranging from media engagement, hosting public events and initiatives to exchange programmes. Public Diplomacy aims at both testing and shaping public attitudes to government policies overseas.[3]

Amid the 2017 Gulf Crisis public diplomacy has played a major role in alleviating the effects of the crisis on Qatar and its people. Although, there are some gaps in its public diplomacy techniques that have made the country vulnerable to issues triggered by the crisis, Qatar has been successful in continuing to execute its sovereign foreign and security policy largely independently. To counter the crisis, Qatar has used many public diplomacy tools such as political engagement, digital diplomacy, cultural diplomacy, sport and science diplomacy, economic diplomacy, citizen's diplomacy and others. This chapter will explain how public diplomacy has been applied by the Qatari government as a strategic communication tool to counter securitisation efforts by the blockading countries to portray Qatar as a threat to regional peace and security. In so doing, this chapter draws on original qualitative empirical research to explore the different types of public diplomacy employed by the state of Qatar since June 2017. The empirical findings were collected through qualitative interviews with ten participants (P1–P10)[4] who are engaged one way or the other in Qatar's public diplomacy effort.

---

[3] Leonard, M. (2002). *Public Diplomacy*. London, UK: Foreign Policy Centre.

[4] P1: Interview with a public diplomacy professional, GCC affairs and security studies in London, UK, 2 May 2018.

P2: Interview with a British Member of parliament in London, UK, 1 May 2018.

P3: interview with a British advisor, who is working as an advisor to the Qatari world cup committee, London UK, 13 May 2018.

P4: Interview with an American diplomat and a public diplomacy officer, London, UK, 13 May 2018.

P5: Interview with US foreign and security policy advisor in Washington, DC, USA, 12 May 2018 via skype.

P6: Interview with a Qatari ambassador in London, UK, 30 May 2018.

P7: Interview with a Qatari researcher and expert in GCC affairs, 21 May 2018.

P8: Interview with one of the Qatari public diplomacy leaders and current ambassador in Spain, 16 May 2018.

P9: Interview with a Qatari diplomate and expert in digital diplomacy, 25 May 2018.

P10: Interview with a senior Qatari official from the government communication office of Qatar, 27 May 2018.

PUBLIC DIPLOMACY AS A SOFT POWER TOOL

According to Roselle and O'Loughlin[5]

> Diplomacy is discussed as another soft power tool, both in its traditional government to-government form, and in the public diplomacy form associated with government-to publics interactions. Much has been written on soft power and public diplomacy as Public diplomacy can, under certain circumstances, serve to amplify soft power resources, strengthening the 'attraction' of a country.

As a strategic tool of communication, public diplomacy is an essential means to build relationships between governmental entities and foreign publics.[6] In fact, these public relationships have long been proven as effective supplements to conventional diplomacy. In an ever more interconnected, globalised world, formal and informal transnational networks between state and non-state actors have become increasingly important.[7]

Public diplomacy enables public diplomats to understand the desires, needs and grievances of foreign publics.[8] By tapping into foreign public spheres, public diplomats can nurture intimate relationships with public discourse overseas increasing their ability to understand attitudes and opinions—something that can help policymakers to tailor their policies to the individual requirements of audiences overseas. They also help manage conflicting diplomatic goals, mostly by balancing foreign and domestic interests. In this capacity, public diplomats are considered the conscience of their Foreign Ministry—those who help develop an understanding of policy and decisions, while considering the interests and

---

[5] Roselle, L. and Loughlin, O. (2014). A. Strategic Narrative: A New Means to Understand Soft Power. *Media, War & Conflict*, 7:1.

[6] Fitzpatrick, K. (2017). Public Diplomacy in the Public Interest. *The Journal of Public Interest Communications*, 1:1.

[7] Fitzpatrick, K. (2010). *The Future of U.S. Public Diplomacy: An Uncertain Fate.* Leiden, The Netherlands: Brill.

[8] Alpaslan, C.M., Green, S.E., and Mitroff, I.I. (2009). Corporate Governance in the Context of Crises: Towards a Stakeholder Theory of Crisis Management. *Journal of Contingencies and Crisis Management*, 17:1.

concerns of involved stakeholders.[9] More importantly, as a report by the Centre for Strategic and International Studies on US public diplomacy indicates, public diplomacy when increasingly fused with disinformation and covert media campaigns can help foreign entities to actively shape public opinion according to their liking.[10]

As one of the first, Olsson[11] suggested that public diplomacy can be used as a tool for management of transnational crisis extrapolating cultural, geographical and religious boundaries. As a crisis management tool, public diplomacy can prepare the ground for a better understanding of the advocating country by explaining its norms, interests and values to an overseas public potentially increasing understanding and receptiveness to the advocating country's messages. At the same time, the interactive nature of public diplomacy as a two-way street, helps advocating states to adapt either their policies or their messaging in direct response to changing attitudes of public discourse overseas.[12]

Communication as power, thereby, fits neatly into Nye's concept of soft power moving beyond narrow dimensions of military power.[13] According to Roselle and O'Loughlin[14] *"scholars and politicians often say that soft power is the ability to influence others through the attraction of culture, values, and policies—which are viewed as soft power resources"*. The role of narratives, as discussed in Chapter 6 to influence public perceptions about the reality of crisis, thereby, often becomes equivalent to real events. Because as Nye argues, in today's world, international affairs have become a matter of 'whose story wins'.[15] Defeat and victory are merely perceptions.

[9] Fitzpatrick, K., Fullerton, J., and Kendrick, A. (2013). Public Relations and Public Diplomacy: Conceptual and Practical Connections. *Public Relations Journal*, 7:4.

[10] Brown, K.A., Green, S.N., and Wang, J. (2017). *Public Diplomacy and National Security in 2017: Building Alliances, Fighting Extremism, and Dispelling Disinformation.* Washington, DC: Centre for Strategic and International Studies.

[11] Olsson, E. (2013). Public Diplomacy as a Crisis Communication Tool. *Journal of International Communication*, 19:2.

[12] Brown, R. (2002). Information Operations, Public Diplomacy and Spin. *Journal of Information Warfare*, 1:3.

[13] See Nye, Jr. J. (2011). *The Future of Power.* New York: Public Affairs.

[14] Roselle, 'A Strategic Narrative'.

[15] Nye, J.S. (2014). The Information Revolution and Soft Power. *Current History*, 113:759 (pp. 19–22).

By suitably positioning the above-mentioned concepts of public diplomacy and strategic communication, this chapter will focus upon the impact of Qatar's public diplomacy effort on changing the discourse on Qatar and the crisis in the West. In particular, this chapter will look at political engagement, digital diplomacy, cultural diplomacy, sports and science diplomacy, citizen diplomacy and economic diplomacy.

POLITICAL ENGAGEMENT

Political interactions, relationships and engagement between states on bilateral terms are the fundamentals of traditional diplomacy.[16] Within the context of Public Diplomacy, political engagement in its non-traditional format has the ability to operate in a far more innovative, creative and contemporary manner.[17] Unlike traditional diplomacy, officials and diplomats use the tools of public diplomacy to engage with non-governmental actors such as private individuals, civil society, corporates, Non-Governmental Organizations (NGOs), think tanks, journalists, and others.[18] Since the beginning of the 2017 Gulf Cooperation Council (GCC) crisis, Qatar has engaged states by first, countering the unsubstantiated claims made by the blockading countries that it was sponsoring terrorism; and second, that it has been a long-time ally of America and the West.[19]

The onset of the Gulf security crisis resulted in a rapid and unprecedented process of public diplomacy's political engagement undertaken by the Qatari government. For instance, an article published by Foreign Policy[20] outlined that Qatar invested in a very effective political engagement campaign. They stated—"*rather than convincing commentators and politicians in the West that Qatar had serious problems it needed to address, the effect has largely been the opposite. This development gave Doha credit in the eyes of its erstwhile critics in the West*". Participant 6 revealed how

[16]Yilmazkuday, D. and Yilmazkuday, H. (2014). Bilateral Versus Multilateral Free Trade Agreements: A Welfare Analysis. *Review of International Economics*, 22:3.

[17]Cull, N.J. (2008). Public Diplomacy: Taxonomies and Histories. *The Annals of the American Academy of Political and Social Science*, 616 (pp. 31–54).

[18]Brown, 'Information Operations'.

[19]Bayoumi, A. (2017). Gulf Crisis: Qatar Has Championed a Modern Approach to Diplomacy. *The New Arab*, 2 August 2017.

[20]Hassan, H. (2018). Qatar Won the Saudi Blockade. *Foreign Policy*, 4 June 2018.

the government engaged with UK Members of Parliament (MPs), state officials and non-state and civil society actors in the United Kingdom, reached out to media representatives, and arranged roundtable discussions with think tanks and other political institutions. Additionally, participant 6 noted that the Qatari foreign minister held a conference in London to discuss policies for countering terrorism, while other state officials met with human rights groups to address longstanding concerns about economic, social and cultural rights. Participant 10, a senior official at the Government Communication Office in Doha, corroborated this position by outlining the huge number of official engagements that have been undertaken with political actors and media representatives to project a benevolent and more factually accurate depiction of Qatar. Participant 10 noted that where, before the crisis the Government Communication Office, would have had up to three foreign journalists visiting per month, in just the first two months after the onset of the crisis, there were over 500 such engagements.

Participant 2, who is a Member of the British Parliament, also noted the various ways in which the Qatari state mobilised its diplomatic resources to open channels of communication with political actors in the UK. MPs from across the political spectrum have met with the Qatari ambassador to the UK and state diplomats. Furthermore, some MPs have visited the Emir in Qatar. As a consequence, those MPs engaged by Qatar's public diplomats in London were exposed to Qatar's side of this war over narratives reinforced by the highest echelons of power in Doha—something that seemed to have affected political discourse in the UK Parliament during the Westminster Hall Debate.[21]

In Washington, DC, Qatar's public diplomacy campaign was even more extensive. As participant 5, a visiting scholar at the American Enterprise Institute (AEI), highlights, public speeches by senior Qatari ministers, most notably Qatar's Minister of Foreign Affairs, at renowned think tanks, were an important part of countering the narratives disseminated by the blockading countries. As participant 5 argues, the relatively low-key visit of Qatar's Emir to the United States was intended to stand in stark contrast to the pomp and pageantry of the visit of Saudi's Crown Prince MbS. Qatar's focus was not so much based on overwhelming America's public with tailored narratives, but more on a substantiated

---

[21] House of Commons. (2018). *Westminster Hall Parliamentary Debates*, 641:144, Wednesday, 23 May 2018.

engagement of the Emir with selected Congressmen and the President. Here, personal rapport between the Qatari monarch and U.S. leaders was at the centre of an effort to alleviate American fears about an escalating security crisis in the Gulf—a crisis that under the impression of Qatar's public diplomacy efforts was increasingly perceived in Washington as man-made and avoidable.[22]

Digital Diplomacy

Digital diplomacy has enabled diplomats to employ innovative, effective, efficient and inclusive ways for engaging in diplomatic activities and devising foreign policy.[23] During the diplomatic crisis, Qatar launched its media diplomacy in the form of both traditional and social media. As this crisis has so far been a digital media war,[24] Qatar had to activate its traditional and new media links to counter the narratives of the blockading countries. Krieg[25] said, "*taken by surprise, Doha had to play catch-up after having neglected its strategic communication for years, to counter the well-planted, yet unsubstantiated, accusations*". The Al Jazeera media network, directly attacked by the blockading countries for their liberal narrative challenging regional authoritarianism naturally moved to the forefront of Qatar's media war to counter its neighbour's allegations.[26] According to *The Guardian*,[27] Qatar used the media to gain international sympathy, releasing statements and news articles to show how the diplomatic blockade affected its people.

Participant 9, a Qatari diplomat, noted that Qatar used Twitter to communicate directly with its citizens and members of the general public. This, according to participant 6, enabled the Qatari government to

[22] Reuters. (2018). Trump, Welcoming Qatar's al Thani, Says U.S.-Qatar Ties Working Well. *Reuters*, 10 April 2018.

[23] Vanc, A. (2012). Post 9/11 US Public Diplomacy in Eastern Europe: Dialogue Via New Technologies or Face-to-Face Communication? *Global Media Journal*, 11:3.

[24] Pinnell, O. (2018). The Online War Between Qatar and Saudi Arabia. *BBC Trending*, 3 June 2018.

[25] Krieg, A. (2018). The Gulf Crisi and Qatari Blockade—A Feud Maintained by an Information War. *Opinion Internationale*, 28 March 2018.

[26] Allagui, I. (2017). Qatar's Crisis Management Comms: The Game Plan. *US Center on Public Diplomacy*, 24 June 2017.

[27] Khanfar, W. (2018). Al-Jazeera Gave Arab Youth a Voice: Gulf Regimes Must Not Silence It. *The Guardian*, 26 June 2017.

"*reach large numbers of the audience with a single message*". This is an immensely important issue to address in the early twenty-first century, where, as participant 7 notes, the far-reaching changes brought about the proliferation of digital technologies that have radically altered the concept of public diplomacy and elevated the expectations of citizens.

Participant 10 stated that "*you had other countries, who would have digital armies with fake accounts, who would just tweet random stuff online*". Amid the crisis Qatar then found itself not only confronted with the strategic problems engendered from the economic blockade, but equally important with issues relating to global public perception as a result of what participant 7 refers to as "fake news" campaigns undertaken by Qatar's regional neighbours. Digital diplomacy presented an ideal vehicle through which the Qatari government, the Qatari public, experts and scholars were able to combat fake news disseminated online, challenging the monopoly of the anti-Qatar narrative of the blockading countries

An example of this is presented by participant 10 with the work undertaken by Georgetown University as part of Qatar's Education City. Here, citizen groups undertook corrective measures, such as responding to misinformed comments by providing links to credible news channels. This represents a diffuse, "bottom-up" approach to digital communication undertaken by non-state actors in defence of the values, interests and norms of the state.

According to participant 1, Qatar was able to retain an upper hand in the digital media war because it did not engage in the smear tactics used by the blockading powers. Rather than seeking to undermine the credibility of its rivals and disseminate fake news, Qatar sought to affirm the social and political reality in the Middle East and defended its integrity and status in the international arena. As participant 1 noted, digital diplomacy undertaken by the Qatari government and its representatives concentrated on "*deeply felt*" convictions about the regime and the country, rather than the "*widely felt*" beliefs. Qatar preferred to communicate via recourse to universal truths as opposed to abstract logic. Digital diplomacy, therefore, was able to help Qatar to reaffirm the ideas and norms transmitted through orthodox diplomatic channels.

CULTURAL DIPLOMACY

Cultural diplomacy refers to the exchange of information, art, ideas and other forms of culture among countries, with the aim of enhancing mutual understanding between them.[28] On several occasions, cultural diplomacy is referred to as *"the linchpin of diplomacy"* (ibid.). Clarke also argues that the main objective of cultural diplomacy is to enable countries to understand foreign institutions and ideals with the aim of building broad support for political and economic benefits. As part of a state's public diplomacy effort to enhance "understanding", societal values, traditions and culture are integral ingredients.

Participant 8, Qatar's Ambassador to Spain and one of the pioneers of Qatari public diplomacy, reiterates cultural diplomacy as a form of soft power, which entails cultural exchange of information, ideas and shared values between countries. He notes that the West and Qatar have a long tradition of cultural diplomacy. This includes conscious state-directed diplomacy through investment in art, film and education, and unconscious non-state diplomacy, where individual actors and organisations reinforce ideas, values and norms of Qatar via individual cultural endeavours. Participant 10 states

> there was a big and artistic image of the Emir that went viral within the country and abroad. It was to show that Qatar is united and stands behind the Emir and that was important, as fake news in the local media in the blockading countries were pushing the other side of the story. Also, there were some Qatari singers, who released songs that pushed for GCC unity to try to bring unity among the people in the GCC.

Thus, as participant 10 notes, citizens played as important a role as the state in promoting Qatari culture. The story of the artistic image of the Emir of Qatar subtitled *"Tamim Al Majed"* (Glorious Tamim) not only went viral in Qatar but made it into Western news stories as a symbol of the emirate's socio-political integrity.[29] The artist who drew the image said, *"I'm thankful God gave me the chance to create this sort of work ... which expresses my love for the Emir"* (ibid.).

[28] Clarke, D. (2016). Theorising the Role of Cultural Products in Cultural Diplomacy from a Cultural Studies Perspective. *International Journal of Cultural Policy*, 22:2.

[29] Daily Mail. (2017). With Qatar in Crisis, Tamim the Glorious Rises as National Emblem. *The Daily Mail*, 3 August 2017.

Many participants acknowledged the intrinsic links between Qatari cultural diplomacy and Islamic cultural identity. Participant 4, for example, discussed "*the promotion of Islamic culture through the museum of Islamic art*" as an example of cultural diplomacy. Qatar, therefore, understands the importance of presenting a favourable image of all Muslims, rather than concentrating solely upon Qatar and its strategic goals. The participants who discussed cultural diplomacy outlined the crucial role of culture in diffusing tension at the onset of the Gulf security crisis. Participant 7, for instance, discussed an interactive art exhibition held in London by a Qatari student, which allowed all Gulf citizens, regardless of their nationality, to participate. This underlined the distinction between Qatar and the blockading countries. Whereas the blockading countries focused upon division between the Gulf states, Qatari cultural diplomacy emphasised the importance of working together, shared interests, cultural ideals and experiences of youth. As Qatar's ambassador to the UK (P6) mentioned, Qatar's governmental organisations, such as the Ministry of Culture and the Supreme Committee for Art and Museums, have used art diplomacy during the 2017 GCC crisis to communicate to the global audience that they can never forget about Qatar's art and culture. Participant 9 also added that Qatari artists used art to clearly illustrate to the world the harmful effects of the GCC crisis. Many of these young artists travelled around the world and visited major cities, such as London, Paris or Washington, to promote their workArt can offer a strong presentation of foreign culture that remains ingrained in the memory of the audience.[30]

Sport and Science Diplomacy

Science has been another important vehicle for Qatar to promote a favourable image of itself among Western powers. Participant 4 highlights the role of Qatar's Science and Technology Park in promoting Qatar as a regional leader in science. Both Participant 6 and 8 highlight that the promotion of science and technology through public diplomacy offers a wide array of opportunities to empower aspiring academics, scientists and entrepreneurs—particularly when well-endowed organisations such as Qatar Foundation became important sponsors of science

---

[30]Brown, J. (2009). Art Diplomacy, the Neglected Aspect of Cultural Diplomacy. In *The Routledge Handbook of Public Diplomacy*. Abingdon, UK: Routledge (pp. 57–59).

projects. Participant 8 said, Qatar has done its best to collaborate with other countries to advance the causes of science and research, although the recent diplomatic crisis has affected research collaborations in the region. Qatar, in recent years, has increased funds for its science and research programmes, and the current diplomatic crisis has not dampened its support for these programmes.[31] Participant 9, a Qatari public diplomacy expert, said that although Qatar is under siege, the Emir went ahead to patronise and inaugurate the Qatar National Library before an international audience of dignitaries, scholars, artists and journalists.[32] Equally important has been Education Above All, a charitable NGO founded by Sheikha Moza, the Emir's mother, which has been able to educate more than 10 million children worldwide—an achievement that participant 8 says helped promote Qatar's leadership in education across the region.

Lately, Qatari sports diplomacy has also gained considerable prominence within the country's public diplomacy effort. Almost all interviewees alluded in some capacity to the FIFA World Cup, scheduled to be held in Qatar in 2022, as a major source of soft power. Hosting the World Cup, the largest and most well-known sporting event, allows Qatar to engage in sport-related diplomacy. Participant 3, for example, discussed a joint venture between Qatar's ambassador in London, the Secretary-General of the 2022 World Cup organising committee and the English football association to *"help support grassroots sport and encourage young people to stay fit and healthy"*. Furthermore, participants 1 and 6 discussed a joint venture with London's Chelsea Football Club to celebrate Qatar's National Sports Day in early 2018. This, according to participant 1, furthered Qatar's position as *"the leading nation in the Middle East for sport and also citizens' engagement in sports"*. These ventures also enabled Qatar to demonstrate why the small Gulf state was selected to host the World Cup. It must be noted that while sports diplomacy can raise the profile of Qatar, and thus counter the narratives expounded by the blockading powers, it can also undermine the image of the country by exposing persistent human rights violations towards labourers constructing the venues. In addition, while sports diplomacy has raised Qatar's profile in the West, it has done little to improve

---

[31]Adams, T. (2018). From Qatar's Blockade, a Bold, Unexpected New Vision Is Emerging. *The Guardian*, 6 May 2018.

[32]QNA. (2018). Emir to Open Qatar National Library. *Qatar Tribune*, 16 April 2018.

relations between Doha and other blockading powers. In many ways, Qatar's sports diplomacy has been tailed towards building Qatar's brand in the West as a sporting hub without using it to reconcile with neighbouring countries where Qatar's ambitions were perceived as a challenge and competition. Participant 10, for instance, notes that blockading countries did not want to play against Qatar in the annual Arabian Gulf Cup. Sport, therefore, has the propensity to enhance existing political divisions.

Economic Diplomacy

Economic diplomacy is the deployment of economic tools by a nation in a bid to achieve its economic interests.[33] When economic diplomacy is mentioned, economic activities, such as developing export and import routes, attracting investments, securing grants and free trade agreements come into play (ibid.). In the midst of the diplomatic crisis, Qatar used its economic diplomacy to reduce the impact of the crisis on its economy. Qatar Airways, for instance, was able to immediately secure alternative routes for its flights to bypass the blockade of air space. Qatar was also able to tab into existing trade links with Turkey and Iran to ensure the country food and water security.[34]

Qatar also engaged in economic diplomacy to reassure the numerous stakeholders and investors affected by the Gulf divide.[35] Qatar reiterated its commitment towards its partners and investors, ensuring that the government would provide financial securities for any potential losses. Qatar's commitment to existing trade deals was an important message that the emirate would put business before politics. Qatar went even that far as to abstain from suspending its gas supplies to the UAE—the primary instigator of the 2017 crisis. Doha's reputation as a reliable business partner was essential in buying credibility and loyalty among

[33] Omelyanenko, V. (2018). Economic Diplomacy in the Innovation Global Value Chains as the National Security Providing Strategy Component. *Traektoriá Nauki*, 3:3.

[34] Wintour, P. (2017). Land of Milk and Money: Qatar Looks to Farms to Beat the Gulf Boycott. *The Guardian*, 20 October 2017.

[35] Aldroubi, M. (2017). Bahrain Says Qatar's Media Is Making Diplomatic Crisis Worse. *The National*, 15 August 2017.

investors and European countries who were fearful that European companies could lose their investments due to the blockade.[36]

In Britain, Qatar presented itself as a guarantor of stability amid the uncertainty of the post-Brexit vote. As participant 3 observes Qatar offered to invest billions in the British economy to demonstrate support for its strategically, and to reaffirm cultural and historical bonds between the two countries. Participant 7 also reveals how Qatar has drawn upon its significant economic resources to counter the blockade since 2017. According to participant 7, Qatar utilised *"all of its capacities to strengthen and promote national manufactured products, and strongly diversified its resources using its strong commercial infrastructure"*. Similarly, participant 1 underlines the importance of economic diversification and foreign direct investment as a diplomatic means of managing the ongoing Gulf security crisis. In an opinion piece published by the New York Times, the Qatari foreign minister outlined how Qatar managed a successful economic plan after the crisis took place. He said

> in the weeks and months that followed, we signed new, long-term contracts for economic cooperation, at the same time accelerating plans to diversify our economy by diminishing our reliance on our hydrocarbon resources.[37]

There is, therefore, consensus that resource wealth is an intrinsic part of Qatar's identity; one that enables the state to navigate a diplomatic pathway through security crises.

Citizen Diplomacy

According to Gregory,[38] the concept of "citizen diplomacy" only became popular more recently after being used by Hillary Clinton. It is difficult to ascertain yet whether citizen diplomacy merely entails engagement of ordinary citizens in cross-border relationships, or also involves

---

[36] Adams, *From Qatar's Blockade, a Bold, Unexpected New Vision Is Emerging*, Sergie, M. (2018). Embattled Qatar Is Rich Enough to Get by for Another 100 Years. *Bloomberg*, 7 June 2018.

[37] Al Thani, M.A. (2018). End the Blockade of Qatar. *The New York Times*, 5 June 2018.

[38] Gregory, B. (2005). Public Diplomacy as Strategic Communication. *Conference Paper presented to American Political Science Association*, 31 August 2005.

their meaningful involvement in diplomatic activities. Citizen diplomacy is an important feature of public diplomacy in the contemporary era, as it reveals how a state interacts with and is represented by its people.[39] The rapid pace of evolution in diplomatic practice has given rise to discussions on the increasing role of citizen diplomacy versus the traditional forms of diplomacy (ibid.).

Both the Qatari ambassador to London (P6) and the Qatari ambassador to Spain (P8) highlight that Engagement with societies and communities at home and overseas is one of the essential features of public diplomacy. This type of interaction is created to offer a direct channel of communication and engagement between the general public and communities of a target state and the diplomatic mission. The Qatari government has done its best to reassure its citizens amidst the diplomatic crisis that their interests would be protected and that they would weather through the crisis.[40]

After the blockade Qatari citizens had an immediate choice to make—whether they support the blockade for a regime change or stand by their leadership. There was an absolute consensus to stand by their leadership, which went beyond just stagnation.[41] They proactively rallied around the leadership of the Emir with a visual campaign, both in Qatar and globally (P1). As participant 10 highlights, it is important to also consider the expats' reaction in Qatar towards the blockade, and their decision to support the leadership. Absolute rejection of the blockade was by far the single most important action taken to minimise the impact of the crisis, and place Qatar in a stronger position. As Qatari citizens rallied together in unity, it sent a distinct message to the blockading countries and Qatari partner alike that despite the blockade, the country remains one of the most resilient in the region.

Qatar was able to control the narrative of the impact of diplomatic crisis on its people. It helped ensure public trust and support towards their leaders. Citizens used hashtags such as #TamimAlMajd (Glorious Tamim) and #WeAreAllTamim, which trended globally, to reassure

[39] Tyler, M. C. and Beyerinck, C. (2016). Citizen Diplomacy. In C.M. Constantinou, P. Kerr, and P. Sharp (eds.), *The Sage Handbook of Diplomacy*. London: Sage.

[40] AlJazeera, (2017). Gulf Diplomatic Crisis: Qatar's Reaction in Full. *Al Jazeera*, 6 June 2017.

[41] Daily Mail, 'With Qatar in Crisis'.

Qatar's leadership of the people's support.[42] Participant 7 points out that Qatar was able to withstand the blockade *"because both its citizens and residents stood with the government"*. In particular, the Qatari youth played a crucial role in mobilising support for the emir. This leads participant 7 to hypothesise that Qatar's youth, rather than its oil, represents the true source of the state's power and national identity.

ACCESSING THE IMPORTANCE OF PUBLIC DIPLOMACY

Many public diplomacy scholars have discussed ways to evaluate and measure the effectiveness of public diplomacy initiatives and the challenges that policymakers face during its evaluation process.[43] It remains hard to assess the outcome of public diplomacy engagements as the concept itself is highly contested. However, one way of looking at the outcome of public diplomacy is by looking at how international media outlets have looked at the GCC crisis one year on.

On average, the international media was overwhelmingly positive in adopting the Qatari narrative disseminated by Qatar's public diplomats through their various channels. In the wake of the first anniversary of the Crisis, Western newspapers published a range of articles on the crisis, describing the harsh act performed by the blockading countries. For instance, the Financial Times wrote *"the continuing blockade of Qatar makes no sense"*.[44] Also, The New York Times published an article titled *"Pompeo's Message to Saudis? Enough Is Enough: Stop Qatar Blockade"*.[45] In this article Gardiner Harris said, *"Secretary of State, Mike Pompeo, arrived in Riyadh on his first overseas trip as the nation's top diplomat with a simple message: Enough is enough"* (ibid.). An article published in the French newspaper, *Le Figaro*, examined how the blockading countries

[42] Allagui, 'Qatar's Crisis Management'; Pinnell, 'The Online War Between Qatar and Saudi Arabia'.

[43] Fitzpatrick, 'The Future of U.S. Public Diplomacy'; Johnson, J. (2006). How Does Public Diplomacy Measure Up? *Foreign Service Journal*, 83:12; Kelley, J. (2005). *U.S. Public Diplomacy: A Cold War Success Story?* 2005–2006 Cold War Studies Centre Seminar Series, Department of International Relations, LSE, 2 November 2005: 1–29; Pahlavi, C. (2007). Evaluating Public Diplomacy Programmes. *The Hague Journal of Diplomacy*, 2:3.

[44] FT. (2018). The Continuing Blockade of Qatar Makes No Sense. *Financial Times*, 19 April 2018

[45] Harris, G. (2018). Pompeo's Message to Saudis? Enough Is Enough: Stop Qatar Blockade. *The New York Times*, 28 April 2018.

have struggled to isolate Qatar during the year-long blockade. The piece illustrated Qatar's victory in what they described as the *"public relations battle"*, which helped Doha resist the blockade.[46] Hassan explains that Qatar had invested in public relation campaigns that successfully and positively influenced Western audience: *"A year on, however, Qatar has not only weathered the storm—it also appears to have emerged as the main winner of the conflict".*[47] In an op-ed for *Foreign Affairs*[48] Ulrichsen argues that the illegal blockade has failed, with Qatar *"outplaying its rivals"* and *"proving more resilient than most people anticipated"*. The *Economist* [49]also published an article titled, *"The siege of Qatar isn't working"*. It outlined the measures the country *took to counter the harmful impact of this crisis.* Additionally, Richard Spencer from The Times *said "The wealthy Gulf state has made friends in high places and stayed one step ahead of its neighbours'* attempts to ostracise it".[50] Finally, an article published in the French outlet *Jeune Afrique*[51] details the one-year-old blockade of Qatar, claiming that Qatar is on an *"offensive to restore its image"* and asserted that allegations of Qatar's support for terrorism are *"false"*.

The Qatari government has been successful in countering the securitisation effort by Saudi Arabia and the UAE portraying Qatar as a threat to regional security. Through public diplomacy, Qatar tried to divert attention towards the Western public to avoid being drawn into a highly polarised misinformation campaign shaped by a discourse of unsubstantiated and sometimes outright false statements. This informed move by the Qatar government enabled them to seize the opportunity to preserve the moral high ground amidst what was to become an offensive and emotional campaign directed at demeaning the Qatari leadership. Qatar's sober and facts-based public diplomacy effort sought to return

[46]Malbrunot, G. (2018). L'Arabie saoudite peine à faire plier le Qatar. *Le Figaro*, 3 June 2018.

[47]Hassan, H. (2018). Qatar Won the Saudi Blockade. *Foreign Policy*, 4 June 2018.

[48]Ulrichsen, K.C. (2018). How Qatar Weathered the Gulf Crisis. *Foreign Affairs*, 11 June 2018.

[49]The Economist. (2017). The Siege of Qatar Isn't Working. *The Economist*, 15 June 2017.

[50]Spencer, R. (2018). Splendid Isolation: How Qatar Is Beating the Blockade. *The Times*, 18 June 2018.

[51]Gillion, J. (2018). Financement du terrorisme: le Qatar à l'offensive pour redorer son image. *Jeune Afrique*, 11 June 2018.

the crisis and its discourse to the realm of conventional and conservative diplomacy.

As mentioned by Roselle and O'Loughlin,[52] public diplomacy is best understood as a form of soft power, which enables governments to engage in a process of social and cultural persuasion. Participant 6, for instance, suggested that public diplomacy is an important soft power tools for Qatar because it allowed the government to disseminate the core values, interests and ideas that define the state, its people and political leadership. Participant 1 interpreted this in terms of building "brand trust" through international cultural projects, such as the Al-Jazeera network. Understood in this way, public diplomacy is important, because it links countries to the wider international political and economic system. This is a particularly important issue to recognise for a small state such as Qatar whose identity, values and strategic interests have historically been intertwined with that of the GCC.

Most interviewees acknowledged the crucial role that public diplomacy has played in allowing the Qatari government to manage the Gulf Crisis. For instance, participant 10 noted that public diplomacy has enabled the Qatari government to, firstly, react to the digital information war initiated by the four blockading actors and, secondly, undertake a proactive public communication campaign to depict Qatar in a more favourable light. The dual function of public diplomacy as a proactive and a reactive tool of public communication was also supported by participants 1 and 10. They highlight that while proactive public diplomacy is now embedded in foreign policy institutions of Qatar, the de-securitisation of the GCC crisis has been facilitated by reactive diplomatic efforts introduced to counter anti-Qatar narratives disseminated by the blockading countries.

This was reaffirmed by participants 2, 6, 7 and 8, all highlighting the attempt from the four blockading countries to undermine Qatar's image by disseminating unsubstantiated accusations on its alleged links to international terrorism. Public diplomacy has therefore allowed the state to defend its sovereignty and interests while exposing the mistruths of its Gulf rivals. Where the blockading powers attempted to portray Qatar as the midwife of Islamic extremism, public diplomacy showed Qatar as an open, tolerant and progressive society. Therefore, as Participant 7 concludes, in the aftermath of a high-profile public diplomacy campaign, *"the world can clearly see where Qatar stands and where the four siege countries are."*

---

[52] Roselle, 'A. Strategic Narrative'.

Conclusion

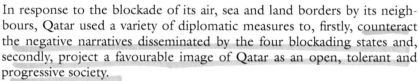

In response to the blockade of its air, sea and land borders by its neighbours, Qatar used a variety of diplomatic measures to, firstly, counteract the negative narratives disseminated by the four blockading states and, secondly, project a favourable image of Qatar as an open, tolerant and progressive society.

The qualitative research on which this chapter is based, has clearly illustrated how effective public diplomacy has been for Qatar to diffuse tensions with its Western partners, which escalated during the GCC crisis. In particular, a combination of reactive and proactive approaches to public diplomacy projected shared ideas, identities, values and interests of Qatar to the international community. This underlined considerable distinction between the narratives disseminated by the quartet and the political reality in the Gulf.

Public diplomacy is thus a great tool that made Qatar more resilient to the communication onslaught of the UAE and Saudi Arabia during and just prior to 5 June 2017. While Qatar's public diplomacy may not have reached a wider audience, it assisted in offering an alternative view of Qatar, especially to those who had long been fed with narratives from Qatar's immediate neighbours. Public diplomacy has proven to be a significant force multiplier to conventional diplomacy that can be used to build direct links between the Qatari government and Western diplomats, policymakers, journalists and other stakeholders.

Also, through public diplomacy, Qatar has been able to prevent other countries from declaring a blockade against it. Situations could have been worse for Qatar without the use of public diplomacy as a strategic communication tool. As it were, Qatar moved quickly and efficiently to secure its diplomatic links with other countries, ensuring that their lines of communication were open, and business as usual could continue for Qatar and its partners. Qatar also took advantage of the media (both traditional and social media) to clarify its position and to disseminate more accurate and useful information to the public. Under these adverse conditions, Qatar has been able to overcome its traditional inhibition to engage proactively in public diplomacy. Although there is room for improvement in Qatar's public diplomacy effort, the enduring Gulf divide has triggered the country.

CHAPTER 15

Making Sense of Europe's Response to the Gulf Crisis

Jeremias Kettner

INTRODUCTION

When we look at the reactions of major European powers toward the Gulf Crisis, it is astonishing that while Germany showed unusual strong support for Qatar, France and the United Kingdom (UK) followed a rather neutral approach.

To analyze the different responses of these three European powers to the blockade of Qatar, this chapter will look at the various factors that shape their respective policies in the Gulf region. Such a holistic approach combines both internal and external factors. The main driving forces assumed to have shaped the responses of these three European governments are first economic interests; second, security interests, both military and energy; third, domestic public opinion; fourth ideology and finally personal interests of leading politicians as well as relations between the country's leaders.

Consequently, the main question of this chapter is twofold: First, what interests informed the European states' responses to the Gulf Crisis?

J. Kettner (✉)
Free University Berlin, Berlin, Germany
e-mail: jeremias.kettner@fu-berlin.de

A. Krieg (ed.), *Divided Gulf*, Contemporary Gulf Studies,
https://doi.org/10.1007/978-981-13-6314-6_15

Second, to what extent were the Gulf states able to rely on their soft power to transform money into political influence?

This chapter will take a case by case look at German, French and UK relations with the three main protagonists of the Gulf divide: Qatar, the UAE and Saudi Arabia.

Understanding the German Response to the Gulf Crisis

Berlin's position on the crisis has been patently clear from the beginning. At the time, German Foreign Minister Sigmar Gabriel was the first Western politician to initiate shuttle diplomacy and called for the lifting of the blockade on Qatar, which he described as detrimental to efforts to combat terrorism.[1] It was also him who hosted his counterpart Qatari Foreign Minister Abdulrahman Al Thani in Germany only a few days after the crisis started. Germany called for greater diplomatic efforts to resolve the regional rift and said Arab states should lift their blockade of the small Gulf state and avoid any escalation into violence.[2] Foreign Minister Gabriel said that some of the demands put upon Qatar by the blockading states clearly challenged its sovereignty, while it would be tough for Qatar to accept all 13 items on what he described as "*a very provocative list*".[3] Berlin's reaction was backed by Chancellor Angela Merkel, who received Qatari Emir Sheikh Tamim Al Thani in Berlin in September 2017, where she stressed that although Germany is not party to this conflict, it is in line with its values to help resolve it. She urged the actors involved to identify fair compromises and said that "*no party should lose face*".[4] This approach did not even change when Saudi Arabia withdrew its Ambassador from Germany in November 2017 over

---

[1] Reuters. (2017). Germany Calls for Diplomacy to Resolve Qatar Standoff, Turns Down Mediator Role. *Deutsche Welle*, 9 June 2017.

[2] Reuters. (2017). Germany Urges Diplomatic Solution to Qatar Crisis. *Reuters*, 9 June 2017.

[3] Shalal, A. (2017). Saudi Demands from Qatar 'Very Provocative': Germany. *Reuters*, 26 June 2017.

[4] The German Federal Government. (2017). Qatar Conflict Should Be Swiftly Resolved. *Federal Government*, 15 September 2017. https://www.bundesregierung.de/Content/EN/Artikel/2017/09_en/2017-09-15-merkel-emir-katar_en.html.

critical comments by Foreign Minister Gabriel[5] and imposed a boycott on German businesses wishing to strike deals with the Saudi state.[6]

Since Berlin for a long time did not have a Middle East policy at all—except maybe positions with regards to Iran and Israel—Berlin's strong reaction on the Qatar crisis is untypical and needs further explanation. The German position on the crisis came in part as a reaction to President Trump's policies in the Gulf region.[7] In remarks to the newspaper Handelsblatt, Foreign Minister Gabriel warned of the "Trumpification" of relations between the Gulf States.[8] After displaying a more assertive stance in the JCPOA negotiations,[9] Germany's reaction to the Qatar crisis is yet another example of the country's ambition to defend and outline its own interests in the Gulf region more clearly. But what are these interests and how can they explain Germanys response on the Qatar crisis?

Looking at Qatari-German relations for the past 15 years, they were mainly shaped by economic interests.[10] Consequently some commentators argued that Berlin's reaction toward the Qatar crisis can be best explained by the 35 billion Euro Doha had invested in Germany and was feared to withdraw to stabilize its own economy.[11] In addition, Berlin was concerned that German companies could be forced by the blockading countries to choose a preferred place to do business in the GCC. Indeed, given Germany's wide-reaching economic interests in the Gulf a more reserved and neutral reaction from Berlin should have been expected in the first place. The UAE is Germany's biggest export market

[5] Reuters. (2017). Saudi Arabia Recalls Ambassador to Germany Over Gabriel Comments. *Reuters*, 9 June 2017.

[6] Nereim, V., Nair, D., Martin, M., and Carey, G. (2018). Saudi Arabia Blocks Some German Business Over Rift. *Bloomberg*, 18 March 2018.

[7] AFP. (2018). Germany Warns Gulf Crisis Exacerbates Middle East 'Powder Keg'. *Deutsche Welle*, 7 June 2017.

[8] Sigmund, T., Brüggmann, M., and Fockenbrock, D. (2017). Foreign Minister Supports Qatar, Bashes Trump. *Handelsblatt Global Edition*, 6 June 2017.

[9] Kettner, J. (2010). *Ein vergeblicher Versuch der Einbindung: deutsche Außen- und Sicherheitspolitik gegenüber dem Iran*. Berlin: Freie Universität Berlin.

[10] Kettner, J. (2017). *Deutsch-katarische Beziehungen von 1999–2014: Außenpolitik im Spannungsfeld zwischen wirtschaftlichen Interessen und politischen und gesellschaftlichen Rahmenbedingungen*. Berlin: Freie Universität Berlin (238).

[11] Brüggmann, M. (2017). The German Business Stake in Qatar. *Handelsblatt Global Edition*, 8 June 2017.

in the Middle East, with exports worth approximately 14.5 billion Euro in 2016, and imports of 0.9 billion Euro the same year.[12] Saudi Arabia comes in second with a bilateral trade volume of 7.3 billion Euro in 2016[13] and Qatar only third with a bilateral trade volume of 2.52 billion Euro in 2017.[14]

Although important, commercial interests cannot be said to be the sole explanatory factor for Germany's reaction to the crisis. This is shown by Sigmar Gabriel's comments, who primarily appealed to security interests by saying that a destabilized Gulf cannot be in anyone's interest.[15] A divided GCC would clearly run against Germany's main concern in the region—the multilateral cooperation to fight global terrorism.[16] In this regard, the GCC is seen as an island of stability in a war-torn region that had now become threatened by a crisis that Berlin could only describe as arbitrary. The existence of German security interests in the Gulf is confirmed by the bilateral defense cooperation agreements between Doha and Berlin involving arms sales and capacity building efforts that are unique for Germany's otherwise restrictive security engagement with the Gulf.[17] Although never made public, Berlin's authorization of the extensive Leopard II tank deal with Qatar must have been inspired by a belief that the chance of Qatar using these tanks either against its own people or in regional conflicts is less than with the other GCC states where Germany often sees its values being less respected than in Doha.[18]

Another factor assumed to have played a role is public opinion. In this regard the narrative of the beleaguered tiny Qatar has certainly helped German politicians to stand by Qatar with the German public for whom the blockade of West Berlin during the Cold War remains in living

---

[12] Federal German Foreign Office. (2018). *United Arab Emirates.* https://www.auswaertiges-amt.de/de/aussenpolitik/laender/vereinigtearabischeemirate-node/vereinigtearabischeemiratesicherheit/202332.

[13] Germany Trade and Invest. (2018). *Wirtschaftsdaten Kompakt Saudi Arabien.* https://www.gtai.de/GTAI/Navigation/DE/Trade/Maerkte/Wirtschaftsklima/wirtschaftsdaten-kompakt,t=wirtschaftsdaten-kompakt--saudiarabien,did=1584882.html.

[14] German Federal Foreign Office. (2018). *Beziehungen zu Deutschland.* https://www.auswaertiges-amt.de/de/aussenpolitik/laender/katar-node/-/202286.

[15] Sigmund, T. 'Foreign Minister Supports Qatar'.

[16] German Federal Government, 'Qatar Conflict Should Be Swiftly Resolved'.

[17] DPA. (2009). Deutsche Spürpanzer für die Arabischen Emirate. *Der Merkur*, 14 April 2009.

[18] Kettner, 'Deutsch-katarische Beziehungen' (pp. 100ff).

memory. In addition, Saudi Arabia and the UAE are highly criticized for their military campaign in Yemen by German NGOs and newspapers, which led to the blockade of all arm sales to countries involved in the Yemen war by the German government.[19]

The next factor has certainly been ideology. Sigmar Gabriel emphasized repeatedly that diplomacy was the only suitable instrument to solve the Qatar crisis. This strengthens the argument of a value-based German foreign policy after 1945, which is characterized by military restraint and relies on non-interventionist, multilateral conflict resolution. Thus, Germany's behavior after 5 June 2017, besides economic and security interests, can be best explained with the fact that Germany and Qatar alike are following a similar foreign policy approach which puts soft power at the core of their international relations. In addition, both states share a strong preference for peaceful conflict resolution. With Germany being a relatively new player in Middle Eastern affairs, and with no colonial past, its reaction can be seen as a natural extension of the country's increasing bilateral relations with Qatar since 1999. Doha presented itself as a more flexible partner and alternative to the regional heavy weight Saudi Arabia, which is constrained by the fact that it is a conservative theocracy. The UAE might be an important partner as well, but it follows a regional policy approach which stands at odds with the German one. Doha simply corresponded better with Germany's preferred role as a mediator and broker in the past. From a value-based approach, Qatar's support for change during the Arab Spring aligned closer with Berlin than the narrative of authoritarian stability propagated by Saudi Arabia and the UAE. Qatar's more liberal-leaning foreign policy approach has helped Berlin taking a more supportive stance toward Qatar even at the expense of Saudi Arabia and the UAE as equally important partners.

A final factor might have been the personal interests of Gabriel, Germany's Foreign Minister. The Qatar crisis offered him a chance to portray himself as a leading European politician with strong foreign policy credentials by further differentiating Germany's policy toward the region from the US approach. Consequently, Berlin's unusually strong reaction can be traced back, to a certain extent, to his personal political interests prior to an upcoming federal election in 2017 where he intended to position himself as a leader of Germany's labor party SPD.

[19] DPA. (2018). Saudi Arabia Minister Tells Germany It Will Find Weapons Elsewhere. *Deutsche Welle*, 23 February 2018.

Falling victim to an internal party power reshuffle, Gabriel's political calculus did not seem to materialize. Nonetheless, the Merkel administration has remained Qatar's most important ally in Europe—all that, when Germany's soft power-led foreign policy could do little to coerce the blockading countries to come to the negotiation table.

UNDERSTANDING THE FRENCH RESPONSE TO THE GULF CRISIS

In comparison to Germany, France reacted slightly later and followed a more neutral approach in the Gulf divide. On 15 and 16 July 2017 French Foreign Minister Jean-Yves Le Drian visited Qatar, Saudi Arabia, Kuwait and the UAE in an effort to ease tensions in the region.[20] On September 5, 2017 France appointed a special envoy Bertrand Besancenot.[21] France positioned itself as a major player to resolve the conflict with newly elected French president Emanuel Macron being personally involved in the mediation efforts.[22] Recognizing the threats that this crisis posed to France's interests, not only did Macron fly to Morocco to discuss future diplomatic proceedings over the Qatar crisis, but he urged GCC officials multiple times to reconcile their differences within the crisis' first 48 hours.[23] On September 15, 2017 he met the Emir of Qatar in Paris, where he called for the blockade *"to be lifted as quickly as possible"*. He also expressed *"his concern over the tensions that threaten regional stability, undermining the political resolution of crises and our collective fight against terrorism."*[24] The following November Macron visited the UAE and Saudi Arabia to meet with Saudi Crown Prince Mohammed Bin Salman and the leadership of the UAE to discuss the strengthening of economic cooperation as well as the military

[20] AFP. (2018). France Wants to Help Mediate Gulf Crisis, Foreign Minister Says. *France 24*, 16 July 2018.

[21] M'tiri, H. (2017). France Appoints Envoy to Mediate in Gulf Crisis. *The Peninsula*, 5 September 2017.

[22] Salacanin, S. (2017). *Europe and the Gulf Crisis*. Doha: Al Jazeera Center for Studies, 4 September 2017.

[23] AFP. (2017). Macron in Morocco to Discuss Libya, Qatar Crisis. *Daily Mail*, 14 June 2017.

[24] The New Arab. (2017). French President Macron Urges Lifting of Qatar Blockade. *The New Arab*, 15 September 2017.

conflict in Yemen and the Qatar crisis.[25] In December Macron was received by Qatar's Emir in Doha where he visited French soldiers at Al Udeid airbase and signed deals worth 12 billion Euro.[26] France quickly became the most active European power in the Gulf crisis and President Macron visibly tried to take a lead.

Applying the main motivating factors on the reaction of France to the Qatar crisis it becomes obvious that economic interests played a major role. Given how much French-Qatari trade and defense cooperation has increased in recent years, Paris, not surprisingly, maintained a "neutral" position in the crisis that recognized the need for a dialogue between the two sides. With its increased investment in the Middle East, France stands to lose much from any deepening of this feud. Like in Germany and the UK, Qatar is a major foreign investor in France holding over 30 billion Euro in investments. Although the French government has signed financial and tax agreements with other Gulf states, its deals with Doha are especially favorable to Qatari investments in France.[27] In addition, there are strong relations in the field of energy with the French company Total first setting up operations in Qatar in 1938 and is operating in most areas of production, on the key liquid natural gas (LNG) projects and in the country's petrochemical activities.[28] Yet, France also maintains strategic economic relations with the blockading states. Especially the defense sector is crucial for the French president's promise to secure jobs at home and reform the French industrial sector. France's biggest defense firms have major contracts in the Gulf. In 2016, licenses potentially worth 45 billion Euro to the UAE and Saudi Arabia were approved with deliveries worth about 2 billion Euro.[29] Paris has already reached military deals worth around 20 billion Euro with Saudi Arabia alone.[30]

[25] Al Arabiya English. (2017). Macron Arrives in Saudi Arabia, Meets Crown Prince Mohammed Bin Salman. *Al Arabiya*, 9 November 2017.

[26] Reuters. (2017). Macron Secures €12 Billion in Deals on Qatar Visit. *France 24*, 7 December 2017.

[27] Tertrais, B. and Gadel, A. (2018). Qatar Remains an Important French Partner in the Gulf, but It's Not the Only One. *World Politics Review*, 16 January 2018.

[28] Boniface, P. and Mattellys, S. (2016). *France and Qatar: Mutual Economic Benefits*. Paris: Institut de Relations Internationales et Stratégiques: IRIS, March 2016 (44).

[29] Irish, J. and Louet, S. (2018). Pressure Mounts on Macron Over Arms Sales to Saudi Arabia, UAE. *Reuters*, 19 June 2018.

[30] Press TV. (2018). France, Saudi Arabia Sign Multiple Contracts Worth $18bn. *Press TV*, 10 April 2018.

At the same time France has secured a major contract with Doha in 2015 for the purchase of 24 Rafale fighter aircraft, and the activation of the option for 12 additional fighters in December 2017.

These economic considerations are closely tied to French security interests in the Gulf region. Unlike Germany, France follows an active foreign policy in the region and is militarily involved, be it in Mali, Libya, Syria or Yemen, where contributions of the Gulf states became crucial for France's success.[31] Given how the crisis is undermining international efforts to combat violent jihadist forces such as ISIS, which have inspired or conducted deadly terrorist attacks throughout France in recent years, the security dimension is one Macron cannot ignore. In the fight against terrorism and its financing a far-reaching Memorandum of Understanding (MoU) has been signed by Qatar and France providing Paris with unprecedentedly intimate access to the emirate's finances.[32] Qatar's potential to serve as a diplomatic bridge between various state and non-state actors across the polarized Middle East is another reason why France has much to gain from Doha and its fellow GCC capitals restoring relations. However, Macron needs to carefully navigate the ongoing crisis in the GCC as France has cultivated close defense relations with countries on both sides of the rift. France has a military presence in the UAE with 700 French soldiers since 2009,[33] while Riyadh and Abu Dhabi have done a lot to boost the country's defense exports since the Saudi-led coalition entered Yemen in 2015 where France has assumed an assisting role to the coalition. Therefore, reinstating calm in the region not only benefits the collective effort to combat terrorism but also sustains the various defense alliances France has in the region.[34]

Public opinion seems to have played a minor role for Frances response on the crisis. Although the Saudi-led campaign in Yemen receives extensive negative coverage—a recent YouGov poll found that seventy-five percent of French people want Macron to suspend arms exports to Saudi

---

[31] Libya Tribune. (2017). Sahel Force: France Obtains Saudi and UAE Support. *Libya Tribune*, 17 December 2017.

[32] Ministry for Europe and Foreign Affairs. (2017). *France and Qatar*. https://www.diplomatie.gouv.fr/en/country-files/qatar/.

[33] Chrisafis, A. (2009). France Opens Military Base in UAE Despite Iranian Concerns. *The Guardian*, 26 May 2009.

[34] Cafiero, G. and Miao, E. (2017). Macron and the Qatar Crisis. *Lob Log*, 17 July 2017.

Arabia and the UAE[35]—the GCC Crisis is a matter of minor public concern. The Gulf has often been simplistically portrayed in France as an ultraconservative, non-liberal and theocratic part of the Middle East with links to local French extremist groups. Consequently, public sympathies to the Gulf remain limited.

Another assumed factor is ideology. French laicism corresponds well with the UAEs anti-Islamic narrative. As Krieg, Ulrichsen and Davidson highlight, the UAE sees all sorts of political Islam as a deep threat to its stability and has exported this narrative to France becoming an important partner of France in the fight against Islamic extremism. Toward Saudi Arabia France holds ideological reservations as the kingdom's raison d'état has long been contradicting French liberalism. Saudi new Crown Prince MbS has so far tried unsuccessfully to woo Macron and convince the new administration in Paris that the kingdom is fundamentally reforming.[36]

Finally, personal interests of leading politicians seemed to have played a role in the French response as well. Close French-Qatari relations in almost every field are based on personal relationships, especially between the former French president Nicolas Sarkozy and the Father Emir Hamad Al Thani.[37] Many leading Qataris with the current Emir on top are francophone and Qatar joined the International Organization of La Francophonie in 2012 as an associate member—the only country in the region to be granted such status.[38] However, President Macron recently improved relations with his counterparts in Riyadh and Abu Dhabi and some think that while Macron has avoided antagonizing both sides in this crisis, he has built a deepening relationship with the country he feels more in tune with: the UAE.[39]

To summarize, it can be said, that France, unlike Germany, has the means—strong energy and military relations—to actively influence its

[35] Reuters. (2018). Poll Shows Most French Oppose Arms Sales to Saudi-Led Yemen Coalition. *Reuters*, 26 March 2018.

[36] Winter, C. (2018). In France, Saudi Crown Prince Seeks to Woo Macron Despite Differences on Iran and Yemen. *Deutsche Welle*, 7 April 2018.

[37] The National. (2009). The Ties That Bind Doha and Paris. *The National*, 18 September 2009.

[38] Ministry for Europe and Foreign Affairs, 'France and Qatar'.

[39] Al Jazeera. (2017). Is France Reinventing Itself as a Kingmaker in the Middle East? *Al Jazeera*, 17 April 2018.

Gulf partners. Yet, on the other hand, France has interests and values it shares with both sides of the Gulf divide equally and cannot afford providing one partner with a more preferential treatment than the other.

Understanding the British Response to the Gulf Crisis

The UK's approach has been different to that of the German and French, as the UK has traditionally been more aligned with US foreign policy. Former Foreign Secretary Boris Johnson flew to Qatar and Kuwait, where he made clear that the UK supports the Kuwaiti efforts to mediate the crisis.[40] After meeting his Qatari counterpart in London, he called on Qatar to do more to clamp down on the funding of extremist groups but also urged Saudi Arabia and other Gulf states to ease their blockade of Qatar.[41] In the middle of July 2017, the UK and the US reportedly proposed a road map to help resolve the standoff between a Saudi-led alliance and Qatar during former Secretary of State Rex Tillerson's trip to the region.[42] The UK's response was the most passive of all three European states analyzed and was even quickly watered down, despite its position as the top importer of Qatari LNG in Europe.[43] However, amid the Brexit negotiations weighing heavy on UK resources, capacity and domestic politics, Britain's response to the crisis has been vague at best.

Britain's relative inaction does not stem from its lack of influence alone. London is wary of antagonizing Saudi Arabia and the UAE, two key British allies spearheading the campaign to isolate Qatar. But the crisis has also shed light on the fact that, however much it invests in its military presence and trade ties, the UK is unlikely to be able to play a

---

[40] Peck, T. (2017). Boris Johnson Flies into Qatar to Discuss Gulf Crisis. *The Independent*, 8 July 2017.

[41] Wintour, P. (2017). Gulf Crisis: Boris Johnson Urges Qatar to Crack Down on Extremists. *The Guardian*, 12 June 2017.

[42] Salacanin, S. (2017). *Europe and the Gulf Crisis*. Doha: Al Jazeera Center for Studies, 4 September 2017.

[43] Vaughan, A. (2017). Qatar Crisis Highlights Rising UK Energy Reliance on Imports. *The Guardian*, 8 June 2017.

significant role in shaping regional developments without the support of Washington.[44]

Again, economic interests played a major role in Britain's response to the crisis. With trade between the UK and the GCC worth more than $40 billion annually, in addition to billions of dollars that various Gulf sovereign wealth funds have invested across the UK, the Qatar crisis came as a political earthquake to London. Facing the threat of a hard Brexit the Gulf rift could not have come at a more inconvenient moment for Britain.[45] Prime Minister Theresa May singled out Qatar as an important trading partner for the UK in the post-Brexit world. A memorandum of understanding recently signed aims to deepen the cooperation between governments and businesses "across a wide range of vital areas". In return, Qatar pledged to invest an extra 5 billion pounds in the UK, on top of the more than 35–40 billion pounds already invested by vehicles such as the Qatar Investment Authority.[46] The British Ambassador to Qatar said in a recent newspaper interview that *"the UK has big ambitions with Qatar and they are continuing, and they have not changed because of this (regional) dispute."*[47] What stands out in UK–Qatari relations is the cooperation in the energy sector. Although gas imports have fallen in recent years—Qatar gas deliveries amounted to 40% of all the UK's imported gas in 2011—Qatar remains the UK's second largest supplier of gas, after Norway.[48] But the blockading states are not any less important to the UK economy. The British government has mapped out investment opportunities in GCC countries across 15 sectors, estimated at a total of 29 billion pounds over the next five years.[49] Like Qatar, Saudi Arabia is a major investor in the UK, owning an estimated £80–90 billion worth of assets and £20 billion worth of government bonds.[50] Both countries

[44] Vagneur-Jones, A. (2017). *Global Britain in the Gulf: Brexit and Relations with the GCC.* Paris: Fondation pour la recherche stratégique (p. 3).

[45] Akkad, D. (2017). Gulf Crisis: A Political Earthquake with Aftershocks in Britain. *Middle East Eye*, 30 June 2017.

[46] Moshinsky, U. (2017). The Crisis in Qatar Has Come at a Terrible Time for the UK. *Business Insider*, 12 June 2018.

[47] Saleem, F. (2018). Qatar–UK Relations Stronger Despite Siege: British Envoy. *The Peninsula*, 11 April 2018.

[48] Vagneur-Jones, 'Global Britain in the Gulf' (p. 4).

[49] Ibid. (p. 3).

[50] Royal Embassy of Saudi Arabia. (2018). *Relations with the United Kingdom.* https://saudiembassyuk.co.uk/uk-saudi-relations/.

recently confirmed and reinforced their relationship by committing to develop a deeper and more strategic partnership to enhance mutual interests. Crown Prince MbS and Prime Minister Theresa May launched an annual "UK–Saudi Strategic Partnership Council" in March 2018 as a key mechanism for discussing and developing all aspects of the bilateral relationship, including UK support for Saudi Arabia's "Vision 2030". Taken together, these opportunities are expected to amount up to 100 billion US-Dollar over a 10-year period.[51] Not less important for British commercial interests is the UAE with the country being the UK's largest export market in the Middle East and the 13th biggest globally today. UK exports to the Emirates amounted to £9.8 billions of goods and services in 2016. This was a 37% increase since 2009.[52]

The outlined trade and investment figures can explain why the years since 2012 have seen an uptick in strategic and commercial agreements with GCC states. Brexit's economic cost, as well as the UK's reduced global influence outside the EU, have augmented the perceived importance of relations with the Gulf. For some analysts, the UK's return "East of Suez" may even be seen as a means of maintaining a degree of geopolitical relevance, as the British government strives to convince America of its ability to take the initiative in forging deep alliances with states in a region of strategic importance.[53]

From the point of view of security, Britain has been deeply concerned with the Gulf divide. Britain is heavily invested militarily in the Middle East and its defense industry plays an equally important role as it does for France. In December 2017 the UK signed a statement of intent with Qatar to supply 24 Typhoon jets and a package of missile and laser-guided bombs, worth a total of £6 billion.[54] In 2016 both countries signed

---

[51] Commonwealth Office. (2018). *United Kingdom-Saudi Arabia Joint Communiqué.* https://www.gov.uk/government/news/united-kingdom-saudi-arabia-joint-communique.

[52] Department for International Trade. (2018). *Doing Business in the United Arab Emirates: UAE Trade and Export Guide.* https://www.gov.uk/government/publications/exporting-to-the-united-arab-emirates/exporting-to-the-united-arab-emirates.

[53] Vagneur-Jones, 'Global Britain in the Gulf' (p. 3).

[54] House of Commons Library. (2018: 4). UK Relations with Qatar. *Parliament.uk,* 21 May 2018.

a bilateral defense agreement[55] and in July 2018 a UK–Qatari Joint Typhoon Squadron was set-up making Qatar the only nation with which the UK has such intimate military relations outside of NATO.[56] At the same time the UK signed a Military and Security Cooperation Agreement with Saudi Arabia last year.[57] Britain's biggest arms manufacturer, BAE Systems, has moved toward completing an order worth billions of pounds from Saudi Arabia for the purchase of 48 Typhoon fighter jets. Since the air campaign against Yemen began in 2015, the UK has authorized the sale of arms worth 4.6 billion pounds to the kingdom.[58] In the UAE, the UK opened a military installation in 2009 to be used by British forces. Having deployed more than 1500 military personnel and seven warships in the Gulf, the UK's regional presence is second only to that of the United States.[59] This shows how important the UK considers the stability of the Gulf region, where it does not only pursuits energy and economic interests, but foremost security interests, which are closely connected to its commercial interests. Like for Berlin and Paris, on top of its security agenda stands the fight against global terrorism and radical extremism, where all Gulf states are equally important partners for London.[60]

A third factor, which is believed to have influenced Britain's response to the Qatar crisis is public opinion. In the case of the UK, however, public opinion did not help any of the conflicting parties in order to shape Britain's response. The questionable human rights records of several GCC states has attracted extensive media coverage but has rarely impacted UK policymaking in the past. The UK's close relationship with Saudi Arabia has drawn much flak in this regard: opposition groups and NGOs have decried Whitehall's tolerance of the House of Saud's authoritarian rule and bloody intervention in Yemen in which the UAE is also a key actor. Successive Prime Ministers, including Tony Blair, David

---

[55] QNA. (2016). Qatar and UK Sign Defense Cooperation Agreement. *The Peninsula*, 25 March 2016.

[56] Ministry of Defense and Williamson, G. (2018). Joint UK-Qatari Typhoon Squadron Stands Up as Defense Relationship Deepens. *Gov.uk*, 24 July 2018.

[57] Ministry of Defence and Fallon, M. (2017). New Agreement Strengthens UK-Saudi Arabia Defence Relationship. *Gov.uk*, 19 September 2017.

[58] MacAskill, E. (2018). UK Moves Closer to Signing Typhoon Jet Deal with Saudis. *The Guardian*, 9 March 2018.

[59] Vagneur-Jones, 'Global Britain in the Gulf' (p. 5).

[60] Al-Otaibi, N. (2018). *Terror Overseas*. London: The Henry Jackson Society.

Cameron and Theresa May, have downplayed Saudi human rights violations, drawing attention to the kingdom's role in fighting terrorism. Another example is concerns regarding the funding of jihadist organizations likely to hinder the UK's Gulf-oriented rapprochement. The government has notably been criticized for failing to publish a report, which aimed to investigate the funding of extremist Islamist organizations in the UK most likely driven by fears that the report would have a negative effect on relations with Saudi Arabia. Mrs. May's government has not indicated that it would address concerns linked to donations to Islamist organizations. As is the case with human rights, the Prime Minister will follow her predecessors' lead; the disquiet expressed concerning Gulf States' jihadist ties will remain unheeded.[61]

Ideology seems to play less of an important role in a post-Brexit Britain where economic interests outside of the Europe are of crucial importance. As Doyle highlights *"British Middle East policy has never been consistent or even ethical. And that is almost certainly an unrealistic goal, but it should aspire to narrow the gap between perceived interests and its proclaimed values."*[62] A less value-based approach by London means that while concerns over looming authoritarianism in Riyadh and Abu Dhabi might be addressed, interests will most likely take precedence in dealing with the Gulf pragmatically.

The personal dimension is probably the most pronounced in the case of the UK. As a recent report by the UK-based NGO *Spinwatch* has revealed, there have been close relations between former Prime Ministers Tony Blair and David Camron and the UAE's Crown Prince Mohammed Bin Zayed.[63] The UAE actively tried to exploit these relationships in order to convince Britain to take a harsher stance toward the Muslim Brotherhood and Qatar, while tying these requests to lucrative economic and military deals—deals the Cameron government was particularly interested in.[64] On the other hand, many royals from the Gulf monarchies maintain close relations with Britain, its military and

---

[61] Vagneur-Jones, 'Global Britain in the Gulf' (p. 5).

[62] Doyle, C. (2017). Neither Consistent Nor Ethical: Britain's Middle East Policy. *The New Arab*, 6 June 2017.

[63] Delmar-Morgan, A. and Miller, D. (2018) *The UAE Lobby: Subverting British Democracy?* London: Spinnwatch (pp. 15, 41).

[64] Donaghy, R. (2015). Muslim Brotherhood Review: A Tale of UK-UAE Relations. *Middle East Eye*, 17 December 2015.

diplomatic institutions as well as its royal family. Qatar's Emir went to military college in the UK as did the UAE's Crown Prince MbZ.[65]

CONCLUSION

In addressing the Gulf Crisis, Germany's stance has been the most proactive and surprising in comparison to France's and the UK's response. In contrast to its European partners, Germany has no colonial history in the MENA region allowing the Federal Republic to act as a more neutral and credible mediator. In addition, Germany, unlike France and the UK, does not maintain strong energy relations with GCC member states nor does it maintain military bases in the region. In a way, this made it easier to adopt a stance which clearly spoke against the blockade. What has often been seen as a shortcoming in Germany's ambition to deepen its ties in the Gulf, has helped Berlin to take a determined stance on the Gulf divide. Maybe the most influential factor motivating Germany's rather partial response has been a deeply anchored, value-based foreign policy personally advanced by the former Foreign Minister Gabriel. While Germany lacks hard power means to influence any of the conflicting parties, the German mediation efforts can be seen as a natural extension of strong relations with Qatar, which are not only based on shared economic and security interests, but also on a common understanding of a multilateral rules-based international order.

The French response was more neutral than the German one because France maintains close commercial and defense ties with all the conflicting states. Having traditionally good relations with Doha, in recent years, Paris deepened its relations with Saudi Arabia and the UAE. For the inexperienced French President Macron, the Gulf divide was another possibility to stress the French role in the Middle East as an alternative to the United States. That is why he was personally engaged in the mediation efforts and took over the European lead from Germany after Berlin became bogged down in a post-electoral stalemate. The UK's response was the weakest of the three analyzed European countries and followed in large parts the United States. As showed, this has mainly been due to economic Brexit uncertainties. London is careful not to antagonize any of the conflicting states which are all potentially important partners for Britain.

---

[65] Popham, P. (2013). Sheikh Tamim bin Hamad al-Thani: The Emir from Sandhurst Who's Been Given the Keys to the Kingdom. *The Independent*, 25 June 2013.

CHAPTER 16

Conclusion

Andreas Krieg

In its second year the most recent Gulf crisis appears to consolidate the Gulf Divide in crasser ways than any previous Gulf feud has. Few had anticipated in June 2017 that the diplomatic rift and the subsequent blockade would last for more than twelve months without any sign of resolution. Today, the two fronts appear to be as eager as they have been in the summer of 2017 to defend their positions—Qatar doing so, knowing that any concession on its sovereignty might transform the emirate into a vassal state. Despite the huge costs the crisis has imposed on both sides, Doha and its neighbours seem to have come to terms with what appears to be the new reality in the Gulf. As Wright explains, Qatar's LNG economy has proven to be highly resilient and immune to the economic blockade, leaving the emirate's centre of gravity widely unaffected. Consequently, the urgency for Qatar to overcome the blockade appears to be gradually waning. The new status quo has been consolidated as amid an ongoing, polarizing war over narratives, the blockaders and the blockaded are preparing for a future apart rather than together. The threshold of what constitutes a 'solution' to the crisis is fairly low. While the quartet does not see any reasons to make concessions to Doha, the Qataris might settle for a relaxation of overflight restrictions for

A. Krieg (✉)
Defence Studies Department, King's College London, London, UK
e-mail: andreas.krieg@kcl.ac.uk

© The Author(s) 2019
A. Krieg (ed.), *Divided Gulf*, Contemporary Gulf Studies,
https://doi.org/10.1007/978-981-13-6314-6_16

Qatar Airways, a liberalization of the freedom of movement for families and an unrestricted access for Qatari citizens to the annual *Hajj*. But a return to a pre-crisis status quo appears to be inconceivable.

Qatar's Foreign Minister told me in a conversation that "*From now on Qatar will be an island*"[1] while Saudi Arabia's Crown Prince referred to the Gulf crisis as a "*very, very, very small issue*" purposefully understating the importance of the 'Qatar Question' for the kingdom.[2] It seems that diplomatically both sides have reached a saturation point whereby little can be done to escalate further without resorting to military force—an option that at this point nobody wants to take as commentators and policymakers worldwide have impressed on both sides that "*enough is enough*."[3]

Meanwhile, there appears to be consensus among regional experts that regardless of the ineffectiveness and naivety of Qatar's foreign and security policy during the Arab Spring, "*the continuing blockade of Qatar makes no sense*".[4] With Qatar increasingly being perceived as the victim of a senseless and often silly communication campaign, some have gone so far as to state that "*Qatar has not only weathered the storm—it also appears to have emerged as the main winner of the conflict*".[5] As Al-Muftah writes, Qatar's public diplomacy effort has been successful in positively shaping Western public opinion amid a media war trying to ostracize the emirate internationally. Yet, winning a multi-million-dollar charm offensive might count for little when the Gulf crisis remains in a stalemate that can be more adequately defined as mutually hurting rather than mutually beneficial.

Because, on the diplomatic surface no breakthrough has so far been achieved as despite Kuwaiti and since April 2018 Omani mediation, the blockading countries have still not accepted Qatar's willingness to enter

[1] Editors conversation with H.E. Sheikh Mohammad bin Abdulrahman al Thani, Foreign Minister of the State of Qatar, in London 6 October 2017.

[2] AlKhshali, H. and Qiblawi, T. (2017). Saudi Crown Prince Calls Qatar Embargo a 'Small Issue'. *CNN*, 26 October 2017. https://edition.cnn.com/2017/10/26/middleeast/saudi-crown-prince-qatar/index.html.

[3] Harris, G. (2018). Pompeo's Message to Saudis? Enough Is Enough: Stop Qatar Blockade. *The New York Times*, 28 April 2018.

[4] FT. (2018). The Continuing Blockade of Qatar Makes No Sense. *Financial Times*, 19 April 2018.

[5] Hassan, H. (2018). Qatar Won the Saudi Blockade. *Foreign Policy*, 4 June 2018.

into dialogue. The vague demands and principles presented to the media by the UAE, Saudi Arabia, Bahrain and Egypt in June 2017, left Qatar with few options to respond. Nonetheless, Qatar's Emir publicly reached out to his neighbours to discuss some of their grievances reasserting, however, that

> Our sovereignty is a red line…They want a regime change, this is obvious. I want this to end. But nothing is above our sovereignty or our dignity. If they are willing to walk one meter towards me I am willing to walk 10,000 miles towards them.[6]

Likewise, international partners widely agree that Qatar has fulfilled its international obligations in regard to countering terror finance. Even President Trump who had been embroiled with the blockading countries' strategic narratives tarnishing Qatar's reputation in early 2017, has made a rhetorical U-turn certifying that Qatar is and has been an important partner for the United States in the fight against terror.[7] The joint strategic dialogue between Washington and Doha thereby nicely complemented the bilateral Memorandum of Understanding (MoU) on countering terror finance, which provided the United States with unprecedented access to Qatar's finances and accounts.[8]

Yet, as the course of the crisis has shown so far, the rift between Qatar and its neighbours runs deeper than diverging interests or personal differences. As the book tried to show the divide that runs through the Gulf is also based on fundamental differences in ideology and worldview, which do not merely draw the Arab Gulf monarchies apart but have created a fault line that divides the region. The conflict over worldviews at the heart of the Gulf Divide has played out on a media battlefield that in the era of 'alternative facts' and 'fake news' has spiralled out of control providing individual influencers, media outlets and policymakers on both sides of the rift with a *carte blanche* to attack the other side in an unprecedentedly intimate and aggressive fashion.

---

[6] CBS. (2017). Qatar's Emir Stands Defiant in Face of Blockade. *60 Minutes*, 29 October 2017. https://www.cbsnews.com/news/qatars-emir-stands-defiant-in-face-of-blockade/.

[7] Reuters. (2018). Trump Thanks Qatar for Efforts to Combat Terrorism. *Reuters*, 15 January 2018.

[8] United States and Qatar Sign Memorandum of Understanding Regarding Terrorism Financing. (2017). *American Journal of International Law*, 111:4 (pp. 1023–1027).

What has started as a disagreement over the role of the Muslim Brotherhood in the Arab world has expanded to a fundamental discussion over political Islam in Arab civil society—a matter highly securitized particularly in the United Arab Emirates as Davidson writes. Qatar's more lenient position towards Islamism both at home and abroad as an integral part of Arab political landscape has been perceived in Abu Dhabi as an existential threat to national security. The securitization of Islamism as a 'terrorist' threat has been promoted by the UAE in the United States and beyond since 2014. Thereby, the offensive use of narratives had targeted neo-conservative circles in Washington with the aim of ostracizing Qatar not just regionally but internationally— something that seemed possible with Trump being elected president in 2016 as Cafiero claims. However, Qatar's heavy investment into the neo-con nexus in Washington following the blockade in 2017 saw much of the UAE's efforts made undone. Qatar has been widely able to convey their version of the story to what had been a highly one-sided discourse. The mobilization of Qatar's soft power in the West has demonstrated to the emirate how important strategic communication has become in an era where subjective perception of reality often replaces objectivity. Kettner's analysis of Qatar's employment of soft power tools in Europe to counter the campaign by the blockading states shows that Doha could tap into an existing pool of resilient relationships to protect its image—something Al-Muftah reiterates in his analysis of Qatar's public diplomacy effort.

The significance of this war over ideologies and narratives cannot be overstated as the ideological rift that comes with it does not only affect the Gulf locally but transpires to the rest of the Arab world. As Ulrichsen explains, the shift of the regional centre of gravity from North Africa and the Levant to the shores of the Persian Gulf has provided the Arab monarchies with extensive reach to export their worldviews to those countries still struggling with the aftermath of the Arab Spring. The disintegration of the old order under the weight of a more empowered Arab public, which has been embraced by Qatar as an opportunity for change, has been securitized in Abu Dhabi and Riyadh as a fundamental threat to regime security. The divide over how to deal with a more emancipated civil society amid the negation of the myth of authoritarian stability during the revolutions and protests of 2010 and 2011, has torn apart a socially, politically, economically and culturally homogenous region. State-imposed nationalism, as Al-Hashemi writes, has politicized those tribal bonds that once constituted the foundation of regional cohesion.

The narcissism of minor differences might have invented national *lieux de memoires*, but at the expense of Gulf cohesion. In particular, Quilliam writes, the transition of power in Riyadh and the accompanying uncertainty it brought with it, has triggered an overly ambitious and impulsive crown prince to play the card of nationalism to not only legitimize his own reign but also to demarcate the Saudi sphere from the Qatari sphere. The rise of MbS as a narcissistic leader amid a context of uncertainty and instability in Saudi Arabia has contributed to the polarization and politicization of the minor differences in the Gulf. Thereby, the exploitation of the transnational tribal networks that had once tied the people of the Gulf together, according to Al-Kuwari, has not only failed to turn Qataris against their emir, but also has undermined the very foundation on which socio-political legitimacy rests in the Gulf. The tribal dimension of this Gulf rift must not be under estimated, particularly in the context of state failure, struggling rentierism and growing socio-political tensions between the ruler and ruled since the Arab Spring.

The ripple effects of this ideological spat over the future direction of the Arab world have first been felt in Libya where the two most prominent rivals, Qatar and the UAE, first clashed in the summer of 2011. As El Gomati explains, the surrogate war against Gadhafi saw both Doha and Abu Dhabi support two opposing sites in the emerging civil war: Qatar more closely aligning with Islamist revolutionaries and the UAE supporting the counterrevolutionary forces under the command of Hafter. The polarized clash over narratives that has defined the Gulf Divide in recent years could be witnessed already in Libya in 2014 with the same patrons empowering two opposing camps and narratives on the ground.

As a consequence of the Gulf becoming a source of regional polarization, the one organization that had long kept the façade of regional integration and unity has meanwhile suffered irreparably from the Gulf Divide. The Gulf Cooperation Council, arguably long been reduced to a mere 'talking shop', has suffered its final blow as the blockading countries chose to bypass the various mechanisms of conflict resolution that its charter provides. Baabood sees the group of six moving further apart as the smaller states are developing ties outside the region while Saudi

Arabia and the UAE have announced their own bilateral alliance.[9] The GCC might ultimately suffer the same fate as the Arab League where meaningless summits and generic speeches do little to address the many regional challenges. Consequently, future regional integration might exceed the boundaries of the Persian Gulf and tie in partners that do not share heritage, language or geographic bonds but common ideologies and interests. The plea by Qatar's Emir during the 2018 Munich Security Conference for a new rules-based regional order[10] stands representatively for the GCC's small states' desire for meaningful regional integration across the Middle East and North Africa where the rights of members could be universal and indivisible. Both Oman and Kuwait have been confronted with an aggressive *realpolitik* of Saudi Arabia and the UAE, which does not seem to be constrained by international law, norms and conventions—an observation that has been the reason for extensive discomfort in Kuwait City and Muscat.[11] For both, the potential fall of Qatar under Saudi and Emirati pressure would have jeopardized their own sovereign standing in the region.

In absence of a credible collective security umbrella, the two economically and geopolitically weaker small states of the GCC fear that they might be subjected to more extensive external meddling by Riyadh and Abu Dhabi. Pressured to abandon their traditional role as neutral mediators, Kuwaitis and Omanis feel that they must choose sides in this spat: whereas opting for the 'quartet' might equal a surrender of their independent foreign policy approach, opting for Qatar means beings exposed to more coercive pressure from the kingdom and the UAE. Thereby, Oman has witnessed an increased involvement of Abu Dhabi in the sultanate's unresolved question of succession allegedly trying to court potential successors and bribing tribesmen for allegiances.[12] In Kuwait, Saudi pressure is more acute as the kingdom has tried to fiddle with the

[9] Krieg, A. (2017). The Saudi-Emirati Axis: United Against Gulf Unity. *Middle East Eye*, 7 December 2017.

[10] The Peninsula. (2018). Speech of Qatar Emir at Munich Security Conference. *The Peninsula*, 16 February 2018.

[11] Cafiero, G. and Karasik, T. (2017). Kuwait, Oman and the Qatar Crisis. *The Middle East Institute*, 22 June 2017. http://www.mei.edu/content/article/kuwait-oman-and-qatar-crisis.

[12] Editor's interview with Omani military officer at the UK Defence Academy, Shrivenham, 24 May 2018.

delicate political balance of power internally, interfering with its leadership succession process and courting parliamentarians.[13]

Amid the bullying from both Riyadh and Abu Dhabi, Kuwait, Qatar and Oman have strengthened their extra-regional links outside of the GCC. Most importantly, Turkey and Iran have been able to capitalize on the Gulf Divide. Bakir writes that Turkey has realized that its military support for Doha amid the absence of a functioning regional security mechanism has helped confirming Turkey's role as a regional player and protector. Erdogan's ambitions in the Gulf are a sensitive balancing act between geo-strategic and economic interests that might have brought the country closer to Kuwait and Qatar but jeopardized the more lucrative economic ties with the United Arab Emirates. According to Boussois, Iran's rapprochement with Qatar has not exceeded the commercial and economic dimensions of their pre-existing relationship. Although Iran's immediate response to Qatar's plea for help in the early days of the blockade was far from altruistic, Doha and Tehran are still on two opposing ends on many of the regional conflicts—in terms of foreign and security policy Qatar and the Islamic Republic have not seen any coordination. Nonetheless, the effects of Saudi's securitization of Iran are wearing off in Kuwait, Qatar and Oman where despite ideological differences, Iran appears as a more reliable partner than the 'big brother' in Riyadh.

Looking towards the future, it is hard to ascertain how long the crisis will continue. What is important to understand, however, is that the latest crisis is just the most recent climax in a much longer lasting clash of interests, personalities, ideologies and narratives in the Gulf. The Gulf Divide will endure regardless of whether Kuwaiti or Omani mediation will ultimately generate a negotiated settlement between the main protagonists. The fact that the UAE have so far declined an invitation by the Trump administration to engage in dialogue with Qatar shows that the battle lines are drawn in the Gulf. Every day that brings further accusations and defamations by one side against the other, widens the gap between both sides of the divide. The geo-strategic reality of the Gulf has changed during the recent crisis in such a way that it will take generations to heal. As Ulrichsen writes

---

[13]Schanzer, J. and Koduvayur, V. (2018). Kuwait and Oman Are Stuck in Arab No Man's Land. *Foreign Policy*, 14 June 2018.

> As with the Iraqi invasion and occupation of Kuwait in 1990, the blockade of Qatar is an era-rupturing event that will reverberate through the regional politics and international relations of the Gulf for years to come.[14]

What distinguishes the 2017 Crisis from previous crises is the fact that it is no longer just a clash between the personalities of monarchs but a rift that has torn the social fabric of the region. As a journalist wrote during the beginning of the crisis in an op-ed, the idea of '*khaliji*' identity had died after years of negative integration and the top-down accentuation of minor differences in the attempt to invent local nationalisms[15]—something Al-Kuwari echoes in her chapter. People and communities now are confronted with an inevitable choice under pressure of draconian fines in Bahrain, Saudi Arabia and UAE, whether they stand with their cousins or the policy of their respective monarch.[16] In Qatar, the blockade has led to an unprecedented rallying around the persona of the young emir Tamim. A nationalism is on the rise that is based on negative integration against those countries perceived as aggressors in Doha.[17] While Qataris are adamant that their nationalism is not toxic and does not intend to exclude, it nonetheless seems to have tainted a *khaliji* sense of togetherness.

Yet, while identity and senses of belonging are dynamic, the geography of the region will not change. Even if the blockading countries might succeed in building a canal to physically cut Qatar off from the Arabian Peninsula, it will not alter the fact that inevitably all countries must find a way to coexist—even if only under the umbrella of a fragile cold peace. In the era of globalization, the construction of border walls, fences and other artificial obstacles are desperate attempts to change a dynamic that no one can control. In the end, the underlying networks and interdependencies in the Gulf will provide a level of integration that no Gulf state can ignore.

---

[14] Ulrichsen, K. (2018). The Gulf Impasse's One Year Anniversary & the Changing Regional Dynamics. *The Gulf International Forum*, 30 May 2018. http://gulfif.com/the-gulf-impasse/.

[15] Al Gergawi, M. (2017). Death of the Khaliji. *Gulf News*, 22 August 2017.

[16] BBC News. (2017). Qatar Crisis: UAE Threatens Sympathizers with Prison. *BBC News*, 7 June 2017. https://www.bbc.co.uk/news/world-middle-east-40192730.

[17] Stratfor. (2017). A Renewed Sense of Nationalism Takes Root in Qatar. *Stratfor Reflections*, 29 December 2017. https://worldview.stratfor.com/article/renewed-sense-nationalism-takes-root-qatar.

INDEX

CPSIA information can be obtained
at www.ICGtesting.com
Printed in the USA
LVHW050345061219
639559LV00006B/390/P